COLLECT BRITISH STAMPS

A STANLEY GIBBONS CHECKLIST OF
THE STAMPS OF GREAT BRITAIN

2002 (53rd) Edition

STANLEY GIBBONS LTD

By Appointment to H.M. the Queen
Stanley Gibbons Ltd, London Philatelists.

London and Ringwood

COLLECT BRITISH STAMPS

The 2002 edition

From the famous Penny Black of 1840 to the absorbing issues of today, the stamps of Great Britain are highly popular with collectors. *Collect British Stamps* has been our message since very early days – but particularly since the First Edition of this checklist in September 1967. This 53rd edition includes all the recent issues. Prices have been carefully revised to reflect today's market. Total sales of *Collect British Stamps* are now over 3¾ million copies.

Collect British Stamps appears in the autumn of each year. A more detailed Great Britain catalogue, the *Concise*, is published each spring. The *Great Britain Concise* incorporates many additional listings covering watermark varieties, phosphor omitted errors, missing colour errors, stamp booklets and special commemorative First Day Cover postmarks. It is ideally suited for the collector who wishes to discover more about GB stamps.

Listings in this edition of *Collect British Stamps* include all 2001 issues which have appeared up to the publication date.

Scope. *Collect British Stamps* comprises:
- All stamps with different watermark (*wmk*) or perforation (*perf*).
- Visible plate numbers on the Victorian issues.
- Graphite-lined and phosphor issues, including variations in the numbers of phosphor bands.
- First Day Covers for Definitives from 1936, Regionals and all Special Issues.
- Presentation, Gift and Souvenir Packs.
- Post Office Yearbooks.
- Regional issues and War Occupation stamps of Guernsey and Jersey.
- Postage Due and Official Stamps.
- Post Office Picture Cards (PHQ cards).
- Commemorative gutter pairs and 'Traffic Light' gutter pairs listed as mint sets.
- Royal Mail Postage Labels priced as sets and on P.O. First Day Cover.

Stamps of the independent postal administrations of Guernsey, Isle of Man and Jersey are contained in *Collect Channel Islands and Isle of Man Stamps.*

Layout. Stamps are set out chronologically by date of issue. In the catalogue lists the first numeral is the Stanley Gibbons catalogue number; the black (boldface) numeral alongside is the type number referring to the respective illustration. A blank in this column implies that the number immediately above is repeated. The denomination and colour of the stamp are then shown. Before February 1971 British currency was:

   £1 = 20s   One pound = twenty shillings *and*
   1s = 12d   One shilling = twelve pence.

Upon decimalisation this became:

   £1 = 100p   One pound = one hundred (new)
                   pence.

The catalogue list then shows two price columns. The left-hand is for unused stamps and the right-hand for used. Corresponding small boxes are provided in which collectors may wish to check off the items in their collection.

Our method of indicating prices is:
Numerals for pence, e.g. 10 denotes 10p (10 pence). Numerals for pounds and pence, e.g. 4·25 denotes £4·25 (4 pounds and 25 pence). For £100 and above, prices are in whole pounds and so include the £ sign and omit the zeros for pence.

Colour illustrations. The colour illustrations of stamps are intended as a guide only; they may differ in shade from the originals.

Size of illustrations. To comply with Post Office regulations stamp illustrations are three-quarters linear side. Separate illustrations of surcharges, overprints and watermarks are actual size.

Prices. Prices quoted in this catalogue are our selling prices at the time the book went to press. They are for stamps in fine condition; in issues where condition varies we may ask more for the superb and less for the sub-standard. The unused prices for stamps of Queen Victoria to King George V are for lightly hinged examples. Unused prices for King Edward VIII to Queen Elizabeth II are for unmounted mint (though when not available unmounted, mounted stamps are often supplied at a lower price). Prices for used stamps refer to postally used copies. All prices are subject to change without prior notice and we give no guarantee to supply all stamps priced, since it is not possible to keep every catalogued item in stock. Individual low value stamps sold at 399, Strand are liable to an additional handling charge. Commemorative issues may only be available in complete sets.

In the price columns:
† = Does not exist.
(—) or blank = Exists, or may exist, but price cannot be quoted.
* = Not normally issued (the so-called 'Abnormals' of 1862–80).

Perforations. The 'perforation' is the number of holes in a length of 2 cm, as measured by the Gibbons *Instanta* gauge. The stamp is viewed against a dark background with the transparent gauge put on top of it. Perforations are quoted to the nearest half. Stamps without perforation are termed 'imperforate'.

From 1992 certain stamps occur with a large elliptical (oval) hole inserted in each line of vertical perforations. The £10 definitive, No. 1658, is unique in having two such holes in the horizontal perforations.

Elliptical perforations

Se-tenant combinations. *Se-tenant* means 'joined together'. Some sets include stamps of different design arranged *se-tenant* as blocks or strips and these are often collected unsevered as issued. Where such combinations exist the stamps are priced both mint and used, as singles or complete sets. The set price for mint refers to the unsevered combination plus singles of any other values in the set. The used set price is for single stamps of all values.

First day covers. Prices for first day covers are for complete sets used on plain covers (Nos. 430/8, 453/60, 462/78b, 485/90, and 503/12) or on special covers (Nos. 461, 479/84, 491/502 and 513 onwards), the stamps of which are cancelled with ordinary operational postmarks (1924–1962) or by the *standard* 'First Day of Issue' postmarks (1963 onwards). The British Post Office did not provide 'First Day' treatment for every definitive issued after 1963. Where the stamps in a set were issued on different days, prices are for a cover from each day.

Presentation Packs. Special packs comprising slip-in cards with printed information inside a protective covering, were introduced for the 1964 Shakespeare issue. Collectors packs, containing commemoratives from the preceding twelve months, were issued from 1967. Some packs with text in German from 1968–69 exist as does a Japanese version of the pack for Nos. 916/17. Yearbooks, hardbound and illustrated in colour within a slip cover, joined the product range in 1984.

PHQ cards. Since 1973 the Post Office has produced a series of picture cards, which can be sent through the post as postcards. Each card shows an enlarged colour reproduction of a current British stamp, either of one or more values from a set or of all values. Cards are priced here in fine mint condition for sets complete as issued. The Post Office gives each card a 'PHQ' serial number, hence the term. The cards are usually on sale shortly before the date of issue of the stamps, but there is no officially designated 'first day'.

Used prices are for cards franked with the stamp depicted, on the obverse or reverse; the stamp being cancelled with an official postmark for first day of issue.

Gutter pairs. All modern Great Britain commemoratives are produced in sheets containing two panes of stamps separated by a blank horizontal or vertical margin known as a gutter. This feature first made its appearance on some supplies of the 1972 Royal Silver Wedding 3p, and marked the introduction of Harrison & Sons' new 'Jumelle' stamp-printing press. There are advantages for both the printer and the Post Office in such a layout which has now been used for almost all commemorative issues since 1974.

The term 'gutter pair' is used for a pair of stamps separated by part of the blank gutter margin.

Traffic light gutter pair

Gutter pair

Most printers include some form of colour check device on the sheet margins, in addition to the cylinder or plate numbers. Harrison & Sons used round 'dabs' or spots of colour, resembling traffic lights. For the period from the 1972 Royal Silver Wedding until the end of 1979 these colour dabs appeared in the gutter margin. Gutter pairs showing these 'traffic lights' are worth considerably more than the normal version.

Catalogue numbers used. The checklist uses the same catalogue numbers as the Stanley Gibbons *British Commonwealth* Catalogue (Part 1), 2002 edition.

Latest issue date for stamps recorded in this edition is 6 November 2001.

STANLEY GIBBONS LTD

Head Office: 399 Strand, London WC2R OLX.
Auction Room and Specialist Stamp Departments–
    Open Monday–Friday 9.30 a.m. to 5 p.m.
Shop – Open Monday to Friday 9 a.m. to 5.30 p.m.
    and Saturday 9.30 a.m. to 5.30 p.m.
Telephone 0207-836 8444 for all departments
E-mail: enquiries@stanleygibbons.co.uk
Website: www.stangib.com

Stanley Gibbons Publications:
    5 Parkside, Christchurch Road, Ringwood, Hants
    BH24 3SH. Telephone: 01425 472363
    Publications Mail Order, FREEPHONE: 0800 611622
    E-mail: info@stanleygibbons.co.uk

ISBN: 0-85259-518-2
© Stanley Gibbons Ltd 2001

QUEEN VICTORIA

1837 (20 June)–1901 (22 Jan.)

IDENTIFICATION. In this checklist Victorian stamps are classified firstly according to which printing method was used –line-engraving, embossing or surface-printing.

Corner letters. Numerous stamps also have letters in all four, or just the lower corners. These were an anti-forgery device and the letters differ from stamp to stamp. If present in all four corners the upper pair are the reverse of the lower. Note the importance of these corner letters in the way the checklist is arranged.

Watermarks. Further classification depends on watermarks: these are illustrated in normal position, with stamps priced accordingly.

1 Line-engraved Issues

1

1a

1b

3 White lines added above and below head

2 Small Crown watermark

4 Large Crown watermark

Letters in lower corners

1840 *Wmk Small Crown Type* **2** *Imperforate*

Cat No.	Type		Unused	Used		
2	1	1d black	£3500	£200	☐	☐
5	1a	2d blue	£6500	£425	☐	☐

1841

8	1b	1d red-brown	£180	15·00	☐	☐
14	3	2d blue	£1500	60·00	☐	☐

1854–57 (*i*) *Wmk Small Crown Type* **2** *Perf* 16

17	1b	1d red-brown	£190	15·00	☐	☐
19	3	2d blue	£1800	85·00	☐	☐

(*ii*) *Wmk Small Crown Type* **2** *Perf* 14

24	1b	1d red-brown	£350	45·00	☐	☐
23	3	2d blue	£2250	£180	☐	☐

(*iii*) *Wmk Large Crown Type* **4** *Perf* 16

26	1b	1d red	£650	60·00	☐	☐
27	3	2d blue	£2750	£200	☐	☐

(*iv*) *Wmk Large Crown Type* **4** *Perf* 14

40	1b	1d red	40·00	9·00	☐	☐
34	3	2d blue	£1500	50·00	☐	☐

7

5

8

6

9 Watermark extending over three stamps

Letters in all four corners

Plate numbers. Stamps included a 'plate number' in their design and this affects valuation. The cheapest plates are priced here; see complete list of plate numbers overleaf.

1858–70 (*i*) *Wmk Type* **9** *Perf* 14

48	7	½d red	70·00	15·00	☐	☐

(*ii*) *Wmk Large Crown Type* **4** *Perf* 14

43	5	1d red	10·00	2·00	☐	☐
51	8	1½d red	£250	45·00	☐	☐
45	6	2d blue	£225	10·00	☐	☐

Positions of Plate Numbers

Shows Plate 9 (½d)

Shows Plate 170 (1d, 2d)

Shows Plate 3 (1½d)

HALFPENNY VALUE (S.G. 48)

Plate	Un.	Used			Plate	Un.	Used		
1	£150	70·00	□	□	11	70·00	15·00	□	□
3	80·00	25·00	□	□	12	70·00	15·00	□	□
4	£110	20·00	□	□	13	70·00	15·00	□	□
5	75·00	15·00	□	□	14	70·00	15·00	□	□
6	70·00	15·00	□	□	15	80·00	22·00	□	□
8	£130	70·00	□	□	19	£130	40·00	□	□
9	£2500	£400	□	□	20	£150	60·00	□	□
10	£110	15·00	□	□					

Plates 2, 7, 16, 17 and 18 were not completed, while Plates 21 and 22 though made were not used. Plate 9 was a reserve plate, not greatly used.

PENNY VALUE (S.G. 43)

Plate	Un.	Used			Plate	Un.	Used			Plate	Un.	Used			Plate	Un.	Used		
71	25·00	3·00	□	□	112	45·00	2·25	□	□	154	20·00	2·00	□	□	190	20·00	6·00	□	□
72	30·00	4·00	□	□	113	20·00	12·00	□	□	155	20·00	2·25	□	□	191	10·00	7·00	□	□
73	25·00	3·00	□	□	114	£250	12·00	□	□	156	20·00	2·00	□	□	192	25·00	2·00	□	□
74	20·00	2·00	□	□	115	90·00	2·25	□	□	157	20·00	2·00	□	□	193	10·00	2·00	□	□
76	35·00	2·00	□	□	116	75·00	9·00	□	□	158	10·00	2·00	□	□	194	20·00	8·00	□	□
77	£100000	£80000	□	□	117	20·00	2·00	□	□	159	10·00	2·00	□	□	195	20·00	8·00	□	□
78	90·00	2·00	□	□	118	25·00	2·00	□	□	160	10·00	2·00	□	□	196	18·00	5·00	□	□
79	30·00	2·00	□	□	119	18·00	2·00	□	□	161	28·00	7·00	□	□	197	20·00	9·00	□	□
80	22·00	2·00	□	□	120	10·00	2·00	□	□	162	20·00	7·00	□	□	198	12·00	6·00	□	□
81	45·00	2·25	□	□	121	32·00	9·50	□	□	163	20·00	3·00	□	□	199	22·00	6·00	□	□
82	90·00	4·00	□	□	122	10·00	2·00	□	□	164	20·00	3·00	□	□	200	22·00	2·00	□	□
83	£110	7·00	□	□	123	18·00	2·00	□	□	165	22·00	2·00	□	□	201	10·00	5·00	□	□
84	45·00	2·25	□	□	124	18·00	2·00	□	□	166	20·00	6·00	□	□	202	20·00	8·00	□	□
85	25·00	2·25	□	□	125	18·00	2·00	□	□	167	18·00	2·00	□	□	203	10·00	16·00	□	□
86	30·00	4·00	□	□	127	30·00	2·25	□	□	168	18·00	8·00	□	□	204	18·00	2·25	□	□
87	10·00	2·00	□	□	129	18·00	8·00	□	□	169	30·00	7·00	□	□	205	18·00	3·00	□	□
88	£130	8·00	□	□	130	22·00	2·25	□	□	170	18·00	2·00	□	□	206	18·00	9·00	□	□
89	35·00	2·00	□	□	131	60·00	16·00	□	□	171	10·00	2·00	□	□	207	18·00	9·00	□	□
90	28·00	2·00	□	□	132	90·00	22·00	□	□	172	10·00	2·00	□	□	208	18·00	16·00	□	□
91	35·00	6·00	□	□	133	80·00	9·00	□	□	173	40·00	9·00	□	□	209	20·00	9·00	□	□
92	18·00	2·00	□	□	134	10·00	2·00	□	□	174	10·00	2·00	□	□	210	22·00	12·00	□	□
93	35·00	2·00	□	□	135	90·00	26·00	□	□	175	30·00	3·50	□	□	211	38·00	20·00	□	□
94	35·00	5·00	□	□	136	90·00	20·00	□	□	176	25·00	2·25	□	□	212	20·00	11·00	□	□
95	25·00	2·00	□	□	137	20·00	2·25	□	□	177	18·00	2·00	□	□	213	20·00	11·00	□	□
96	28·00	2·00	□	□	138	18·00	2·00	□	□	178	20·00	3·50	□	□	214	25·00	18·00	□	□
97	20·00	3·50	□	□	139	30·00	16·00	□	□	179	20·00	2·25	□	□	215	25·00	18·00	□	□
98	20·00	6·00	□	□	140	18·00	2·00	□	□	180	20·00	5·00	□	□	216	25·00	18·00	□	□
99	25·00	5·00	□	□	141	£110	9·00	□	□	181	20·00	2·00	□	□	217	22·00	7·00	□	□
100	30·00	2·25	□	□	142	40·00	24·00	□	□	182	75·00	5·00	□	□	218	18·00	8·00	□	□
101	40·00	9·00	□	□	143	30·00	15·00	□	□	183	25·00	3·00	□	□	219	45·00	70·00	□	□
102	22·00	2·00	□	□	144	90·00	20·00	□	□	184	10·00	2·25	□	□	220	10·00	7·00	□	□
103	22·00	3·50	□	□	145	10·00	2·25	□	□	185	20·00	3·00	□	□	221	30·00	16·00	□	□
104	28·00	5·00	□	□	146	18·00	6·00	□	□	186	30·00	2·25	□	□	222	40·00	40·00	□	□
105	50·00	7·00	□	□	147	22·00	3·00	□	□	187	18·00	2·00	□	□	223	45·00	60·00	□	□
106	30·00	2·00	□	□	148	22·00	3·00	□	□	188	22·00	10·00	□	□	224	50·00	50·00	□	□
107	35·00	7·00	□	□	149	20·00	6·00	□	□	189	30·00	7·00	□	□	225	£1250	£400	□	□
108	30·00	2·25	□	□	150	10·00	2·00	□	□										
109	60·00	3·50	□	□	151	25·00	9·00	□	□										
110	22·00	9·00	□	□	152	22·00	5·50	□	□										
111	30·00	2·25	□	□	153	60·00	9·00	□	□										

Plates 69, 70, 75, 77, 126 and 128 were prepared but rejected. No stamps therefore exist, except for a very few from Plate 77 which somehow reached the public. Plate 177 stamps, by accident or design, are sometimes passed off as the rare Plate 77.

THREE-HALFPENNY VALUE (S.G. 51)

Plate	Un.	Used			Plate	Un.	Used		
(1)	£450	65·00	□	□	3	£250	45·00	□	□

Plate 1 did *not* have the plate number in the design. Plate 2 was not completed and no stamps exist.

TWOPENNY VALUE (S.G. 45)

Plate	Un.	Used			Plate	Un.	Used		
7	£550	40·00	□	□	13	£250	20·00	□	□
8	£600	32·00	□	□	14	£300	25·00	□	□
9	£225	10·00	□	□	15	£250	25·00	□	□
12	£1000	£110	□	□					

Plates 10 and 11 were prepared but rejected.

2 Embossed Issues

Prices are for stamps cut square and with average to fine embossing. Stamps with exceptionally clear embossing are worth more.

12   **11**   **10**

13

1847–54 *Wmk* **13** *(6d), no wmk (others) Imperforate*

59	12	6d lilac	£3750	£550	☐ ☐
57	11	10d brown	£3750	£725	☐ ☐
54	10	1s green	£4000	£500	☐ ☐

3 Surface-printed Issues

IDENTIFICATION. Check first whether the design includes corner letters or not, as mentioned for 'Line-engraved Issues'. The checklist is divided up according to whether any letters are small or large, also whether they are white (uncoloured) or printed in the colour of the stamp. Further identification then depends on watermark.

PERFORATION. Except for Nos. 126/9 all the following issues of Queen Victoria are perf 14.

14

15 Small Garter   **16** Medium Garter   **17** Large Garter

18   **19**   **20** Emblems

No corner letters

1855–57 (*i*) *Wmk Small Garter Type* **15**

62	14	4d red	£3250	£325	☐ ☐

(*ii*) *Wmk Medium Garter Type* **16**

64	14	4d red	£2750	£300	☐ ☐

(*iii*) *Wmk Large Garter Type* **17**

66a	14	4d red	£900	75·00	☐ ☐

(*iv*) *Wmk Emblems Type* **20**

70	18	6d lilac	£675	80·00	☐ ☐
72	19	1s green	£800	£225	☐ ☐

Plate numbers. Stamps Nos. 90/163 should be checked for the 'plate numbers' indicated, as this affects valuation (the cheapest plates are priced here). The mark *'Pl.'* shows that several numbers exist, priced in separate list overleaf.

Plate numbers are the small numerals appearing in duplicate in some part of the frame design or adjacent to the lower corner letters (in the 5s value a single numeral above the lower inscription).

21   **22**   **23**

24   **25**

Small white corner letters

1862–64 *Wmk Emblems Type* **20**, *except* 4d (*Large Garter Type* **17**)

76	21	3d red	£1000	£200	☐ ☐
80	22	4d red	£900	80·00	☐ ☐
84	23	6d lilac	£1000	80·00	☐ ☐
87	24	9d bistre	£1900	£225	☐ ☐
90	25	1s green *Pl.*	£1100	£140	☐ ☐

26   **27**   **28** (hyphen in SIX-PENCE)   **32**   **33** Spray of Rose   **34**

29   **30**   **31**

Large white corner letters

1865–67 Wmk Emblems Type 20 *except* 4d *(Large Garter Type* 17*)*

92	**26**	3d red (Plate 4)	. . . .	£600	80·00	☐	☐
94	**27**	4d vermilion *Pl.*	. . . . .	£375	45·00	☐	☐
97	**28**	6d lilac *Pl.*	. . . .	£500	70·00	☐	☐
98	**29**	9d straw *Pl.*	. . . .	£1000	£350	☐	☐
99	**30**	10d brown (Plate 1)	. . .	† £15000		☐	
101	**31**	1s green (Plate 4)	. . . .	£950	£130	☐	☐

1867–80 Wmk Spray of Rose Type 33

103	**26**	3d red *Pl.*	. . . .	£325	40·00	☐	☐
105	**28**	6d lilac (with hyphen) (Plate 6)	. . . . . .	£725	70·00	☐	☐
109		6d mauve (without hyphen) *Pl.*	. . . . . .	£400	65·00	☐	☐
110	**29**	9d straw (Plate 4)	. . . .	£800	£180	☐	☐
112	**30**	10d brown *Pl.*	. . . .	£1500	£250	☐	☐
117	**31**	1s green *Pl.*	. . . .	£550	28·00	☐	☐
119	**32**	2s blue *Pl.*	. . . .	£1500	£110	☐	☐
121		2s brown (Plate 1)	. . .	£8000	£1700	☐	☐

1872–73 Wmk Spray of Rose Type 33

122b	**34**	6d brown *Pl.*	. . . .	£475	40·00	☐	☐
125		6d grey (Plate 12)	. . . .	£1000	£190	☐	☐

PLATE NUMBERS
on stamps of 1862–83

Cat No.		Plate No.	Un.	Used		

Small White Corner Letters (1862–64)

90	1s green	2	£1100	£140	☐	☐
		3	£13000		☐	☐

Plate 2 is actually numbered as '1' and Plate 3 as '2' on the stamps.

Large White Corner Letters (1865–83)

103	3d red	4	£425	£100	☐	☐
		5	£325	40·00	☐	☐
		6	£350	40·00	☐	☐
		7	£425	45·00	☐	☐
		8	£375	45·00	☐	☐
		9	£375	50·00	☐	☐
		10	£425	80·00	☐	☐
94	4d verm	7	£450	50·00	☐	☐
		8	£400	50·00	☐	☐
		9	£400	50·00	☐	☐
		10	£450	70·00	☐	☐
		11	£450	45·00	☐	☐
		12	£375	50·00	☐	☐
		13	£400	50·00	☐	☐
		14	£450	80·00	☐	☐
97	6d lilac	5	£500	70·00	☐	☐
		6	£1500	£130	☐	☐
109	6d mauve	8	£400	65·00	☐	☐
		9	£400	65·00	☐	☐
		10	*	£15000		☐
122b	6d brown	11	£475	40·00	☐	☐
		12	£1100	£130	☐	☐
98	9d straw	4	£1000	£350	☐	☐
		5	£14000		☐	☐

112	10d brown	1	£1500	£250	☐	☐
		2	£15000	£3500	☐	☐
117	1s green	4	£550	32·00	☐	☐
		5	£600	30·00	☐	☐
		6	£750	28·00	☐	☐
		7	£750	60·00	☐	☐
119	2s blue	1	£1500	£110	☐	☐
		3	*	£4000	☐	☐
126	5s red	1	£3750	£400	☐	☐
		2	£4750	£500	☐	☐

Large Coloured Corner Letters (1873–83)

139	2½d mauve	1	£350	65·00	☐	☐
		2	£350	65·00	☐	☐
		3	£550	70·00	☐	☐
141	2½d mauve	3	£675	70·00	☐	☐
		4	£325	35·00	☐	☐
		5	£325	40·00	☐	☐
		6	£325	35·00	☐	☐
		7	£325	35·00	☐	☐
		8	£325	40·00	☐	☐
		9	£325	35·00	☐	☐
		10	£375	50·00	☐	☐
		11	£325	35·00	☐	☐
		12	£325	40·00	☐	☐
		13	£325	40·00	☐	☐
		14	£325	35·00	☐	☐
		15	£325	35·00	☐	☐
		16	£325	35·00	☐	☐
		17	£750	£160	☐	☐
142	2½d blue	17	£275	40·00	☐	☐
		18	£325	32·00	☐	☐
		19	£275	30·00	☐	☐
		20	£275	30·00	☐	☐

157	2½d blue	21	£325	28·00	☐	☐
		22	£275	28·00	☐	☐
		23	£275	20·00	☐	☐
143	3d red	11	£275	30·00	☐	☐
		12	£325	30·00	☐	☐
		14	£350	32·00	☐	☐
		15	£275	30·00	☐	☐
		16	£275	30·00	☐	☐
		17	£325	30·00	☐	☐
		18	£325	30·00	☐	☐
		19	£275	30·00	☐	☐
		20	£275	50·00	☐	☐
158	3d red	20	£375	80·00	☐	☐
		21	£325	60·00	☐	☐
152	4d verm	15	£1000	£275	☐	☐
		16	*	£14000	☐	☐
153	4d green	15	£625	£200	☐	☐
		16	£550	£180	☐	☐
		17	*	£9000	☐	☐
160	4d brown	17	£275	45·00	☐	☐
		18	£275	45·00	☐	☐
147	6d grey	13	£325	40·00	☐	☐
		14	£325	40·00	☐	☐
		15	£325	40·00	☐	☐
		16	£325	40·00	☐	☐
		17	£425	65·00	☐	☐
161	6d grey	17	£275	50·00	☐	☐
		18	£250	50·00	☐	☐
150	1s green	8	£450	65·00	☐	☐
		9	£450	65·00	☐	☐
		10	£425	70·00	☐	☐
		11	£425	70·00	☐	☐
		12	£375	50·00	☐	☐
		13	£325	50·00	☐	☐
		14	*	£14000	☐	☐
163	1s brown	13	£400	£100	☐	☐
		14	£350	£100	☐	☐

35

36

37

38

39 Maltese Cross

40 Large Anchor

1867–83 (*i*) *Wmk Maltese Cross Type* **39** *Perf* 15½ × 15
126	**35**	5s red *Pl.*	£3750	£400	□ □
128	**36**	10s grey (Plate 1)	£28000	£1300	□ □
129	**37**	£1 brown (Plate 1) . . .	£32000	£1900	□ □

     (*ii*) *Wmk Large Anchor Type* **40** *Perf* 14
134	**35**	5s red (Plate 4)	£7500	£1400	□ □
131	**36**	10s grey (Plate 1)	£34000	£2100	□ □
132	**37**	£1 brown (Plate 1) . . .	£40000	£3750	□ □
137	**38**	£5 orange (Plate 1) . . .	£6000	£1800	□ □

41

42

43

44

45

46

47 Small Anchor

48 Orb

Large coloured corner letters

1873–80 (*i*) *Wmk Small Anchor Type* **47**
139	**41**	2½d mauve *Pl.*	£350	65·00	□ □

     (*ii*) *Wmk Orb Type* **48**
141	**41**	2½d mauve *Pl.*	£325	35·00	□ □
142		2½d blue *Pl.*	£275	30·00	□ □

     (*iii*) *Wmk Spray of Rose Type* **33**
143	**42**	3d red *Pl.*	£275	30·00	□ □
145	**43**	6d pale buff (Plate 13) .	*	£6000	□ □
147		6d grey *Pl.*	£325	40·00	□ □
150	**44**	1s green *Pl.*	£375	50·00	□ □
151		1s brown (Plate 13) . . .	£1750	£350	□ □

     (*iv*) *Wmk Large Garter Type* **17**
152	**45**	4d vermilion *Pl.*	£1000	£275	□ □
153		4d green *Pl.*	£550	£180	□ □
154		4d brown (Plate 17) . . .	£800	£300	□ □
156	**46**	8d orange (Plate 1) . . .	£750	£225	□ □

3d   6d

49 Imperial Crown   **(50)** Surcharges in red **(51)**

1880–83 *Wmk Imperial Crown Type* **49**
157	**41**	2½d blue *Pl.*	£275	20·00	□ □
158	**42**	3d red *Pl.*	£325	60·00	□ □
159		3d on 3d lilac (surch			
		Type **50**)	£325	£110	□ □
160	**45**	4d brown *Pl.*	£275	45·00	□ □
161	**43**	6d grey *Pl.*	£250	50·00	□ □
162		6d on 6d lilac (surch			
		Type **51**)	£275	£110	□ □
163	**44**	1s brown *Pl.*	£350	£100	□ □

5

52

53

54

55

56

1880–81 *Wmk Imperial Crown Type* **49**

164	52	½d green	. . . .	40·00	10·00	□	□
166	53	1d brown	. . . .	15·00	10·00	□	□
167	54	1½d brown	. . . .	£140	35·00	□	□
168	55	2d red	. . . .	£175	70·00	□	□
169	56	5d indigo	. . . .	£475	90·00	□	□

57

Die I

Die II

1881 *Wmk Imperial Crown Type* **49**

(a) 14 *dots in each corner, Die I*

171	57	1d lilac	. . . .	£110	25·00	□	□

(b) 16 *dots in each corner, Die II*

174	57	1d mauve	. . . .	2·50	1·50	□	□

58

59

60

Coloured letters in the corners

1883–84 *Wmk Anchor Type* **40**

179	58	2s 6d deep lilac	. . . .	£350	£110	□	□
181	59	5s red	. . . .	£550	£140	□	□
183	60	10s blue	. . . .	£1250	£375	□	□

61

1884 *Wmk 3 Imperial Crowns Type* **49**

185	61	£1 brown	. . . .	£15000	£1400	□	□

1888 *Wmk 3 Orbs Type* **48**

186	61	£1 brown	. . . .	£28000	£2500	□	□

1891 *Wmk 3 Imperial Crowns Type* **49**

212	61	£1 green	. . . .	£2500	£425	□	□

62

63

64

65

66

1883–84 *Wmk Imperial Crown Type* **49** (*sideways on horiz designs*)

187	52	½d blue	. . . .	17·00	7·00	□	□
188	62	1½d lilac	. . . .	85·00	35·00	□	□
189	63	2d lilac	. . . .	£140	65·00	□	□
190	64	2½d lilac	. . . .	70·00	12·00	□	□
191	65	3d lilac	. . . .	£175	85·00	□	□
192	66	4d dull green	. . . . . .	£400	£175	□	□
193	62	5d dull green	. . . . . .	£400	£175	□	□
194	63	6d dull green	. . . . . .	£425	£200	□	□
195	64	9d dull green	. . . . . .	£750	£375	□	□
196	65	1s dull green	. . . . . .	£550	£200	□	□

The above prices are for stamps in the true dull green colour. Stamps which have been soaked, causing the colour to run are virtually worthless.

71   72   73

74   75   76

77   78   79

80   81   82

'Jubilee' issue

1887–1900 *The bicoloured stamps have the value tablets, or the frames including the value tablets, in the second colour. Wmk Imperial Crown Type* **49**

197e	**71**	½d vermilion	1·50	1·00	□	□
213		½d green*	1·75	2·00	□	□
198	**72**	1½d purple and green . .	15·00	7·00	□	□
200	**73**	2d green and red	28·00	12·00	□	□
201	**74**	2½d purple on blue	22·00	3·00	□	□
203	**75**	3d purple on yellow . .	22·00	3·25	□	□
205	**76**	4d green and brown . .	30·00	13·00	□	□
206	**77**	4½d green and red	10·00	40·00	□	□
207a	**78**	5d purple and blue	35·00	11·00	□	□
208	**79**	6d purple on red	30·00	10·00	□	□
209	**80**	9d purple and blue	60·00	40·00	□	□
210	**81**	10d purple and red	45·00	38·00	□	□
211	**82**	1s green	£200	60·00	□	□
214		1s green and red	50·00	£125	□	□
		Set of 14	£500	£325	□	□

*The ½d No. 213 in blue is a colour changeling.

KING EDWARD VII

1901 (22 Jan.)–1910 (6 May)

83   84   85

86   87   88

89   90   91

92   93

94   95   96

97

1902–13 *Wmks Imperial Crown Type* **49** (½*d to* 1*s*)*, Anchor Type* **40** (2*s* 6*d to* 10*s*)*, Three Crowns Type* **49** (£1) (*a*) *Perf* 14

215	83	½d blue-green	2·00	1·50 □ □
217		½d yellow-green	2·00	1·50 □ □
219		1d red	2·00	1·50 □ □
221	84	1½d purple and green . .	32·00	15·00 □ □
291	85	2d green and red	25·00	15·00 □ □
231	86	2½d blue	18·00	7·00 □ □
234	87	3d purple on yellow . .	30·00	12·00 □ □
238	88	4d green and brown . .	40·00	13·00 □ □
240		4d orange	20·00	15·00 □ □
294	89	5d purple and blue . . .	28·00	15·00 □ □
245	83	6d purple	30·00	15·00 □ □
249	90	7d grey	10·00	12·00 □ □
307	91	9d purple and blue . . .	50·00	50·00 □ □
311	92	10d purple and red	60·00	50·00 □ □
314	93	1s green and red	50·00	30·00 □ □
260	94	2s 6d purple	£180	75·00 □ □
263	95	5s red	£180	£110 □ □
265	96	10s blue	£500	£300 □ □
266	97	£1 green	£1100	£450 □ □
		Set of 15 (*to* 1*s*)	£350	£225 □ □

(*b*) *Perf* 15 × 14

279	83	½d green	40·00	45·00 □ □
281		1d red	15·00	15·00 □ □
283	86	2½d blue	22·00	12·00 □ □
285	87	3d purple on yellow . .	40·00	15·00 □ □
286	88	4d orange	30·00	15·00 □ □
		Set of 5	£130	80·00 □ □

KING GEORGE V

1910 (6 May)–1936 (20 Jan.)

PERFORATION. All the following issues are Perf 15 × 14 except vertical commemorative stamps which are 14 × 15, unless otherwise stated.

98 (Hair dark)   **99** (Lion unshaded)   **100**

1911–12 *Wmk Imperial Crown Type* **49**

325	98	½d green	4·50	1·50 □ □
327	99	1d red	4·50	2·50 □ □

1912 *Wmk Royal Cypher* ('*Simple*') *Type* **100**

335	98	½d green	40·00	40·00 □ □
336	99	1d red	30·00	30·00 □ □

101 (Hair light)   **102** (Lion shaded)   **103**

1912 *Wmk Imperial Crown Type* **49**

339	101	½d green	15·00	8·00 □ □
341	102	1d red	4·00	2·00 □ □

1912 *Wmk Royal Cypher* ('*Simple*') *Type* **100**

344	101	½d green	7·00	3·00 □ □
345	102	1d red	8·00	2·50 □ □

1912 *Wmk Royal Cypher* ('*Multiple*') *Type* **103**

347	101	½d green	11·00	8·00 □ □
350	102	1d red	11·00	8·00 □ □

104   **105**   **106**

107

108

111

1912–24 *Wmk Royal Cypher Type* **100**

351	**105**	½d green	1·00	1·00	□	□
357	**104**	1d red	1·00	1·00	□	□
362	**105**	1½d brown	4·00	1·50	□	□
369	**106**	2d orange	5·00	3·00	□	□
371	**104**	2½d blue	12·00	4·00	□	□
377	**106**	3d violet	7·00	2·00	□	□
379		4d grey-green	12·00	2·00	□	□
381	**107**	5d brown	10·00	5·00	□	□
385		6d purple	15·00	7·00	□	□
		a. Perf 14	90·00	£110	□	□
387		7d olive-green	20·00	10·00	□	□
390		8d black on yellow . . .	32·00	11·00	□	□
392	**108**	9d black	18·00	6·00	□	□
393*a*		9d olive-green	£100	30·00	□	□
394		10d blue	22·00	20·00	□	□
395		1s brown	20·00	4·00	□	□
	Set of 15	. . . .	£250	£100	□	□

1913 *Wmk Royal Cypher ('Multiple') Type* **103**

397	**105**	½d green	£150	£180	□	□
398	**104**	1d red	£225	£225	□	□

See also Nos. 418/29.

109

110

T 109. Background around portrait consists of horizontal lines

1913–18 *Wmk Single Cypher Type* **110** *Perf* 11 × 12

413*a*	**109**	2s 6d brown	90·00	60·00	□	□
416		5s red	£210	90·00	□	□
417		10s blue	£300	£140	□	□
403		£1 green	£1300	£800	□	□
	Set of 4	. . . .	£1700	£950	□	□

See also Nos. 450/2.

1924–26 *Wmk Block Cypher Type* **111**

418	**105**	½d green	1·00	1·00	□	□
419	**104**	1d red	1·00	1·00	□	□
420	**105**	1½d brown	1·00	1·00	□	□
421	**106**	2d orange	2·50	2·50	□	□
422	**104**	2½d blue	5·00	3·00	□	□
423	**106**	3d violet	10·00	2·50	□	□
424		4d grey-green	12·00	2·50	□	□
425	**107**	5d brown	20·00	3·00	□	□
426*a*		6d purple	3·00	1·50	□	□
427	**108**	9d olive-green	12·00	3·50	□	□
428		10d blue	35·00	40·00	□	□
429		1s brown	22·00	3·00	□	□
	Set of 12	. . . .	£110	60·00	□	□

112

112a

British Empire Exhibition

1924–25 *Wmk* **111** *Perf* 14 (*a*) 23.4.24. *Dated* '1924'

430	**112**	1d red	10·00	11·00	□	□
431	**112a**	1½d brown	15·00	15·00	□	□
	First Day Cover		£375		□

(*b*) 9.5.25. *Dated* '1925'

432	**112**	1d red	15·00	25·00	□	□
433	**112a**	1½d brown	40·00	65·00	□	□
	First Day Cover		£1300		□

113

114

115

116 St George and the Dragon

117

Ninth Universal Postal Union Congress
1929 (10 MAY) (a) Wmk **111**

434	**113**	½d green	2·25	2·25	□ □
435	**114**	1d red	2·25	2·25	□ □
436		1½d brown	2·25	1·75	□ □
437	**115**	2½d blue	10·00	10·00	□ □

(b) Wmk **117** Perf 12

438	**116**	£1 black	£750	£550	□ □
434/7 Set of 4		. . . .	15·00	14·50	□ □
434/7 First Day Cover (4 vals.)		. . . . .		£500	□
434/8 First Day Cover (5 vals.)		. . . . .		£6000	□

118   **119**   **120**

121   **122**

1934–36 Wmk **111**

439	**118**	½d green	30	40	□ □
440	**119**	1d red	30	40	□ □
441	**118**	1½d brown	30	40	□ □
442	**120**	2d orange	50	75	□ □
443	**119**	2½d blue	1·50	1·25	□ □
444	**120**	3d violet	1·50	1·25	□ □
445		4d grey-green	2·00	1·25	□ □
446	**121**	5d brown	6·00	2·75	□ □
447	**122**	9d olive-green	12·00	2·25	□ □
448		10d blue	15·00	10·00	□ □
449		1s brown	15·00	1·25	□ □
	Set of 11	. . . .	48·00	18·00	□ □

T 109 (re-engraved). Background around portrait consists of horizontal and diagonal lines
1934 Wmk **110** Perf 11 × 12

450	**109**	2s 6d brown	65·00	35·00	□ □
451		5s red	£150	80·00	□ □
452		10s blue	£325	75·00	□ □
	Set of 3	. . . .	£475	£180	□ □

123   **123a**

123b   **123c**

Silver Jubilee
1935 (7 MAY) Wmk **111**

453	**123**	½d green	75	50	□ □
454	**123a**	1d red	1·25	1·50	□ □
455	**123b**	1½d brown	75	50	□ □
456	**123c**	2½d blue	4·50	5·50	□ □
	Set of 4	. . . .	6·00	7·00	□ □
	First Day Cover	. . . .		£600	□

KING EDWARD VIII

1936 (20 Jan.–10 Dec.)

124

125

1936 *Wmk* **125**

457	**124**	½d green	30	30	□	□
458		1d red	60	40	□	□
459		1½d brown	30	30	□	□
460		2½d blue	30	75	□	□
	Set of 4	. . . .	1·25	1·60	□	□

First Day Covers

1 Sept. 1936	Nos. 457, 459/60	£150	□
14 Sept. 1936	No. 458	£160	□

KING GEORGE VI

1936 (11 Dec.)–1952 (6 Feb.)

126   King George VI   127
      and Queen Elizabeth

Coronation

1937 (13 MAY) *Wmk* **127**

461	**126**	1½d brown	30	30	□	□
	First Day Cover		35·00		□

128   129   130

King George VI and National Emblems

1937–47 *Wmk* **127**

462	**128**	½d green	20	25	□	□
463		1d scarlet	20	25	□	□
464		1½d brown	20	25	□	□
465		2d orange	75	50	□	□
466		2½d blue	25	25	□	□
467		3d violet	3·75	1·00	□	□
468	**129**	4d green	60	60	□	□
469		5d brown	2·50	75	□	□
470		6d purple	1·25	60	□	□
471	**130**	7d green	3·75	60	□	□
472		8d red	3·75	70	□	□
473		9d deep green	5·50	80	□	□
474		10d blue	5·50	80	□	□
474*a*		11d plum	2·00	2·50	□	□
475		1s brown	6·00	75	□	□
	Set of 15	. . . .	30·00	9·00	□	□

First Day Covers

10 May 1937	Nos. 462/3, 466	5·00	□
30 July 1937	No. 464	5·00	□
31 Jan. 1938	Nos. 465, 467	22·00	□
21 Nov. 1938	Nos. 468/9	40·00	□
30 Jan. 1939	No. 470	40·00	□
27 Feb. 1939	Nos. 471/2	55·00	□
1 May 1939	Nos. 473/4, 475	£400	□
29 Dec. 1947	No. 474*a*	40·00	□

For later printings of the lower values in apparently lighter shades and different colours, see Nos. 485/90 and 503/8.

130a King George VI   **131**

132   **132a**

133

Centenary of First Adhesive Postage Stamps
1940 (6 MAY) *Wmk* **127** *Perf* 14½ × 14

479	**134**	½d green	30	30 □ □
480		1d red	1·00	40 □ □
481		1½d brown	50	75 □ □
482		2d orange	50	40 □ □
483		2½d blue	2·25	50 □ □
484		3d violet	3·00	3·50 □ □
	Set of 6		6·50	5·25 □ □
	First Day Cover			50·00 □

Head as Nos. 462–7, but lighter background
1941–42 *Wmk* **127**

485	**128**	½d pale green	30	30 □ □
486		1d pale red	30	30 □ □
487		1½d pale brown	50	70 □ □
488		2d pale orange	50	50 □ □
489		2½d light blue	30	30 □ □
490		3d pale violet	2·00	1·00 □ □
	Set of 6		3·50	2·75 □ □

First Day Covers

21 July 1941	No. 489	35·00 □
11 Aug. 1941	No. 486	17·00 □
1 Sept. 1941	No. 485	17·00 □
6 Oct. 1941	No. 488	50·00 □
3 Nov. 1941	No. 490	90·00 □
28 Sept. 1942	No. 487	45·00 □

135 Symbols of Peace and Reconstruction   **136** Symbols of Peace and Reconstruction

Victory
1946 (11 JUNE) *Wmk* **127**

491	**135**	2½d blue	20	15 □ □
492	**136**	3d violet	20	40 □ □
	First Day Cover			60·00 □

1939–48 *Wmk* 133 *Perf* 14

476	**130a**	2s 6d brown	35·00	6·00 □ □
476a		2s 6d green	4·50	1·50 □ □
477	**131**	5s red	9·00	2·00 □ □
478	**132**	10s dark blue	£225	20·00 □ □
478a		10s bright blue	20·00	5·00 □ □
478b	**132a**	£1 brown	7·00	26·00 □ □
	Set of 6		£275	55·00 □ □

First Day Covers

21 Aug. 1939	No. 477	£600 □
4 Sept. 1939	No. 476	£1000 □
30 Oct. 1939	No. 478	£1800 □
9 Mar. 1942	No. 476a	£1000 □
30 Nov. 1942	No. 478a	£2250 □
1 Oct. 1948	No. 478b	£225 □

137 King George VI and Queen Elizabeth   **138** King George VI and Queen Elizabeth

Royal Silver Wedding
1948 (26 APR.) *Wmk* **127**

493	**137**	2½d blue	35	20 □ □
494	**138**	£1 blue	38·00	38·00 □ □
	First Day Cover			£400 □

134 Queen Victoria and King George VI

1948 (10 MAY)

Stamps of 1d and 2½d showing seaweed-gathering were on sale at eight Head Post Offices elsewhere in Great Britain, but were primarily for use in the Channel Islands and are listed there (see after Regional Issues).

139   Globe and Laurel Wreath

140   Speed

141   Olympic Symbol

142   Winged Victory

Olympic Games

1948 (29 JULY) *Wmk* **127**

495	**139**	2½d blue	. . . .	30	10	□	□
496	**140**	3d violet	. . . .	30	45	□	□
497	**141**	6d purple	. . . .	60	35	□	□
498	**142**	1s brown	. . . .	1·25	1·50	□	□
	Set of 4		. . . .	2·00	2·25	□	□
	First Day Cover	. . . .		38·00		□	

143   Two Hemispheres

144   U.P.U. Monument, Berne

145   Goddess Concordia, Globe and Points of Compass

146   Posthorn and Globe

75th Anniversary of Universal Postal Union

1949 (10 OCT.) *Wmk* **127**

499	**143**	2½d blue	. . . .	15	10	□	□
500	**144**	3d violet	. . . .	15	50	□	□
501	**145**	6d purple	. . . .	25	50	□	□
502	**146**	1s brown	. . . .	60	1·25	□	□
	Set of 4		. . . .	1·00	2·10	□	□
	First Day Cover	. . . .		70·00		□	

4d as No. 468 and others as Nos. 485/9, but colours changed

1950–51 *Wmk* **127**

503	**128**	½d pale orange	. . . . .	30	30	□	□
504		1d light blue	. . . . . .	30	30	□	□
505		1½d pale green	. . . . . .	50	60	□	□
506		2d pale brown	. . . . . .	50	40	□	□
507		2½d pale red	. . . . . .	50	40	□	□
508	**129**	4d light blue	. . . .	2·00	1·75	□	□
	Set of 6		. . . .	3·75	3·25	□	□

First Day Covers

2 Oct. 1950	No. 508	. . . .	£100	□
3 May 1951	Nos. 503/7	. . . .	45·00	□

147   HMS *Victory*

148   White Cliffs of Dover

149   St George and the Dragon

150   Royal Coat of Arms

1951 (3 MAY) *Wmk* **133** *Perf* 11 × 12

509	**147**	2s 6d green	. . . .	3·00	1·00	□	□
510	**148**	5s red	. . . .	38·00	1·50	□	□
511	**149**	10s blue	. . . .	12·00	8·50	□	□
512	**150**	£1 brown	. . . .	45·00	20·00	□	□
	Set of 4		. . . .	85·00	25·00	□	□
	First Day Cover	. . . .		£800		□	

151   Commerce and Prosperity

152   Festival Symbol

Festival of Britain

1951 (3 MAY) *Wmk* **127**

513	**151**	2½d red	. . . .	15	20	□	□
514	**152**	4d blue	. . . .	30	65	□	□
	First Day Cover	. . . .		30·00		□	

QUEEN ELIZABETH II
6 February, 1952

153 Tudor Crown

154

155

156

157

158

159   160

1952–54 *Wmk* **153**

515	**154**	½d orange	10	15	☐	☐
516		1d blue	20	20	☐	☐
517		1½d green	10	15	☐	☐
518		2d brown	20	15	☐	☐
519	**155**	2½d red	10	15	☐	☐
520		3d lilac	75	70	☐	☐
521	**156**	4d blue	3·50	1·10	☐	☐
		4½d (*See Nos. 577, 594, 609 and* 616b)				
522	**157**	5d brown	75	3·75	☐	☐
523		6d purple	3·75	90	☐	☐
524		7d green	10·00	6·50	☐	☐
525	**158**	8d magenta	80	80	☐	☐
526		9d bronze-green	25·00	4·25	☐	☐
527		10d blue	14·00	4·25	☐	☐
528		11d plum	30·00	17·00	☐	☐
529	**159**	1s bistre	90	60	☐	☐
530	**160**	1s 3d green	4·25	3·50	☐	☐
531	**159**	1s 6d indigo	12·00	4·00	☐	☐
		Set of 17	95·00	45·00	☐	☐

First Day Covers

5 Dec. 1952	Nos. 517, 519	14·00	☐
6 July 1953	Nos. 522, 525, 529	45·00	☐
31 Aug. 1953	Nos. 515/16, 518	45·00	☐
2 Nov. 1953	Nos. 521, 530/1	£160	☐
18 Jan. 1954	Nos. 520, 523/4	£100	☐
8 Feb. 1954	Nos. 526/8	£200	☐

See also Nos. 540/56, 561/6, 570/94 and 599/618a and for stamps as Type **157** with face values in decimal currency see Nos. 2031/3.

161

162

163

164

Coronation

1953 (3 JUNE) *Wmk* **153**

532	**161**	2½d red	10	25	☐	☐
533	**162**	4d blue	70	2·25	☐	☐
534	**163**	1s 3d green	3·50	3·75	☐	☐
535	**164**	1s 6d blue	7·00	4·25	☐	☐
		Set of 4	10·00	9·50	☐	☐
		First Day Cover	60·00			☐

For a £1 value as Type **163** see No. **MS**2147.

165 St Edward's Crown

166 Carrickfergus Castle

167 Caernarvon Castle

168 Edinburgh Castle   169 Windsor Castle

1955 (1–23 SEPT.) *Wmk* **165** *Perf* 11 × 12

536	**166**	2s 6d brown	10·00	2·00	☐	☐
537	**167**	5s red	30·00	4·25	☐	☐

14

538	168	10s blue	80·00	15·00	☐	☐
539	169	£1 black	£130	40·00	☐	☐
		Set of 4	£225	55·00	☐	☐
		First Day Cover (Nos. 538/9)				
		(1 Sept.)		£750	☐	
		First Day Cover (Nos. 536/7)				
		(23 Sept.)		£550	☐	

See also Nos. 595*a*/8*a* and 759/62.

1955–58 *Wmk* **165**

540	154	½d orange	10	15	☐	☐
541		1d blue	30	15	☐	☐
542		1½d green	30	30	☐	☐
543		2d red-brown	25	30	☐	☐
543*b*		2d light red-brown . . .	20	20	☐	☐
544	155	2½d red	20	25	☐	☐
545		3d lilac	25	30	☐	☐
546	156	4d blue	1·25	40	☐	☐
547	157	5d brown	5·50	5·50	☐	☐
548		6d purple	4·00	1·10	☐	☐
549		7d green	45·00	9·00	☐	☐
550	158	8d magenta	5·50	1·10	☐	☐
551		9d bronze-green	20·00	2·50	☐	☐
552		10d blue	18·00	2·50	☐	☐
553		11d plum	50	1·50	☐	☐
554	159	1s bistre	18·00	60	☐	☐
555	160	1s 3d green	32·00	1·50	☐	☐
556	159	1s 6d indigo	22·00	1·60	☐	☐
		Set of 18	£160	26·00	☐	☐

170 Scout Badge and 'Rolling Hitch'

171 'Scouts coming to Britain'

172 Globe within a Compass

173

World Scout Jubilee Jamboree
1957 (1 Aug.) *Wmk* **165**

557	170	2½d red	15	20	☐	☐
558	171	4d blue	35	1·00	☐	☐
559	172	1s 3d green	3·50	4·00	☐	☐
		Set of 3	3·50	4·75	☐	☐
		First Day Cover		22·00	☐	

46th Inter Parliamentary Union Conference
1957 (12 Sept.) *Wmk* **165**

560	173	4d blue	90	1·25	☐	☐
		First Day Cover		95·00	☐	

Graphite-lined and Phosphor Issues

These are used in connection with automatic sorting machinery, originally experimentally at Southampton but now also operating elsewhere. In such areas these stamps were the normal issue, but from mid 1967 *all* low-value stamps bear phosphor markings.

The graphite lines were printed in black on the back, beneath the gum; two lines per stamp except for the 2d *(see below)*.

174   175   (2d only)
(Stamps viewed from back)

In November 1959, phosphor bands, printed on the front, replaced the graphite. They are wider than the graphite, not easy to see, but show as broad vertical bands at certain angles to the light.

Values representing the rate for printed papers (and second class mail from 1968) have one band and others have two, three or four bands according to size and format. From 1972 onwards some commemorative stamps were printed with 'all-over' phosphor.

In the small stamps the bands are on each side with the single band at left (except where otherwise stated). In the large-size commemorative stamps the single band may be at left, centre or right varying in different issues. The bands are vertical on both horizontal and vertical designs except where otherwise stated.

See also notes on page 37.

Graphite-lined issue
1957 (19 Nov.) *Two graphite lines on the back, except* 2d *value, which has one line. Wmk* **165**

561	154	½d orange	25	25	☐	☐
562		1d blue	25	45	☐	☐
563		1½d green	1·00	1·50	☐	☐
564		2d light red-brown . . .	1·50	2·50	☐	☐
565	155	2½d red	7·75	7·00	☐	☐
566		3d lilac	55	60	☐	☐
		Set of 6	10·00	11·00	☐	☐
		First Day Cover		80·00	☐	

See also Nos. 587/94.

176   Welsh Dragon   177   Flag and Games Emblem

178   Welsh Dragon

Sixth British Empire and Commonwealth Games, Cardiff
1958 (18 JULY) *Wmk* **165**

567	**176**	3d lilac	20	20 ☐ ☐
568	**177**	6d mauve	45	50 ☐ ☐
569	**178**	1s 3d green	2·40	2·50 ☐ ☐
	Set of 3	. . . .	2·75	2·75 ☐ ☐
	First Day Cover		65·00 ☐

179   Multiple Crowns

WATERMARK. All the following issues to No. 755 are Watermark **179** (sideways on the vertical commemorative stamps) unless otherwise stated.

1958–65 *Wmk* **179**

570	**154**	½d orange	10	10 ☐ ☐
571		1d blue	10	10 ☐ ☐
572		1½d green	10	15 ☐ ☐
573		2d light red-brown . . .	10	10 ☐ ☐
574	**155**	2½d red	10	20 ☐ ☐
575		3d lilac	10	20 ☐ ☐
576a	**156**	4d blue	15	15 ☐ ☐
577		4½d brown	10	25 ☐ ☐
578	**157**	5d brown	30	40 ☐ ☐
579		6d purple	40	25 ☐ ☐
580		7d green	45	50 ☐ ☐
581	**158**	8d magenta	50	45 ☐ ☐
582		9d bronze-green	50	45 ☐ ☐
583		10d blue	1·00	50 ☐ ☐
584	**159**	1s bistre	45	35 ☐ ☐
585	**160**	1s 3d green	40	35 ☐ ☐
586	**159**	1s 6d indigo	4·00	55 ☐ ☐
	Set of 17	. . . .	8·00	4·50 ☐ ☐
	First Day Cover (*No.* 577)			
	(9 Feb. 1959)		£200 ☐

For full information on all future British issues, collectors should write to Royal Mail, Freepost EH3647, 21 South Gyle Crescent, Edinburgh EH12 9PE.

Graphite-lined issue
1958–59 *Two graphite lines on the back, except* 2d *value, which has one line.* Wmk **179**

587	**154**	½d orange	3·25	3·75 ☐ ☐
588		1d blue	1·25	1·40 ☐ ☐
589		1½d green	38·00	38·00 ☐ ☐
590		2d light red-brown . . .	6·25	3·00 ☐ ☐
591	**155**	2½d red	7·50	9·00 ☐ ☐
592		3d lilac	50	55 ☐ ☐
593	**156**	4d blue	4·00	4·75 ☐ ☐
594		4½d brown	6·00	4·75 ☐ ☐
	Set of 8	. . . .	60·00	60·00 ☐ ☐

The prices quoted for Nos. 587 and 589 are for examples with inverted watermark. Stamps with upright watermark are priced at: ½d £7 *mint*, £8 *used* and 1½d £90 *mint*, £80 *used*.

1959–63 *Wmk* **179**   *Perf* 11 × 12

595a	**166**	2s 6d brown	40	30 ☐ ☐
596a	**167**	5s red	90	45 ☐ ☐
597a	**168**	10s blue	3·25	3·75 ☐ ☐
598a	**169**	£1 black	10·00	5·75 ☐ ☐
	Set of 4	. . . .	13·00	9·50 ☐ ☐

Phosphor-Graphite issue
1959 (18 Nov.) *Two phosphor bands on front and two graphite lines on back, except* 2d *value, which has one band on front and one line on back* (a) Wmk **165**

599	**154**	½d orange	3·00	3·50 ☐ ☐
600		1d blue	7·50	7·50 ☐ ☐
601		1½d green	3·00	3·00 ☐ ☐
		(b) *Wmk* **179**		
605	**154**	2d light red-brown		
		(1 band)	4·00	4·00 ☐ ☐
606	**155**	2½d red	16·00	14·00 ☐ ☐
607		3d lilac	8·00	6·50 ☐ ☐
608	**156**	4d blue	14·00	16·00 ☐ ☐
609		4½d brown	24·00	18·00 ☐ ☐
	Set of 8	. . . .	70·00	65·00 ☐ ☐

Phosphor issue
1960–67 *Two phosphor bands on front, except where otherwise stated.* Wmk **179**

610	**154**	½d orange	10	15 ☐ ☐
611		1d blue	10	10 ☐ ☐
612		1½d green	10	15 ☐ ☐
613		2d light red-brown		
		(1 band)	18·00	20·00 ☐ ☐
613a		2d light red-brown		
		(2 bands)	10	10 ☐ ☐
614	**155**	2½d red (2 bands)	10	30 ☐ ☐
614a		2½d red (1 band)	30	60 ☐ ☐
615		3d lilac (2 bands)	50	60 ☐ ☐
615c		3d lilac (1 side band) . .	50	60 ☐ ☐
615e		3d lilac (1 centre band) .	40	45 ☐ ☐
616a	**156**	4d blue	25	25 ☐ ☐
616b		4½d brown	20	25 ☐ ☐

16

616c	**157**	5d brown	30	35 ☐	☐
617		6d purple	30	25 ☐	☐
617a		7d green	50	40 ☐	☐
617b	**158**	8d magenta	45	40 ☐	☐
617c		9d bronze-green	55	50 ☐	☐
617d		10d blue	75	50 ☐	☐
617e	**159**	1s bistre	35	35 ☐	☐
618	**160**	1s 3d green	1·90	2·50 ☐	☐
618a	**159**	1s 6d indigo	1·90	1·60 ☐	☐
		Set of 17 (one of each value) . .	7·50	7·75 ☐	☐

No. 615c exists with the phosphor band at the left or right of the stamp.

180 Postboy of 1660   **181** Posthorn of 1660

Tercentenary of Establishment of 'General Letter Office'
1960 (7 JULY)

619	**180**	3d lilac	20	20 ☐	☐
620	**181**	1s 3d green	3·00	3·00 ☐	☐
		Set of 2	3·00	3·00 ☐	☐
		First Day Cover		45·00	☐

182 Conference Emblem

First Anniversary of European Postal and Telecommunications Conference
1960 (19 SEPT.)

621	**182**	6d green and purple . .	50	50 ☐	☐
622		1s 6d brown and blue . . .	6·50	5·00 ☐	☐
		Set of 2	7·00	5·50 ☐	☐
		First Day Cover		50·00	☐

183 Thrift Plant   **184** 'Growth of Savings'

185 Thrift Plant

Centenary of Post Office Savings Bank
1961 (28 AUG.)

623A	**183**	2½d black and red	30	25 ☐	☐
624A	**184**	3d orange-brown and violet	25	20 ☐	☐
625A	**185**	1s 6d red and blue	2·50	2·25 ☐	☐
		Set of 3	2·75	2·40 ☐	☐
		First Day Cover		65·00	☐

186 C.E.P.T. Emblem   **187** Doves and Emblem

188 Doves and Emblem

European Postal and Telecommunications (C.E.P.T.) Conference, Torquay
1961 (18 SEPT.)

626	**186**	2d orange, pink and brown	20	25 ☐	☐
627	**187**	4d buff, mauve and ultramarine	20	25 ☐	☐
628	**188**	10d turquoise, green and blue	20	85 ☐	☐
		Set of 3	50	1·25 ☐	☐
		First Day Cover		7·00	☐

189 Hammer Beam Roof,   **190** Palace of
Westminster Hall   Westminster

Seventh Commonwealth Parliamentary Conference
1961 (25 Sept.)

629	**189**	6d purple and gold . . .	30	30	☐	☐
630	**190**	1s 3d green and blue . . .	2·50	2·75	☐	☐
		Set of 2	2·75	3·00	☐	☐
		First Day Cover		35·00		☐

191 'Units of Productivity'   **192** 'National Productivity'

193 'Unified Productivity'

National Productivity Year
1962 (14 Nov.) *Wmk* **179** (*inverted on* 2½d *and* 3d)

631	**191**	2½d green and red	20	15	☐	☐
		p. Phosphor	70	60	☐	☐
632	**192**	3d blue and violet	25	15	☐	☐
		p. Phosphor	1·75	90	☐	☐
633	**193**	1s 3d red, blue and green .	1·75	2·00	☐	☐
		p. Phosphor	35·00	22·00	☐	☐
		Set of 3 (Ordinary)	2·00	2·10	☐	☐
		Set of 3 (Phosphor)	35·00	22·00	☐	☐
		First Day Cover (Ordinary)		55·00		☐
		First Day Cover (Phosphor) . . .		£100		☐

194 Campaign Emblem   **195** Children of Three Races
and Family

Freedom from Hunger
1963 (21 Mar.) *Wmk* **179** (*inverted*)

634	**194**	2½d crimson and pink . .	10	10	☐	☐
		p. Phosphor	3·00	1·50	☐	☐
635	**195**	1s 3d brown and yellow . .	2·00	2·50	☐	☐
		p. Phosphor	32·00	24·00	☐	☐
		Set of 2 (Ordinary)	2·00	2·50	☐	☐
		Set of 2 (Phosphor)	35·00	25·00	☐	☐
		First Day Cover (Ordinary)		35·00		☐
		First Day Cover (Phosphor) . . .		40·00		☐

196 'Paris Conference'

Paris Postal Conference Centenary
1963 (7 May) *Wmk* **179** (*inverted*)

636	**196**	6d green and mauve . .	35	40	☐	☐
		p. Phosphor	6·50	6·50	☐	☐
		First Day Cover (Ordinary)		15·00		☐
		First Day Cover (Phosphor) . . .		28·00		☐

197 Posy of Flowers   **198** Woodland Life

National Nature Week
1963 (16 May)

637	**197**	3d multicoloured	15	10	☐	☐
		p. Phosphor	75	55	☐	☐
638	**198**	4½d multicoloured	20	35	☐	☐
		p. Phosphor	2·25	2·50	☐	☐
		Set of 2 (Ordinary)	35	45	☐	☐
		Set of 2 (Phosphor)	3·00	3·00	☐	☐
		First Day Cover (Ordinary)		20·00		☐
		First Day Cover (Phosphor) . . .		28·00		☐

199 Rescue at Sea   **200** 19th-century Lifeboat

201 Lifeboatmen

Ninth International Lifeboat Conference, Edinburgh
1963 (31 May)

639	**199**	2½d blue, black and red .	15	20	☐	☐
		p. Phosphor	50	60	☐	☐
640	**200**	4d multicoloured	45	50	☐	☐
		p. Phosphor	50	60	☐	☐

641	201	1s 6d sepia, yellow and				
		blue	2·50	2·75	☐	☐
		p. Phosphor	45·00	28·00	☐	☐
		Set of 3 (Ordinary)	2·75	3·00	☐	☐
		Set of 3 (Phosphor)	45·00	28·00	☐	☐
		First Day Cover (Ordinary)		38·00		☐
		First Day Cover (Phosphor) . . .		48·00		☐

202 Red Cross   203

204

Red Cross Centenary Congress
1963 (15 Aug.)

642	202	3d red and lilac	15	15	☐	☐
		p. Phosphor	1·10	85	☐	☐
643	203	1s 3d red, blue and grey . .	2·75	3·00	☐	☐
		p. Phosphor	35·00	32·00	☐	☐
644	204	1s 6d red, blue and bistre .	2·75	2·75	☐	☐
		p. Phosphor	32·00	27·00	☐	☐
		Set of 3 (Ordinary)	5·00	5·25	☐	☐
		Set of 3 (Phosphor)	60·00	55·00	☐	☐
		First Day Cover (Ordinary)		38·00		☐
		First Day Cover (Phosphor) . . .		65·00		☐

205   'Commonwealth Cable'

Opening of COMPAC (Trans-Pacific Telephone Cable)
1963 (3 Dec.)

645	205	1s 6d blue and black	2·25	2·25	☐	☐
		p. Phosphor	18·00	18·00	☐	☐
		First Day Cover (Ordinary)		26·00		☐
		First Day Cover (Phosphor) . . .		30·00		☐

206 Puck and Bottom   207 Feste (Twelfth Night)
(A Midsummer
Night's Dream)

208 Balcony Scene   209 'Eve of Agincourt'
(Romeo and Juliet)   (Henry V)

210 Hamlet contemplating
Yorick's skull (Hamlet)
and Queen Elizabeth II

Shakespeare Festival
1964 (23 Apr.) Perf 11 × 12 (2s 6d) or 15 × 14 (others)

646	206	3d bistre, black and				
		violet-blue	15	15	☐	☐
		p. Phosphor	25	25	☐	☐
647	207	6d multicoloured	30	30	☐	☐
		p. Phosphor	75	75	☐	☐
648	208	1s 3d multicoloured	70	90	☐	☐
		p. Phosphor	3·50	6·00	☐	☐
649	209	1s 6d multicoloured	1·00	85	☐	☐
		p. Phosphor	8·50	7·50	☐	☐
650	210	2s 6d deep slate-purple . .	2·50	2·50	☐	☐
		Set of 5 (Ordinary)	4·25	4·25	☐	☐
		Set of 4 (Phosphor)	12·00	13·00	☐	☐
		First Day Cover (Ordinary)		12·00		☐
		First Day Cover (Phosphor) . . .		16·00		☐
		Presentation Pack (Ordinary) . .	15·00			☐

PRESENTATION PACKS were first introduced by the G.P.O. for the Shakespeare Festival issue. The packs include one set of stamps and details of the designs, the designer and the stamp printer. They were issued for almost all later definitive and special issues.

211 Flats near Richmond Park   212 Shipbuilding Yards, Belfast
('Urban Development')   ('Industrial Activity')

213 Beddgelert Forest Park,   214 Nuclear Reactor, Dounreay
Snowdonia ('Forestry')   ('Technological Development')

20th International Geographical Congress, London

1964 (1 JULY)

651	**211**	2½d multicoloured	10	10	☐	☐
		p. Phosphor	40	45	☐	☐
652	**212**	4d multicoloured	35	35	☐	☐
		p. Phosphor	1·25	1·25	☐	☐
653	**213**	8d multicoloured	75	80	☐	☐
		p. Phosphor	2·50	2·00	☐	☐
654	**214**	1s 6d multicoloured	3·00	2·75	☐	☐
		p. Phosphor	26·00	20·00	☐	☐
		Set of 4 (Ordinary)	3·75	3·50	☐	☐
		Set of 4 (Phosphor)	27·00	21·00	☐	☐
		First Day Cover (Ordinary)		20·00		☐
		First Day Cover (Phosphor) . . .		30·00		☐
		Presentation Pack (Ordinary) . . £130			☐	

215 Spring Gentian

216 Dog Rose

217 Honeysuckle

218 Fringed Water Lily

Tenth International Botanical Congress, Edinburgh

1964 (5 AUG.)

655	**215**	3d violet, blue and green	10	10	☐	☐
		p. Phosphor	40	35	☐	☐
656	**216**	6d multicoloured	30	35	☐	☐
		p. Phosphor	2·75	2·75	☐	☐
657	**217**	9d multicoloured	1·40	2·25	☐	☐
		p. Phosphor	3·50	4·00	☐	☐
658	**218**	1s 3d multicoloured	2·00	2·50	☐	☐
		p. Phosphor	24·00	18·00	☐	☐
		Set of 4 (Ordinary)	3·50	4·75	☐	☐
		Set of 4 (Phosphor)	28·00	23·00	☐	☐
		First Day Cover (Ordinary)		24·00		☐
		First Day Cover (Phosphor) . . .		32·00		☐
		Presentation Pack (Ordinary) . . £130			☐	

219 Forth Road Bridge

220 Forth Road and Railway Bridges

Opening of Forth Road Bridge

1964 (4 SEPT.)

659	**219**	3d black, blue and violet	10	10	☐	☐
		p. Phosphor	50	50	☐	☐
660	**220**	6d blackish lilac, blue and red	40	40	☐	☐
		p. Phosphor	3·75	3·75	☐	☐
		Set of 2 (Ordinary)	50	50	☐	☐
		Set of 2 (Phosphor)	4·25	4·25	☐	☐
		First Day Cover (Ordinary)		9·00		☐
		First Day Cover (Phosphor) . . .		12·00		☐
		Presentation Pack (Ordinary) . . £325			☐	

221 Sir Winston Churchill   **221a** Sir Winston Churchill

Churchill Commemoration

1965 (8 JULY)

661	**221**	4d black and drab	15	10	☐	☐
		p. Phosphor	30	30	☐	☐
662	**221a**	1s 3d black and grey	35	40	☐	☐
		p. Phosphor	2·75	3·75	☐	☐
		Set of 2 (Ordinary)	50	50	☐	☐
		Set of 2 (Phosphor)	3·00	4·00	☐	☐
		First Day Cover (Ordinary)		6·00		☐
		First Day Cover (Phosphor) . . .		8·00		☐
		Presentation Pack (Ordinary) . . 20·00			☐	

222 Simon de Montfort's Seal

223 Parliament Buildings
(after engraving by Hollar, 1647)

700th Anniversary of Simon de Montfort's Parliament

1965 (19 JULY)

663	**222**	6d green	20	20	☐	☐
		p. Phosphor	75	90	☐	☐
664	**223**	2s 6d black, grey and drab	1·00	1·25	☐	☐
		Set of 2 (Ordinary)	1·10	1·25	☐	☐
		First Day Cover (Ordinary)		14·00		☐
		First Day Cover (Phosphor) . . .		18·00		☐
		Presentation Pack (Ordinary) . . 45·00			☐	

224 Bandsmen and Banner

225 Three Salvationists

Salvation Army Centenary
1965 (9 Aug.)

665	**224**	3d multicoloured	10	15 □ □
		p. Phosphor	40	55 □ □
666	**225**	1s 6d multicoloured	75	1·25 □ □
		p. Phosphor	2·75	2·75 □ □
		Set of 2 (Ordinary)	85	1·40 □ □
		Set of 2 (Phosphor)	3·00	3·25 □ □
		First Day Cover (Ordinary)		24·00 □
		First Day Cover (Phosphor) . . .		30·00 □

226 Lister's Carbolic Spray

227 Lister and Chemical Symbols

Centenary of Joseph Lister's Discovery of Antiseptic Surgery
1965 (1 Sept.)

667	**226**	4d indigo, chestnut and grey	10	15 □ □
		p. Phosphor	30	30 □ □
668	**227**	1s black, purple and blue	80	1·25 □ □
		p. Phosphor	2·50	2·50 □ □
		Set of 2 (Ordinary)	90	1·40 □ □
		Set of 2 (Phosphor)	2·75	2·75 □ □
		First Day Cover (Ordinary)		20·00 □
		First Day Cover (Phosphor) . . .		20·00 □

228 Trinidad Carnival Dancers   **229** Canadian Folk Dancers

Commonwealth Arts Festival
1965 (1 Sept.)

669	**228**	6d black and orange . .	20	20 □ □
		p. Phosphor	40	40 □ □
670	**229**	1s 6d black and violet . . .	90	1·25 □ □
		p. Phosphor	2·75	2·75 □ □
		Set of 2 (Ordinary)	1·10	1·40 □ □
		Set of 2 (Phosphor)	3·00	3·00 □ □
		First Day Cover (Ordinary)		18·00 □
		First Day Cover (Phosphor) . . .		22·00 □

230 Flight of Supermarine Spitfires

231 Pilot in Hawker Hurricane Mk I

232 Wing-tips of Supermarine Spitfire and Messerschmitt Bf 109

233 Supermarine Spitfires attacking Heinkel HE 111H Bomber

234 Supermarine Spitfire attacking Junkers Ju 87B 'Stuka' Dive-bomber

235 Hawker Hurricanes Mk I over Wreck of Dornier Do-17Z Bomber

The above were issued together *se-tenant* in blocks of six (3 × 2) within the sheet.

236 Anti-aircraft Artillery in Action

237 Air Battle over St Paul's Cathedral

25th Anniversary of Battle of Britain
1965 (13 Sept.)

671	**230**	4d olive and black	50	50 □ □
		a. Block of 6. Nos. 671/6	8·00	10·00 □ □
		p. Phosphor	90	1·00 □ □
		pa. Block of 6. Nos. 671p/6p	12·00	15·00 □ □
672	**231**	4d olive, blackish olive and black	50	50 □ □
		p. Phosphor	90	1·00 □ □
673	**232**	4d multicoloured	50	50 □ □
		p. Phosphor	90	1·00 □ □
674	**233**	4d olive and black	50	50 □ □
		p. Phosphor	90	1·00 □ □
675	**234**	4d olive and black	50	50 □ □
		p. Phosphor	90	1·00 □ □

676	235	4d multicoloured	50	50 □ □
		p. Phosphor	90	1·00 □ □
677	236	9d violet, orange and purple	1·25	1·25 □ □
		p. Phosphor	1·25	1·25 □ □
678	237	1s 3d multicoloured	1·25	1·25 □ □
		p. Phosphor	1·25	1·25 □ □
		Set of 8 (Ordinary)	9·50	5·00 □ □
		Set of 8 (Phosphor)	13·00	7·75 □ □
		First Day Cover (Ordinary)		28·00 □
		First Day Cover (Phosphor) . . .		29·00 □
		Presentation Pack (Ordinary) . .		50·00 □

238 Tower and Georgian Buildings
239 Tower and Nash Terrace, Regent's Park

Opening of Post Office Tower
1965 (8 Oct.)

679	238	3d yellow, blue and green	10	15 □ □
		p. Phosphor	15	15 □ □
680	239	1s 3d green and blue . . .	35	60 □ □
		p. Phosphor	30	55 □ □
		Set of 2 (Ordinary)	45	75 □ □
		Set of 2 (Phosphor)	45	70 □ □
		First Day Cover (Ordinary)		10·00 □
		First Day Cover (Phosphor) . . .		10·00 □
		Presentation Pack (Ordinary) . .		4·00 □
		Presentation Pack (Phosphor) . .		4·00 □

240 U.N. Emblem
241 I.C.Y. Emblem

20th Anniversary of UNO and International Co-operation Year
1965 (25 Oct.)

681	240	3d black, orange and blue	15	20 □ □
		p. Phosphor	25	30 □ □
682	241	1s 6d black, purple and blue	90	1·00 □ □
		p. Phosphor	3·00	3·25 □ □
		Set of 2 (Ordinary)	1·00	1·10 □ □
		Set of 2 (Phosphor)	3·25	3·50 □ □
		First Day Cover (Ordinary)		12·00 □
		First Day Cover (Phosphor) . . .		18·00 □

242 Telecommunications Network
243 Radio Waves and Switchboard

I.T.U. Centenary
1965 (15 Nov.)

683	242	9d multicoloured	35	40 □ □
		p. Phosphor	65	65 □ □
684	243	1s 6d multicoloured	1·25	1·50 □ □
		p. Phosphor	4·50	4·50 □ □
		Set of 2 (Ordinary)	1·60	1·90 □ □
		Set of 2 (Phosphor)	5·00	5·00 □ □
		First Day Cover (Ordinary)		20·00 □
		First Day Cover (Phosphor) . . .		22·00 □

244 Robert Burns (after Skirving chalk drawing)
245 Robert Burns (after Nasmyth portrait)

Burns Commemoration
1965 (25 Jan.)

685	244	4d black, indigo and blue	15	15 □ □
		p. Phosphor	25	40 □ □
686	245	1s 3d black, blue and orange	35	70 □ □
		p. Phosphor	2·00	2·00 □ □
		Set of 2 (Ordinary)	40	85 □ □
		Set of 2 (Phosphor)	2·25	2·40 □ □
		First Day Cover (Ordinary)		7·00 □
		First Day Cover (Phosphor) . . .		8·00 □
		Presentation Pack (Ordinary) . .		42·00 □

246 Westminster Abbey
247 Fan Vaulting, Henry VII Chapel

900th Anniversary of Westminster Abbey
1966 (28 Feb.) *Perf* 15 × 14 (3d) *or* 11 × 12 (2s 6d)

| 687 | 246 | 3d black, brown and blue . . . . | 15 | 20 □ □ |
| | | p. Phosphor . . . . | 30 | 35 □ □ |

688	247	2s 6d black	75	1·00	□	□
		Set of 2	90	1·10	□	□
		First Day Cover (Ordinary) . . .		10·00		□
		First Day Cover (Phosphor) . . .		15·00		□
		Presentation Pack (Ordinary) . .	19·00			□

248 View near Hassocks, Sussex   **249** Antrim, Northern Ireland

250 Harlech Castle, Wales   **251** Cairngorm Mountains, Scotland

Landscapes
1966 (2 MAY)

689	248	4d black, yellow-green and blue	10	15	□	□
		p. Phosphor	10	15	□	□
690	249	6d black, green and blue	15	20	□	□
		p. Phosphor	15	20	□	□
691	250	1s 3d black, yellow and blue	25	45	□	□
		p. Phosphor	25	45	□	□
692	251	1s 6d black, orange and blue	40	60	□	□
		p. Phosphor	40	60	□	□
		Set of 4 (Ordinary)	80	1·25	□	□
		Set of 4 (Phosphor)	80	1·25	□	□
		First Day Cover (Ordinary)		9·00		□
		First Day Cover (Phosphor) . . .		9·00		□

252 Players with Ball

253 Goalmouth Mêlée   **254** Goalkeeper saving Goal

World Cup Football Championship
1966 (1 JUNE)

693	252	4d multicoloured	10	10	□	□
		p. Phosphor	10	10	□	□
694	253	6d multicoloured	15	25	□	□
		p. Phosphor	15	25	□	□
695	254	1s 3d multicoloured	50	70	□	□
		p. Phosphor	50	70	□	□
		Set of 3 (Ordinary)	70	95	□	□
		Set of 3 (Phosphor)	70	95	□	□
		First Day Cover (Ordinary)		15·00		□
		First Day Cover (Phosphor) . . .		20·00		□
		Presentation Pack (Ordinary) . .	16·00			□

255 Black-headed Gull   **256** Blue Tit

257 European Robin   **258** Blackbird

The above were issued *se-tenant* in blocks of four within the sheet.

British Birds
1966 (8 AUG.)

696	255	4d multicoloured	10	15	□	□
		a. Block of 4. Nos. 696/9	1·00	2·00	□	□
		p. Phosphor	10	15	□	□
		pa. Block of 4. Nos. 696p/9p	70	2·00	□	□
697	256	4d multicoloured	10	15	□	□
		p. Phosphor	10	15	□	□
698	257	4d multicoloured	10	15	□	□
		p. Phosphor	10	15	□	□
699	258	4d multicoloured	10	15	□	□
		p. Phosphor	10	15	□	□
		Set of 4 (Ordinary)	1·00	55	□	□
		Set of 4 (Phosphor)	70	55	□	□
		First Day Cover (Ordinary)		15·00		□
		First Day Cover (Phosphor) . . .		15·00		□
		Presentation Pack (Ordinary) . .	10·00			□

259 Cup Winners

England's World Cup Football Victory
1966 (18 Aug.)

700	259	4d multicoloured	20	20	□	□
		First Day Cover		11·00		□

260 Jodrell Bank Radio Telescope

261 British Motor-cars

262 SR N6 Hovercraft

263 Windscale Reactor

British Technology
1966 (19 Sept.)

701	**260**	4d black and lemon . . .	10	10	□	□
		p. Phosphor	10	10	□	□
702	**261**	6d red, blue and orange	15	20	□	□
		p. Phosphor	15	25	□	□
703	**262**	1s 3d multicoloured	25	40	□	□
		p. Phosphor	40	50	□	□
704	**263**	1s 6d multicoloured	40	60	□	□
		p. Phosphor	55	70	□	□
		Set of 4 (Ordinary)	80	1·10	□	□
		Set of 4 (Phosphor)	1·10	1·40	□	□
		First Day Cover (Ordinary)		10·00		□
		First Day Cover (Phosphor) . . .		10·00		□
		Presentation Pack (Ordinary) . .	11·00			□

264

265

266

267

268

269

The above show battle scenes, they were issued together *se-tenant* in horizontal strips of six within the sheet.

270 Norman Ship

271 Norman Horsemen attacking Harold's Troops

900th Anniversary of Battle of Hastings
1966 (14 Oct.) *Designs show scenes from Bayeux Tapestry*
Wmk **179** (*sideways on 1s 3d*)

705	**264**	4d multicoloured	10	15	□	□
		a. Strip of 6. Nos. 705/10	2·00	6·00	□	□
		p. Phosphor	10	25	□	□
		pa. Strip of 6. Nos. 705p/10p	2·00	6·00	□	□
706	**265**	4d multicoloured	10	15	□	□
		p. Phosphor	10	25	□	□
707	**266**	4d multicoloured	10	15	□	□
		p. Phosphor	10	25	□	□
708	**267**	4d multicoloured	10	15	□	□
		p. Phosphor	10	25	□	□
709	**268**	4d multicoloured	10	15	□	□
		p. Phosphor	10	25	□	□
710	**269**	4d multicoloured	10	15	□	□
		p. Phosphor	10	25	□	□

711	**270**	6d multicoloured	10	15 □	□
		p. Phosphor	10	15 □	□
712	**271**	1s 3d multicoloured	20	30 □	□
		p. Phosphor	20	30 □	□
		Set of 8 (Ordinary)	2·10	1·25 □	□
		Set of 8 (Phosphor)	2·10	1·75 □	□
		First Day Cover (Ordinary)		10·00	□
		First Day Cover (Phosphor) . . .		10·00	□
		Presentation Pack (Ordinary) . .	13·00		□

272 King of the Orient **273** Snowman

Christmas
1966 (1 Dec.) Wmk **179** (upright on 1s 6d)

713	**272**	3d multicoloured	10	10 □	□
		p. Phosphor	10	10 □	□
714	**273**	1s 6d multicoloured	35	40 □	□
		p. Phosphor	35	40 □	□
		Set of 2 (Ordinary)	45	50 □	□
		Set of 2 (Phosphor)	45	50 □	□
		First Day Cover (Ordinary)		5·00	□
		First Day Cover (Phosphor) . . .		5·00	□
		Presentation Pack (Ordinary) . .	10·00		□

274 Sea Freight **275** Air Freight

European Free Trade Association (EFTA)
1967 (20 Feb.)

715	**274**	9d multicoloured	20	25 □	□
		p. Phosphor	20	25 □	□
716	**275**	1s 6d multicoloured	30	45 □	□
		p. Phosphor	30	45 □	□
		Set of 2 (Ordinary)	50	70 □	□
		Set of 2 (Phosphor)	50	70 □	□
		First Day Cover (Ordinary)		5·00	□
		First Day Cover (Phosphor) . . .		5·00	□
		Presentation Pack (Ordinary) . .	4·00		□

276 Hawthorn and Bramble **277** Larger Bindweed and Viper's Bugloss

278 Ox-eye Daisy, Coltsfoot and Buttercup **279** Bluebell, Red Campion and Wood Anemone

The above sheet were issued together se-tenant in blocks of four within the sheet.

280 Dog Violet **281** Primroses

British Wild Flowers
1967 (24 Apr.)

717	**276**	4d multicoloured	15	15 □	□
		a. Block of 4. Nos. 717/20	1·40	2·75 □	□
		p. Phosphor	10	10 □	□
		pa Block of 4. Nos. 717p/20p	50	2·50 □	□
718	**277**	4d multicoloured	15	15 □	□
		p. Phosphor	10	10 □	□
719	**278**	4d multicoloured	15	15 □	□
		p. Phosphor	10	10 □	□
720	**279**	4d multicoloured	15	15 □	□
		p. Phosphor	10	10 □	□
721	**280**	9d multicoloured	15	20 □	□
		p. Phosphor	10	15 □	□
722	**281**	1s 9d multicoloured	20	30 □	□
		p. Phosphor	25	25 □	□
		Set of 6 (Ordinary)	1·50	1·00 □	□
		Set of 6 (Phosphor)	75	70 □	□
		First Day Cover (Ordinary)		8·00	□
		First Day Cover (Phosphor) . . .		10·00	□
		Presentation Pack (Ordinary) . .	5·50		□
		Presentation Pack (Phosphor) . .	5·50		□

282 (value at left)   **282a** (value at right)

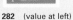

I   II

Two *types* of the 2d.
I. Value spaced away from left side of stamp.
II. Value close to left side from new multi-positive. This results in the portrait appearing in the centre, thus conforming with the other values.

1967–69 *Two phosphor bands, except where otherwise stated. No wmk.*

723	**282**	⅓d orange-brown	10	20	☐	☐
724		1d olive (2 bands)	10	10	☐	☐
725		1d olive (1 centre band)	25	30	☐	☐
726		2d lake-brown (Type I) (2 bands)	10	15	☐	☐
727		2d lake-brown (Type II) (2 bands)	15	15	☐	☐
728		2d lake-brown (Type II) (1 centre band) . . .	70	1·00	☐	☐
729		3d violet (1 centre band)	10	10	☐	☐
730		3d violet (2 bands) . . .	30	30	☐	☐
731		4d sepia (2 bands) . . .	10	10	☐	☐
732		4d olive-brown (1 centre band)	10	10	☐	☐
733		4d vermilion (1 centre band)	10	10	☐	☐
734		4d vermilion (1 side band)	1·50	1·75	☐	☐
735		5d blue	10	10	☐	☐
736		6d purple	20	20	☐	☐
737	**282a**	7d emerald	40	30	☐	☐
738		8d vermilion	20	50	☐	☐
739		8d turquoise-blue	60	75	☐	☐
740		9d green	50	25	☐	☐
741	**282**	10d drab	55	40	☐	☐
742		1s violet	50	25	☐	☐
743		1s 6d blue and deep blue .	50	35	☐	☐
		c. *Phosphorised paper* .	80	90	☐	☐
744		1s 9d orange and black . .	50	40	☐	☐
		Set of 16 (one of each value and colour)	4·25	4·50	☐	☐
		Presentation Pack (one of each value)	8·00		☐	
		Presentation Pack (German) . . .	40·00		☐	

First Day Covers

5 June 1967	Nos. 731, 742, 744	3·00 ☐
8 Aug. 1967	Nos. 729, 740, 743	3·00 ☐
5 Feb. 1968	Nos. 723/4, 726, 736	3·00 ☐
1 July 1968	Nos. 735, 737/8, 741	3·00 ☐

No. 734 exists with phosphor band at the left or right.

283 'Master Lambton' (Sir Thomas Lawrence)   **284** 'Mares and Foals in a Landscape' (George Stubbs)

285 'Children Coming Out of School' (L. S. Lowry)

British Paintings
1967 (10 JULY) *Two phosphor bands. No wmk*

748	**283**	4d multicoloured	10	10	☐	☐
749	**284**	9d multicoloured	15	20	☐	☐
750	**285**	1s 6d multicoloured	35	40	☐	☐
		Set of 3	50	60	☐	☐
		First Day Cover		5·00		☐
		Presentation Pack	7·00		☐	

286 *Gipsy Moth IV*

Sir Francis Chichester's World Voyage
1967 (24 JULY) *Three phosphor bands. No wmk*

751	**286**	1s 9d multicoloured	25	25	☐	☐
		First Day Cover		2·75		☐

287 Radar Screen   **288** *Penicillium notatum*

289 Vickers VC-10 Jet Engines   **290** Television Equipment

British Discovery and Invention

1967 (19 SEPT.) *Two phosphor bands* (*except* 4d. *three bands*). *Wmk* **179** (*sideways on* 1s 9d)

752	**287**	4d yellow, black and ver-milion	. . . . . .	10	10	□	□
753	**288**	1s multicoloured	. . . .	10	15	□	□
754	**289**	1s 6d multicoloured	. . . .	25	30	□	□
755	**290**	1s 9d multicoloured	. . . .	25	35	□	□
		Set of 4	. . . .	60	80	□	□
		First Day Cover	. . . .		4·00		□
		Presentation Pack	. . . .	3·00			□

NO WATERMARK. All the following issues are on un-watermarked paper unless otherwise stated.

291 'The Adoration of the Shepherds' (School of Seville)   **292** 'Madonna and Child' (Murillo)

293 'The Adoration of the Shepherds' (Louis Le Nain)

Christmas

1967 *Two phosphor bands* (*except* 3d, *one phosphor band*)

756	**291**	3d multicoloured (27 Nov.)	. . . .	10	15	□	□
757	**292**	4d multicoloured (18 Oct.)	. . . .	10	10	□	□

758	**293**	1s 6d multicoloured (27 Nov.)	. . . .	20	40	□	□
		Set of 3	. . . .	35	60	□	□
		First Day Covers (2)	. . . .		5·00		□

Gift Pack 1967

1967 (27 Nov.) *Comprises Nos.* 715p/22p *and* 748/58

	Gift Pack	. . . .	3·00	□

1967–68 *No wmk. Perf* 11 × 12

759	**166**	2s 6d brown	. . . .	40	50	□	□
760	**167**	5s red	. . . .	1·00	1·00	□	□
761	**168**	10s blue	. . . .	5·50	8·25	□	□
762	**169**	£1 black	. . . .	4·50	6·75	□	□
		Set of 4	. . . .	10·00	15·00	□	□

294 Tarr Steps, Exmoor   **295** Aberfeldy Bridge

296 Menai Bridge   **297** M4 Viaduct

British Bridges

1968 (29 APR.) *Two phosphor bands*

763	**294**	4d multicoloured	. . . .	10	10	□	□
764	**295**	9d multicoloured	. . . .	10	10	□	□
765	**296**	1s 6d multicoloured	. . . .	20	30	□	□
766	**297**	1s 9d multicoloured	. . . .	25	40	□	□
		Set of 4	. . . .	50	80	□	□
		First Day Cover	. . . .		3·50		□
		Presentation Pack	. . . .	2·50			□

298 'TUC' and Trades Unionists   **299** Mrs Emmeline Pankhurst (statue)

300 Sopwith Camel and English Electric Lightning Fighters   **301** Captain Cook's *Endeavour* and Signature

British Anniversaries. Events described on stamps

1968 (29 MAY) *Two phosphor bands*

767	**298**	4d multicoloured	10	10 □ □
768	**299**	9d violet, grey and black	10	15 □ □
769	**300**	1s multicoloured	35	35 □ □
770	**301**	1s 9d ochre and brown . .	40	50 □ □
		Set of 4	85	1·00 □ □
		First Day Cover		8·00 □
		Presentation Pack	3·00	□

302 'Queen Elizabeth I' (Unknown Artist)

303 'Pinkie' (Lawrence)

304 'Ruins of St Mary Le Port' (Piper)

305 'The Hay Wain' (Constable)

British Paintings

1968 (12 AUG.) *Two phosphor bands*

771	**302**	4d multicoloured	10	10 □ □
772	**303**	1s multicoloured	10	20 □ □
773	**304**	1s 6d multicoloured	20	30 □ □
774	**305**	1s 9d multicoloured	25	50 □ □
		Set of 4	50	1·00 □ □
		First Day Cover		3·50 □
		Presentation Pack	3·00	□
		Presentation Pack (German) . . .	6·00	□

Gift Pack 1968

1968 (16 SEPT.) *Comprises Nos. 763/74*

	Gift Pack	8·00	□
	Gift Pack (German)	20·00	□

Collectors Pack 1968

1968 (16 SEPT.) *Comprises Nos. 752/8 and 763/74*

	Collectors Pack	9·00	□

306 Girl and Boy with Rocking Horse

307 Girl with Doll's House

308 Boy with Train Set

Christmas

1968 (25 Nov.) *Two phosphor bands (except 4d, one centre phosphor band)*

775	**306**	4d multicoloured	10	10 □ □
776	**307**	9d multicoloured	15	25 □ □
777	**308**	1s 6d multicoloured	15	40 □ □
		Set of 3	35	65 □ □
		First Day Cover		4·00 □
		Presentation Pack	3·75	□
		Presentation Pack (German) . . .	5·00	□

RMS Queen Elizabeth 2

309 *Queen Elizabeth 2*

310 Elizabethan Galleon

311 East Indiaman

312 *Cutty Sark*

313   *Great Britain*

314   *Mauretania I*

The 9d and 1s values were arranged in horizontal strips of three and pairs respectively throughout the sheet.

British Ships

1969 (15 JAN.) *One horiz phosphor band (5d), two phosphor bands (9d) or two vert phosphor bands at right (1s)*

778	**309**	5d multicoloured	10	10	□	□
779	**310**	9d multicoloured	10	15	□	□
		a. Strip of 3. Nos. 779/81	1·75	3·00	□	□
780	**311**	9d multicoloured	10	15	□	□
781	**312**	9d multicoloured	10	15	□	□
782	**313**	1s multicoloured	40	30	□	□
		a. Pair. Nos. 782/3 . . .	1·50	2·50	□	□
783	**314**	1s multicoloured	40	30	□	□
		Set of 6	2·50	1·00	□	□
		First Day Cover		7·00		□
		Presentation Pack	4·50		□	
		Presentation Pack (German) . . .	20·00		□	

315   Concorde in Flight

316   Plan and Elevation Views

317   Concorde's Nose and Tail

First Flight of Concorde

1969 (3 MAR.) *Two phosphor bands*

784	**315**	4d multicoloured	10	10	□	□
785	**316**	9d multicoloured	15	30	□	□

786	**317**	1s 6d deep blue, grey and light blue	20	40	□	□
		Set of 3	40	70	□	□
		First Day Cover		4·00		□
		Presentation Pack	3·50		□	
		Presentation Pack (German) . . .	15·00		□	

318   (See also Type **357a**)

1969 (5 MAR.) *P 12*

787	**318**	2s 6d brown	50	30	□	□
788		5s lake	2·25	60	□	□
789		10s ultramarine	7·00	6·50	□	□
790		£1 black	3·00	2·00	□	□
		Set of 4	11·50	8·50	□	□
		First Day Cover		10·00		□
		Presentation Pack	18·00		□	
		Presentation Pack (German) . . .	38·00		□	

319   Page from the *Daily Mail,* and Vickers FB-27 Vimy Aircraft

320   Europa and C.E.P.T. Emblems

321   I.L.O. Emblem

322   Flags of N.A.T.O. Countries

323   Vickers FB-27 Vimy Aircraft and Globe showing Flight

Anniversaries. Events described on stamps

1969 (2 APR.) *Two phosphor bands*

791	**319**	5d multicoloured	10	10	□	□
792	**320**	9d multicoloured	15	20	□	□

793	**321**	1s claret, red and blue .	15	20 ☐ ☐
794	**322**	1s 6d multicoloured	15	25 ☐ ☐
795	**323**	1s 9d olive, yellow and		
		turquoise-green . . .	15	30 ☐ ☐
		Set of 5	60	90 ☐ ☐
		First Day Cover		5·50 ☐
		Presentation Pack	3·75	☐
		Presentation Pack (*German*) . . .	40·00	☐

324 Durham Cathedral

325 York Minster

326 St Giles' Cathedral,
Edinburgh

327 Canterbury Cathedral

The above were issued together *se-tenant* in blocks of four within the sheet.

328 St Paul's Cathedral

329 Liverpool Metropolitan Cathedral

British Architecture (Cathedrals)

1969 (28 MAY) *Two phosphor bands*

796	**324**	5d multicoloured	10	10 ☐ ☐
		a. Block of 4. *Nos.* 796/9	85	2·50 ☐ ☐
797	**325**	5d multicoloured	10	10 ☐ ☐
798	**326**	5d multicoloured	10	10 ☐ ☐
799	**327**	5d multicoloured	10	10 ☐ ☐
800	**328**	9d multicoloured	15	15 ☐ ☐
801	**329**	1s 6d multicoloured	15	15 ☐ ☐
		Set of 6	1·00	60 ☐ ☐
		First Day Cover		5·50 ☐
		Presentation Pack	4·00	☐
		Presentation Pack (*German*) . . .	20·00	☐

330 The King's Gate,
Caernarvon Castle

331 The Eagle Tower,
Caernarvon Castle

332 Queen Eleanor's Gate,
Caernarvon Castle

333 Celtic Cross,
Margam Abbey

The 5d values were printed *se-tenant* in strips of three throughout the sheet

334 Prince Charles

Investiture of H.R.H. The Prince of Wales

1969 (1 JULY) *Two phosphor bands*

802	**330**	5d multicoloured	10	10 ☐ ☐
		a. Strip of 3. *Nos.* 802/4	30	1·50 ☐ ☐
803	**331**	5d multicoloured	10	10 ☐ ☐
804	**332**	5d multicoloured	10	10 ☐ ☐
805	**333**	9d multicoloured	15	10 ☐ ☐
806	**334**	1s black and gold	15	10 ☐ ☐
		Set of 5	50	45 ☐ ☐
		First Day Cover		3·00 ☐
		Presentation Pack	3·00	☐
		Presentation Pack (*German*) . . .	16·00	☐

335 Mahatma Gandhi

Gandhi Centenary Year
1969 (13 Aug.) *Two phosphor bands*

807	**335**	1s 6d multicoloured	25	30 ☐	☐
		First Day Cover		2·50	☐

Collectors Pack 1969
1969 (15 Sept.) *Comprises Nos. 775/86 and 791/807*

Collectors Pack	20·00	☐

336 National Giro **337** Telecommunications — International Subscriber Dialling

338 Telecommunications — Pulse Code Modulation **339** Postal Mechanisation — Automatic Sorting

British Post Office Technology
1969 (1 Oct.) *Two phosphor bands. Perf* $13\frac{1}{2} \times 14$

808	**336**	5d multicoloured	10	10 ☐	☐
809	**337**	9d green, blue and black	20	20 ☐	☐
810	**338**	1s green, lavender and black	20	20 ☐	☐
811	**339**	1s 6d multicoloured	25	40 ☐	☐
		Set of 4	70	80 ☐	☐
		First Day Cover		3·00	☐
		Presentation Pack	3·50		☐

340 Herald Angel **341** The Three Shepherds

342 The Three Kings

Christmas
1969 (26 Nov.) *Two phosphor bands (5d, 1s 6d) or one centre band (4d)*

812	**340**	4d multicoloured	10	10 ☐	☐
813	**341**	5d multicoloured	15	20 ☐	☐
814	**342**	1s 6d multicoloured	20	40 ☐	☐
		Set of 3	40	60 ☐	☐
		First Day Cover		2·50	☐
		Presentation Pack	3·00		☐

343 Fife Harling **344** Cotswold Limestone

345 Welsh Stucco **346** Ulster Thatch

British Rural Architecture
1970 (11 Feb.) *Two phosphor bands*

815	**343**	5d multicoloured	10	10 ☐	☐
816	**344**	9d multicoloured	10	20 ☐	☐
817	**345**	1s multicoloured	15	20 ☐	☐
818	**346**	1s 6d multicoloured	20	40 ☐	☐
		Set of 4	50	80 ☐	☐
		First Day Cover		3·50	☐
		Presentation Pack	3·75		☐

347 Signing the Declaration of Arbroath **348** Florence Nightingale attending Patients

349 Signing of International Co-operative Alliance **350** Pilgrims and *Mayflower*

351 Sir William Herschel, Francis
Baily, Sir John Herschel and
Telescope

Anniversaries. Events described on stamps

1970 (1 APR.) *Two phosphor bands*

819	**347**	5d multicoloured	. . . .	10	10 □	□
820	**348**	9d multicoloured	. . . .	15	15 □	□
821	**349**	1s multicoloured	. . . .	25	35 □	□
822	**350**	1s 6d multicoloured	. . . .	25	35 □	□
823	**351**	1s 9d multicoloured	. . . .	25	35 □	□
		Set of 5	. . . .	90	1·10 □	□
		First Day Cover	. . . .		4·50	□
		Presentation Pack	. . . .	3·75		□

| 352 | 'Mr Pickwick and Sam' (*Pickwick Papers*) | 353 | 'Mr and Mrs Micawber' (*David Copperfield*) | 354 | 'David Copperfield and Betsy Trotwood' (*David Copperfield*) |

| 355 | 'Oliver asking for more' (*Oliver Twist*) | 356 | 'Grasmere' (from engraving by J. Farrington, R.A.) |

The 5d values were issued together *se-tenant* in blocks of four within the sheet.

Literary Anniversaries. Events described on stamps

1970 (3 JUNE) *Two phosphor bands*

824	**352**	5d multicoloured	. . . .	10	15 □	□
		a. Block of 4. Nos. 824/7		1·00	2·00 □	□
825	**353**	5d multicoloured	. . . .	10	15 □	□

826	**354**	5d multicoloured	. . . .	10	15 □	□
827	**355**	5d multicoloured	. . . .	10	15 □	□
828	**356**	1s 6d multicoloured	. . . .	20	25 □	□
		Set of 5	. . . .	1·00	75 □	□
		First Day Cover	. . . .		5·00	□
		Presentation Pack	. . . .	4·00		□

356a   357 (Value redrawn)

Decimal Currency

1970 (17 JUNE)–**72** *10p and some printings of the 50p were issued on phosphor paper. Perf 12*

829	**356a**	10p cerise	. . . .	50	75 □	□
830		20p olive-green	. . . . .	50	25 □	□
831		50p ultramarine	. . . . .	1·00	40 □	□
831b	**357**	£1 black (6 Dec. 1972)	. .	5·00	90 □	□
		Set of 4	. . . .	6·25	2·10 □	□
		First Day Cover (Nos. 829/31)	. .		2·75	□
		First Day Cover (No. 831b)	. . . .		3·00	□
		Presentation Pack (P.O Pack No. 18)				
		(Nos. 829/31)	. . . .	9·00		□
		Presentation Pack (P.O Pack No. 38)				
		(Nos. 830/1, 790 or 831b)	. . .	9·50		□

358 Runners   359 Swimmers

360 Cyclists

Ninth British Commonwealth Games, Edinburgh

1970 (15 JULY) *Two phosphor bands. Perf 13½ × 14*

832	**358**	5d pink, emerald, greenish yellow and yellow-green	10	10 □	□
833	**359**	1s 6d greenish blue, lilac, brown and Prussian blue	35	50 □	□

834	**360**	1s 9d yellow-orange, lilac, salmon and red-brown	. . . .	35	50	☐	☐
		Set of 3	. . . .	75	1·00	☐	☐
		First Day Cover	. . . .		2·50		☐
		Presentation Pack	. . . .	3·00		☐	

Collectors Pack 1970

1970 (14 SEPT.) *Comprises Nos. 808/28 and 832/4*

| | Collectors Pack | . . . . | 22·00 | | ☐ |

361 1d Black (1840)

362 1s Green (1847)

363 4d Carmine (1855)

'Philympia 70' Stamp Exhibition

1970 (18 SEPT.) *Two phosphor bands. Perf 14 × 14½*

835	**361**	5d multicoloured	. . . .	10	10	☐	☐
836	**362**	9d multicoloured	. . . .	20	40	☐	☐
837	**363**	1s 6d multicoloured	. . . .	20	50	☐	☐
		Set of 3	. . . .	45	90	☐	☐
		First Day Cover	. . . .		2·75		☐
		Presentation Pack	. . . .	3·00		☐	

364 Shepherds and Apparition of the Angel

365 Mary, Joseph and Christ in the Manger

366 The Wise Men bearing Gifts

Christmas

1970 (25 NOV.) *Two phosphor bands (5d, 1s 6d) or one centre phosphor band (4d)*

838	**364**	4d multicoloured	. . . .	10	10	☐	☐
839	**365**	5d multicoloured	. . . .	15	15	☐	☐
840	**366**	1s 6d multicoloured	. . . .	20	30	☐	☐
		Set of 3	. . . .	40	50	☐	☐
		First Day Cover	. . . .		2·75		☐
		Presentation Pack	. . . .	3·00		☐	

PRINTING PROCESSES

There is a basic distinction between stamps printed by photogravure and those printed by lithography. Sorting the two is not as difficult as it sounds and with a little experience it should become easy to tell which method of production was employed for a particular stamp.

The tiny dots of the printing screen give uneven edges to the values on photogravure stamps (right). Litho values have clean, clear outlines (left).

All you need is a reasonably good glass giving a magnification of ×4 or more (×10 is even better!).

The image on a photogravure stamp is created from a pattern or 'screen', of minute dots which are not evident when looking at the stamp without a glass but show up quite clearly under magnification, especially in the Queen's face and around the margin of the stamp design where it meets the white background of the paper. Now look at the value; here also, what looks to the naked eye like a straight line is in fact made up of rows of tiny little dots.

'Screens' of dots are also used in the production of litho printed stamps but they are only required where the printer is attempting to produce shades and tints as is necessary in the Queen's head portion of the stamp. Where solid colour is used, as in the background of the majority of values, there is no need to resort to a screen of dots and the background is printed as a solid mass of colour. If you look at the margins or the values of stamps produced in this way you will not see any evidence of dots—just a clear clean break between the inked portion of the stamp and the uninked white of the paper.

367

367a

Decimal Currency
1971–96. *Type* **367**

(*a*) *Printed in photogravure by Harrison and Sons (except for some ptgs of Nos. X879 and X913 which were produced by Enschedé) with phosphor bands. Perf* 15 × 14

X841	½p turquoise-blue (2 bands)	10	10	□	□
X842	½p turquoise-blue (1 side band)	45·00	30·00	□	□
X843	½p turquoise-blue (1 centre band)	40	25	□	□
X844	1p crimson (2 bands) . . .	10	15	□	□
X845	1p crimson (1 centre band)	20	15	□	□
X846	1p crimson ('all-over' phosphor)	15	25	□	□
X847	1p crimson (1 side band) .	1·00	1·40	□	□
X848	1½p black (2 bands)	20	20	□	□
X849	2p myrtle-green (face value as in T **367**) (2 bands) .	10	20	□	□
X850	2p myrtle-green (face value as in T **367**) ('all-over' phosphor)	20	25	□	□
X851	2½p magenta (1 centre band)	20	15	□	□
X852	2½p magenta (1 side band) .	1·00	2·00	□	□
X853	2½p magenta (2 bands) . . .	30	60	□	□
X854	2½p rose-red (2 bands) . . .	50	90	□	□
X855	3p ultramarine (2 bands) .	20	15	□	□
X856	3p ultramarine (1 centre band)	15	20	□	□
X857	3p bright magenta (2 bands)	30	45	□	□
X858	3½p olive-grey (2 bands) . .	25	25	□	□
X859	3½p olive-grey (1 centre band)	30	20	□	□
X860	3½p purple-brown (1 centre band)	1·25	1·25	□	□
X861	4p ochre-brown (2 bands)	20	20	□	□
X862	4p greenish blue (2 bands)	1·75	2·00	□	□
X863	4p greenish blue (1 centre band)	1·50	1·90	□	□
X864	4p greenish blue (1 side band)	2·00	2·25	□	□
X865	4½p grey-blue (2 bands) . .	25	30	□	□
X866	5p pale violet (2 bands) . .	15	15	□	□
X867	5p claret (1 centre band) .	1·75	2·25	□	□
X868	5½p violet (2 bands)	25	30	□	□
X869	5½p violet (1 centre band) .	25	30	□	□
X870	6p light emerald (2 bands)	25	20	□	□
X871	6½p greenish blue (2 bands)	35	45	□	□
X872	6½p greenish blue (1 centre band)	30	10	□	□
X873	6½p greenish blue (1 side band)	50	70	□	□
X874	7p purple-brown (2 bands)	40	40	□	□
X875	7p purple-brown (1 centre band)	30	30	□	□
X876	7p purple-brown (1 side band)	45	80	□	□
X877	7½p chestnut (2 bands) . . .	25	30	□	□
X878	8p rosine (2 bands) . . .	25	40	□	□
X879	8p rosine (1 centre band) .	25	40	□	□
X880	8p rosine (1 side band) . .	70	90	□	□
X881	8½p yellowish green (2 bands)	25	25	□	□
X882	9p yellow-orange and black (2 bands)	50	60	□	□
X883	9p deep violet (2 bands) .	35	40	□	□
X884	9½p purple (2 bands)	35	45	□	□
X885	10p orange-brown and chestnut (2 bands) . .	25	25	□	□
X886	10p orange-brown (2 bands)	25	25	□	□
X887	10p orange-brown ('all-over' phosphor)	35	45	□	□
X888	10p orange-brown (1 centre band)	35	35	□	□
X889	10p orange-brown (1 side band)	70	90	□	□
X890	10½p yellow (2 bands)	45	50	□	□
X891	10½p blue (2 bands)	60	60	□	□
X892	11p brown-red (2 bands) . .	50	60	□	□
X893	11½p drab (1 centre band) . .	40	40	□	□
X894	11½p drab (1 side band) . . .	50	75	□	□
X895	12p yellowish green (2 bands)	45	45	□	□
X896	12p bright emerald (1 centre band)	45	45	□	□
X897	12p bright emerald (1 side band)	1·00	1·10	□	□
X898	12½p light emerald (1 centre band)	50	50	□	□
X899	12½p light emerald (1 side band)	80	80	□	□
X900	13p pale chestnut (1 centre band)	35	45	□	□
X901	13p pale chestnut (1 side band)	50	60	□	□
X902	14p grey-blue (2 bands) . .	95	75	□	□
X903	14p deep blue (1 centre band)	50	50	□	□
X904	14p deep blue (1 side band)	3·00	3·50	□	□
X905	15p bright blue (1 centre band)	75	75	□	□
X906	15p bright blue (1 side band)	3·00	3·00	□	□
X907	15½p pale violet (2 bands) . .	70	70	□	□
X908	16p olive-drab (2 bands) . .	1·40	1·50	□	□
X909	17p grey-blue (2 bands) . .	65	65	□	□
X910	17p deep blue (1 centre band)	1·00	1·00	□	□
X911	17p deep blue (1 side band)	1·50	1·50	□	□
X912	18p deep olive-grey (2 bands	75	1·00	□	□
X913	18p bright green (1 centre band)	60	40	□	□

			Un	Used		
X914	19p	bright orange-red (2 bands)	1·50	1·75	□	□
X915	20p	dull purple (2 bands)	1·00	45	□	□
X916	20p	brownish black (2 bands)	1·50	2·25	□	□
X917	22p	bright orange-red (2 bands)	1·25	1·25	□	□
X917a	25p	rose-red (2 bands)	5·00	3·50	□	□
X918	26p	rosine (2 bands)	6·50	8·50	□	□
X919	31p	purple (2 bands)	12·00	12·00	□	□
X920	34p	ochre-brown (2 bands)	6·00	8·00	□	□
X921	50p	ochre-brown (2 bands)	2·00	50	□	□
X922	50p	ochre (2 bands)	5·00	5·50	□	□

(b) *Printed in photogravure by Harrison and Sons on phosphorised paper. Perf* 15 × 14

X924	½p	turquoise-blue	10	15	□	
X925	1p	crimson	10	15	□	□
X926	2p	myrtle-green (face value as in T 367)	10	20	□	□
X927	2p	deep green (smaller value as in T 367a)	10	20	□	□
X928	2p	myrtle-green (smaller value as in T 367a)	2·50	2·50	□	
X929	2½p	rose-red	10	15	□	□
X930	3p	bright magenta	10	30	□	□
X931	3½p	purple-brown	50	60	□	□
X932	4p	greenish blue	60	70	□	□
X933	4p	new blue	20	25	□	□
X934	5p	pale violet	20	20	□	□
X935	5p	dull red-brown	20	30	□	□
X936	6p	yellow-olive	25	30	□	□
X937	7p	brownish red	1·25	2·00	□	□
X938	8½p	yellowish green	40	60	□	□
X939	10p	orange-brown	30	30	□	□
X940	10p	dull orange	50	40	□	□
X941	11p	brown-red	75	90	□	□
X942	11½p	ochre-brown	50	60	□	□
X943	12p	yellowish green	45	45	□	□
X944	13p	olive-grey	45	50	□	□
X945	13½p	purple-brown	50	70	□	□
X946	14p	grey-blue	50	50	□	□
X947	15p	ultramarine	60	60	□	□
X948	15½p	pale violet	60	50	□	□
X949	16p	olive-drab	45	40	□	□
X950	16½p	pale chestnut	85	1·00	□	□
X951	17p	light emerald	70	60	□	□
X952	17p	grey-blue	55	55	□	□
X953	17½p	pale chestnut	70	90	□	□
X954	18p	deep violet	80	80	□	□
X955	18p	deep olive-grey	75	60	□	□
X956	19p	bright orange-red	1·00	70	□	□
X957	19½p	olive-grey	1·60	1·60	□	□
X958	20p	dull purple	85	15	□	□
X959	20p	turquoise-green	1·25	80	□	□
X960	20p	brownish black	90	60	□	□
X961	20½p	ultramarine	1·60	1·50	□	□
X962	22p	blue	85	70	□	□
X963	22p	yellow-green	95	80	□	□
X964	22p	bright orange-red	1·10	90	□	□
X965	23p	brown-red	1·25	80	□	□
X966	23p	bright green	80	80	□	□
X967	24p	violet	1·75	1·25	□	□
X968	24p	Indian red	2·00	1·40	□	□
X969	24p	chestnut	90	50	□	□
X970	25p	purple	1·00	1·00	□	□
X971	26p	rosine	1·25	60	□	□
X972	26p	drab	1·50	1·25	□	□
X973	27p	chestnut	1·40	1·40	□	□
X974	27p	violet	1·50	1·25	□	□
X975	28p	deep violet	1·40	1·40	□	□
X976	28p	ochre	1·50	1·25	□	□
X977	28p	deep bluish grey	1·60	1·25	□	□
X978	29p	ochre-brown	2·00	1·75	□	□
X979	29p	deep mauve	2·40	1·60	□	□
X980	30p	deep olive-grey	1·25	1·25	□	□
X981	31p	purple	1·00	1·50	□	□
X982	31p	ultramarine	1·60	1·50	□	□
X983	32p	greenish blue	1·90	1·75	□	□
X984	33p	light emerald	1·75	1·50	□	□
X985	34p	ochre-brown	1·90	1·90	□	□
X986	34p	deep bluish grey	2·25	1·90	□	□
X987	34p	deep mauve	1·75	1·75	□	□
X988	35p	sepia	1·50	1·25	□	□
X989	35p	yellow	1·75	1·60	□	□
X990	37p	rosine	2·25	1·75	□	□
X991	39p	bright mauve	1·90	1·60	□	□

(c) *Printed in photogravure by Harrison and Sons on ordinary paper. Perf* 15 × 14

X992	50p	ochre-brown	1·50	50	□	□
X993	75p	grey-black (smaller values as T 367a)	2·25	2·00	□	□

(d) *Printed in photogravure by Harrison and Sons on ordinary paper or phosphorised paper. Perf* 15 × 14

X994	50p	ochre	2·00	75	□	□

(e) *Printed in lithography by John Waddington. Perf* 14

X996	4p	greenish blue (2 bands)	20	25	□	□
X997	4p	greenish blue (phosphorised paper)	25	30	□	□
X998	20p	dull purple (2 bands)	1·25	40	□	□
X999	20p	dull purple (phosphorised paper)	1·75	40	□	□

(f) *Printed in lithography by Questa. Perf* 14 (*Nos* X1000, X1003/4 *and* X1023) *or* 15 × 14 (*others*)

X1000	2p	emerald-green (face value as in T 367) (phosphorised paper)	20	20	□	□
		a. Perf 15 × 14	25	25	□	□
X1001	2p	bright green and deep green (smaller value as in T 367a) (phosphorised paper)	75	50	□	□
X1002	4p	greenish blue (phosphorised paper)	60	60	□	□

X1003	5p light violet				
	(phosphorised paper) .	20	20	☐	☐
X1004	5p claret (phosphorised				
	paper)	25	30	☐	☐
	a. Perf 15 × 14	70	50	☐	☐
X1005	13p pale chestnut (1 centre				
	band)	90	90	☐	☐
X1006	13p pale chestnut (1 side				
	band)	1·00	1·00	☐	☐
X1007	14p deep blue (1 centre				
	band)	1·50	1·50	☐	☐
X1008	17p deep blue (1 centre				
	band)	80	80	☐	☐
X1009	18p deep olive-grey				
	(phosphorised paper) .	1·00	70	☐	☐
X1010	18p deep olive-grey (2				
	bands)	6·50	6·50	☐	☐
X1011	18p bright green (1 centre				
	band)	1·25	1·25	☐	☐
X1012	18p bright green (1 side				
	band)	2·00	1·75	☐	☐
X1013	19p bright orange-red				
	(phosphorised paper) .	2·50	2·25	☐	☐
X1014	20p dull purple				
	(phosphorised paper) .	1·75	1·75	☐	☐
X1015	22p yellow-green (2 bands)	9·50	9·50	☐	☐
X1016	22p bright orange-red				
	(phosphorised paper) .	90	1·00	☐	☐
X1017	24p chestnut (phosphorised				
	paper)	1·75	1·75	☐	☐
X1018	24p chestnut (2 bands) . . .	1·90	1·90	☐	☐
X1019	33p light emerald				
	(phosphorised paper) .	2·75	2·00	☐	☐
X1020	33p light emerald (2 bands)	1·10	1·50	☐	☐
X1021	34p bistre-brown (2 bands)	8·00	7·50	☐	☐
X1022	39p bright mauve (2 bands)	1·75	2·50	☐	☐
X1023	75p black (face value as				
	T **367**) (ordinary paper)	2·25	75	☐	☐
	a. Perf 15 × 14	3·00	2·50	☐	☐
X1024	75p brownish grey and				
	black (smaller value as				
	T **367a**) (ordinary paper)	8·00	8·00	☐	☐

(g) Printed in lithography by Walsall. Perf 14

X1050	2p deep green				
	(phosphorised paper) .	1·00	1·25	☐	☐
X1051	14p deep blue (1 side band)	3·75	3·50	☐	☐
X1052	19p bright orange-red (2				
	bands)	2·50	2·25	☐	☐
X1053	24p chestnut (phosphorised				
	paper)	1·10	1·50	☐	☐
X1054	29p deep mauve (2 bands) .	2·75	3·50	☐	☐
X1055	29p deep mauve				
	(phosphorised paper) .	3·75	5·75	☐	☐
X1056	31p ultramarine				
	(phosphorised paper) .	1·75	1·75	☐	☐
X1057	33p light emerald				
	(phosphorised paper) .	1·50	1·60	☐	☐
X1058	39p bright mauve				
	(phosphorised paper) .	1·90	2·00	☐	☐

Presentation Pack (P.O. Pack No. 26)
(*contains* ½p (X841), 1p (X844), 1½p (X848), 2p (X849), 2½p (X851), 3p (X855), 3½p (X858), 4p (X861), 5p (X866), 6p (X870), 7½p (X877), 9p (X882)) . . . . 5·00 ☐

Presentation Pack (*'Scandinavia 71'*) (*contents as above*) . . . . 35·00 ☐

Presentation Pack (P.O. Pack No. 37)
(*contains* ½p (X841), 1p (X844), 1½p (X848), 2p (X849), 2½p (X851), 3p (X855 *or* X856), 3½p (X858 *or* X859), 4p (X861), 4½p (X865), 5p (X866), 5½p (X868 *or* X869), 6p (X870), 6½p (X871 *or* X872), 7p (X874), 7½p (X877), 8p (X878), 9p (X882), 10p (X885)) . . . 5·00 ☐

Presentation Pack (P.O. Pack No. 90)
(*contains* ½p (X841), 1p (X844), 1½p (X848), 2p (X849), 2½p (X851), 3p (X856), 5p (X866), 6½p (X872), 7p (X874 *or* X875), 7½p (X877), 8p (X878), 8½p (X881), 9p (X883), 9½p (X884), 10p (X886), 10½p (X890), 11p (X892), 20p (X915), 50p (X921)) . . . 6·00 ☐

Presentation Pack (P.O. Pack No. 129a)
(*contains* 2½p (X929), 3p (X930), 4p (X996), 10½p (X891), 11½p (X893), 11½p (X942), 12p (X943), 13p (X944), 13½p (X945), 14p (X946), 15p (X947), 15½p (X948), 17p (X951), 17½p (X953), 18p (X954), 22p (X962), 25p (X970), 75p (X1023) . . . . 18·00 ☐

Presentation Pack (P.O. Pack No. 1)
(*contains* ½p (X924), 1p (X925), 2p (X1000), 3p (X930), 3½p (X931), 4p (X997), 5p (X1004), 10p (X888), 12½p (X898), 16p (X949), 16½p (X950), 17p (X952), 20p (X999), 20½p (X961), 23p (X965), 26p (X971), 28p (X975), 31p (X981), 50p (X992), 75p (X1023)) . . 25·00 ☐

Presentation Pack (P.O. Pack No. 5)
(*contains* ½p (X924), 1p (X925), 2p (X1000a), 3p (X930), 4p (X997), 5p (X1004a), 10p (X939), 13p (X900), 16p (X949), 17p (X952), 18p (X955), 20p (X999), 22p (X963), 24p (X967), 26p (X971), 28p (X975), 31p (X981), 34p (X985), 50p (X992), 75p (X1023a)) . . . . 24·00 ☐

Presentation Pack (P.O. Pack No. 9)
(contains 1p (X925), 2p (X1000a), 3p
(X930), 4p (X997), 5p (X1004a), 7p
(X937), 10p (X939), 12p (X896), 13p
(X900), 17p (X952), 18p (X955), 20p
(X999), 22p (X963), 24p (X967), 26p
(X971), 28p (X975), 31p (X981), 34p
(X985), 50p (X992), 75p (X1023a))   25·00   ☐

Presentation Pack (P.O. Pack No. 15)
(contains 14p (X903), 19p (X956),
20p (X959), 23p (X966), 27p (X973),
28p (X976), 32p (X983), 35p (X988))   11·00   ☐

Presentation Pack (P.O. Pack No. 19)
(contains 15p (X905), 20p (X960),
24p (X968), 29p (X979), 30p (X980),
34p (X986), 37p (X990)) . . . .   13·00   ☐

Presentation Pack (P.O. Pack No. 22)
(contains 10p (X940), 17p (X910),
22p (X964), 26p (X972), 27p (X974),
31p (X982), 33p (X984)) . . . .   12·00   ☐

Presentation Pack (P.O. Pack No. 24)
(contains 1p (X925), 2p (X927), 3p
(X930), 4p (X933), 5p (X935), 10p
(X940), 17p (X910), 20p (X959), 22p
(X964), 26p (X972), 27p (X974), 30p
(X980), 31p (X982), 32p (X983), 33p
(X984), 37p (X990), 50p (X994), 75p
(X993)) . . . .   22·00   ☐

Presentation Pack (P.O. Pack No. 25)
(contains 6p (X936), 18p (X913), 24p
(X969), 28p (X977), 34p (X987), 35p
(X989), 39p (X991)) . . . .   12·00   ☐

First Day Covers

15 Feb. 1971	$\frac{1}{2}$p, 1p, 1$\frac{1}{2}$p, 2p, 2$\frac{1}{2}$p, 3p, 3$\frac{1}{2}$p, 4p, 5p, 6p, 7$\frac{1}{2}$p, 9p (Nos. X841, X844, X848/9, X851, X855, X858, X861, X866, X870, X877, X882) (Covers carry 'POSTING DELAYED BY THE POST OFFICE STRIKE 1971' cachet)	2·75	☐
11 Aug. 1971	10p (No. X885)	2·00	☐
24 Oct. 1973	4$\frac{1}{2}$p, 5$\frac{1}{2}$p, 8p (Nos. X865, X868, X878)	2·00	☐
4 Sept. 1974	6$\frac{1}{2}$p (No. X871)	2·00	☐
15 Jan. 1975	7p (No. X874)	2·00	☐
24 Sept. 1975	8$\frac{1}{2}$p (No. X881)	2·00	☐
25 Feb. 1976	9p, 9$\frac{1}{2}$p, 10p, 10$\frac{1}{2}$p, 11p, 20p (Nos. X883/4, X886, X890, X892, X915)	3·00	☐

2 Feb. 1977	50p (No. X921)	2·00	☐
26 April 1978	10$\frac{1}{2}$p (No. X891)	2·00	☐
15 Aug. 1979	11$\frac{1}{2}$p, 13p, 15p (Nos. X942, X944, X947)	2·00	☐
30 Jan. 1980	4p, 12p, 13$\frac{1}{2}$p, 17p, 17$\frac{1}{2}$p, 75p (Nos. X996, X943, X945, X951, X953, X1023)	3·00	☐
22 Oct. 1980	3p, 22p (Nos. X930, X962) . . .	2·00	☐
14 Jan. 1981	2$\frac{1}{2}$p, 11$\frac{1}{2}$p, 14p, 15$\frac{1}{2}$p, 18p, 25p (Nos. X929, X893, X946, X948, X954, X970)	2·00	☐
27 Jan. 1982	5p, 12$\frac{1}{2}$p, 16$\frac{1}{2}$p, 19$\frac{1}{2}$p, 26p, 29p (Nos. X1004, X898, X950, X957, X971, X978)	3·00	☐
30 Mar. 1983	3$\frac{1}{2}$p, 16p, 17p, 20$\frac{1}{2}$p, 23p, 28p, 31p (Nos. X931, X949, X952, X961, X965, X975, X981)	3·00	☐
28 Aug. 1984	13p, 18p, 22p, 24p, 34p (Nos. X900, X955, X963, X967, X985)	3·00	☐
29 Oct. 1985	7p, 12p (Nos. X937, X896) . . .	3·00	☐
23 Aug. 1988	14p, 19p, 20p, 23p, 27p, 28p, 32p, 35p (Nos. X903, X956, X959, X966, X973, X976, X983, X988)	5·00	☐
26 Sept. 1989	15p, 20p, 24p, 29p, 30p, 34p, 37p (Nos. X905, X960, X968, X979/80, X986, X990)	5·00	☐
4 Sept. 1990	10p, 17p, 22p, 26p, 27p, 31p, 33p (Nos. X940, X910, X964, X972, X974, X982, X984)	5·00	☐
10 Sept. 1991	6p, 18p, 24p, 28p, 34p, 35p, 39p (Nos. X936, X913, X969, X977, X987, X989, X991)	5·00	☐

For similar stamps, but with elliptical perforations see Nos. Y1667/1759 in 1993.

PHOSPHOR BANDS. See notes on page 15.
Phosphor bands are applied to the stamps, after the design has been printed, by a separate cylinder. On issues with 'all-over' phosphor the 'band' covers the entire stamp. Parts of the stamp covered by phosphor bands, or the entire surface for 'all-over' phosphor versions, appear matt.

Nos. X847, X852, X864, X873, X876, X880, X889, X894, X897, X899, X901, X906, X911, X1006 and X1012 exist with the phosphor band at the left or right of the stamp.

PHOSPHORISED PAPER. First introduced as an experiment for a limited printing of the 1s 6d value (No. 743c) in 1969, this paper has the phosphor, to activate the automatic sorting machinery, added to the paper coating before the stamps were printed. Issues on this paper have a completely shiny surface. Although not adopted after this first trial further experiments on the 8$\frac{1}{2}$p in 1976 led to this paper being used for new printings of current values.

368 'A Mountain Road'
(T. P. Flanagan)

369 'Deer's Meadow'
(Tom Carr)

370 'Slieve na brock'
(Colin Middleton)

'Ulster '71' Paintings

1971 (16 JUNE) *Two phosphor bands*

881	368	3p multicoloured	10	10 □	□
882	369	7½p multicoloured	45	50 □	□
883	370	9p multicoloured	50	50 □	□
		Set of 3	95	1·00 □	□
		First Day Cover		3·00	□
		Presentation Pack	5·50		□

371 John Keats
(150th Death Anniv)

372 Thomas Gray
(Death Bicentenary)

373 Sir Walter Scott (Birth
Bicentenary)

Literary Anniversaries. Events described above

1971 (28 JULY) *Two phosphor bands*

884	371	3p black, gold and blue . .	10	10 □	□
885	372	5p black, gold and olive .	45	45 □	□
886	373	7½p black, gold and brown	50	50 □	□
		Set of 3	95	95 □	□
		First Day Cover		4·00	□
		Presentation Pack	5·50		□

374 Servicemen and Nurse
of 1921

375 Roman Centurion

376 Rugby Football, 1871

British Anniversaries. Events described on stamps

1971 (25 AUG.) *Two phosphor bands*

887	374	3p multicoloured	10	10 □	□
888	375	7½p multicoloured	50	50 □	□
889	376	9p multicoloured	50	50 □	□
		Set of 3	1·00	1·00 □	□
		First Day Cover		2·25	□
		Presentation Pack	5·50		□

377 Physical Sciences
Building, University
College of Wales,
Aberystwyth

378 Faraday Building,
Southampton
University

379 Engineering Department,
Leicester University

380 Hexagon Restaurant,
Essex University

British Architecture (Modern University Buildings)

1971 (22 SEPT.) *Two phosphor bands*

890	377	3p multicoloured	10	10 □	□
891	378	5p multicoloured	15	20 □	□

892	**379**	7½p ochre, black and				
		purple-brown	45	65	□	□
893	**380**	9p multicoloured	70	90	□	□
		Set of 4	1·25	1·60	□	□
		First Day Cover		4·00		□
		Presentation Pack	6·00		□	

Collectors Pack 1971

1971 (29 Sept.) *Comprises Nos.* 835/40 *and* 881/93

	Collectors Pack	30·00		□

381 Dream of the Wise Men   **382** Adoration of the Magi

383 Ride of the Magi

Christmas

1971 (13 Oct.) *Two phosphor bands* (3p, 7½p) *or one centre phosphor band* (2½p)

894	**381**	2½p multicoloured	15	10	□	□
895	**382**	3p multicoloured	15	10	□	□
896	**383**	7½p multicoloured	80	1·00	□	□
		Set of 3	1·00	1·25	□	□
		First Day Cover		3·50		□
		Presentation Pack	5·00		□	

384 Sir James Clark Ross   **385** Sir Martin Frobisher

386 Henry Hudson   **387** Capt. Robert F. Scott

British Polar Explorers

1972 (16 Feb.) *Two phosphor bands*

897	**384**	3p multicoloured	10	10	□	□
898	**385**	5p multicoloured	15	20	□	□
899	**386**	7½p multicoloured	45	50	□	□
900	**387**	9p multicoloured	70	90	□	□
		Set of 4	1·25	1·50	□	□
		First Day Cover		5·00		□
		Presentation Pack	5·00		□	

388 Statuette of Tutankhamun   **389** 19th-century Coastguard

390 Ralph Vaughan Williams and Score

Anniversaries. Events described on stamps

1972 (26 Apr.) *Two phosphor bands*

901	**388**	3p multicoloured	10	10	□	□
902	**389**	7½p multicoloured	35	50	□	□
903	**390**	9p multicoloured	45	50	□	□
		Set of 3	85	1·00	□	□
		First Day Cover		2·75		□
		Presentation Pack	5·00		□	

For full information on all future British issues, collectors should write to Royal Mail, Freepost EH3647, 21 South Gyle Crescent, Edinburgh EH12 9PE.

391 St Andrew's, Greensted- juxta- Ongar, Essex

392 All Saints, Earls Barton, Northants

393 St Andrew's, Letheringsett, Norfolk

394 St Andrew's, Helpringham, Lincs

395 St Mary the Virgin, Huish Episcopi, Somerset

British Architecture (Village Churches)

1972 (21 JUNE) *Two phosphor bands*

904	**391**	3p multicoloured	. . . . .	10	10	☐	☐
905	**392**	4p multicoloured	. . . . .	15	20	☐	☐
906	**393**	5p multicoloured	. . . . .	15	25	☐	☐
907	**394**	7½p multicoloured	. . . . .	75	80	☐	☐
908	**395**	9p multicoloured	. . . . .	75	90	☐	☐
		Set of 5	. . . .	1·75	2·00	☐	☐
		First Day Cover	. . . .		4·50		☐
		Presentation Pack	. . . .	6·50		☐	

'Belgica '72' Souvenir Pack

1972 (24 JUNE) *Comprises Nos. 894/6 and 904/8*

	Souvenir Pack	. . . .	10·00	☐

396 Microphones, 1924–69

397 Horn Loudspeaker

398 TV Camera, 1972

399 Oscillator and Spark Transmitter, 1897

Broadcasting Anniversaries. Events described on stamps

1972 (13 SEPT.) *Two phosphor bands*

909	**396**	3p multicoloured	. . . . .	10	10	☐	☐
910	**397**	5p multicoloured	. . . . .	10	20	☐	☐
911	**398**	7½p multicoloured	. . . . .	55	60	☐	☐
912	**399**	9p multicoloured	. . . . .	60	70	☐	☐
		Set of 4	. . . .	1·25	1·40	☐	☐
		First Day Cover	. . . .		4·25		☐
		Presentation Pack	. . . .	3·50		☐	

400 Angel holding Trumpet

401 Angel playing Lute

402 Angel playing Harp

Christmas

1972 (18 OCT.) *Two phosphor bands (3p, 7½p) or one centre phosphor band (2½p)*

913	400	2½p multicoloured	10	10 □ □
914	401	3p multicoloured	10	10 □ □
915	402	7½p multicoloured	70	1·10 □ □
		Set of 3	80	1·10 □
		First Day Cover		3·00 □
		Presentation Pack	3·00	□

403 Queen Elizabeth II and Prince Philip

404 Europe

Royal Silver Wedding

1972 (20 NOV.) *3p 'all-over' phosphor, 20p without phosphor*

916	403	3p brownish black, deep blue and silver	25	10 □ □
917		20p brownish black, reddish purple and silver	75	90 □ □
		Set of 2	1·00	1·00 □ □
		First Day Cover		2·75 □
		Presentation Pack	2·50	□
		Presentation Pack (Japanese) . .	4·50	□
		Souvenir Book	5·00	□
		Gutter Pair (3p)	80	□
		Traffic Light Gutter Pair (3p) . . .	16·00	□

Collectors Pack 1972

1972 (20 NOV.) *Comprises Nos. 897/918*

	Collectors Pack	30·00	□

Nos. 920/1 were issued horizontally *se-tenant* throughout the sheet.

Britain's Entry into European Communities

1973 (3 JAN.) *Two phosphor bands*

919	404	3p multicoloured	10	15 □ □
920		5p multicoloured (blue jigsaw)	30	50 □ □
		a. Pair. Nos. 920/1	75	1·50 □ □
921		5p multicoloured (green jigsaw)	30	50 □ □
		Set of 3	75	1·00 □ □
		First Day Cover		2·25 □
		Presentation Pack	2·75	□

405 Oak Tree

British Trees (1st Issue)

1973 (28 FEB.) *Two phosphor bands*

922	405	9p multicoloured	35	50 □ □
		First Day Cover		2·75 □
		Presentation Pack	2·75	□

See also No. 949

406 David Livingstone   407 H. M. Stanley

The above were issued horizontally *se-tenant* throughout the sheet.

408 Sir Francis Drake   409 Sir Walter Raleigh

410 Charles Sturt

British Explorers

1973 (18 APR.) *'All-over' phosphor*

923	406	3p multicoloured	20	10 □ □
		a. Pair. Nos. 923/4	80	1·25 □ □

924	407	3p multicoloured	. . . .	20	10	□	□
925	408	5p multicoloured	. . . .	20	30	□	□
926	409	7½p multicoloured	. . . .	20	30	□	□
927	410	9p multicoloured	. . . .	20	40	□	□
		Set of 5	. . . .	1·25	1·10	□	□
		First Day Cover	. . . .		4·50	□	
		Presentation Pack	. . . .	4·50		□	

411

412

413

County Cricket 1873–1973

1973 (16 MAY) *Designs show sketches of W. G. Grace by Harry Furniss. Queen's head in gold. 'All-over' phosphor*

928	411	3p black and brown	. . . .	10	10	□	□
929	412	7½p black and green	. . . .	70	80	□	□
930	413	9p black and blue	. . . . .	90	1·00	□	□
		Set of 3	. . . .	1·60	1·75	□	□
		First Day Cover	. . . .		4·00	□	
		Presentation Pack	. . . .	3·75		□	
		Souvenir Book	. . . .	7·50		□	
		PHQ Card (No. 928)	. . . .	55·00	£200	□	□

The PHQ Card did not become available until mid-July. The used price quoted is for an example used in July or August 1973.

414 'Self-portrait' (Sir Joshua Reynolds)

415 'Self-portrait' (Sir Henry Raeburn)

416 'Nelly O'Brien' (Sir Joshua Reynolds)

417 'Rev R. Walker (The Skater)' (Sir Henry Raeburn)

Artistic Anniversaries. Events described on stamps

1973 (4 JULY) *'All-over' phosphor*

931	414	3p multicoloured	. . . .	10	10	□	□
932	415	5p multicoloured	. . . .	15	25	□	□
933	416	7½p multicoloured	. . . .	40	50	□	□
934	417	9p multicoloured	. . . .	45	60	□	□
		Set of 4	. . . .	1·00	1·25	□	□
		First Day Cover	. . . .		2·50	□	
		Presentation Pack	. . . .	3·00		□	

418 Court Masque Costumes

419 St Paul's Church, Covent Garden

420 Prince's Lodging, Newmarket

421 Court Masque Stage Scene

The 3p and 5p values were printed horizontally *se-tenant* within the sheet.

400th Anniversary of the Birth of Inigo Jones

1973 (15 AUG.) *'All-over' phosphor*

935	418	3p deep mauve, black and gold	. . . .	10	15	□	□
		a. Pair. Nos. 935/6	. . . .	35	50	□	□
936	419	3p deep brown, black and gold	. . . .	10	15	□	□

937	**420**	5p blue, black and gold ..	40	50 ☐ ☐
		a. Pair. Nos. 937/8	1·25	1·50 ☐ ☐
938	**421**	5p grey-olive, black and gold	40	50 ☐ ☐
		Set of 4	1·50	1·25 ☐ ☐
		First Day Cover		2·75 ☐
		Presentation Pack	4·00	☐
		PHQ Card (No. 936)	£130	90·00 ☐ ☐

422 Palace of Westminster seen from Whitehall
423 Palace of Westminster seen from Millbank

19th Commonwealth Parliamentary Conference

1973 (12 SEPT.) *'All-over' phosphor*

939	**422**	8p black, grey and pale buff	50	60 ☐ ☐
940	**423**	10p gold and black	50	40 ☐ ☐
		Set of 2	1·00	1·00 ☐ ☐
		First Day Cover		2·75 ☐
		Presentation Pack	2·50	☐
		Souvenir Book	5·50	☐
		PHQ Card (No. 939)	38·00	80·00 ☐ ☐

424 Princess Anne and Captain Mark Phillips

Royal Wedding

1973 (14 NOV.) *'All-over' phosphor*

941	**424**	3½p violet and silver	10	10 ☐ ☐
942		20p brown and silver ...	65	80 ☐ ☐
		Set of 2	75	90 ☐ ☐
		First Day Cover		2·50 ☐
		Presentation Pack	2·50	☐
		PHQ Card (No. 941)	7·50	25·00 ☐ ☐
		Set of 2 Gutter Pairs	3·00	☐
		Set of 2 Traffic Light Gutter Pairs	85·00	☐

425   426

427   428

429   **430** 'Good King Wenceslas, the Page and Peasant'

The 3p values depict the carol 'Good King Wenceslas' and were printed horizontally *se-tenant* within the sheet.

Christmas

1973 (28 NOV.) *One phosphor band (3p) or 'all-over' phosphor (3½p)*

943	**425**	3p multicoloured	15	10 ☐ ☐
		a. Strip of 5. Nos. 943/7 .	2·75	4·00 ☐ ☐
944	**426**	3p multicoloured	15	10 ☐ ☐
945	**427**	3p multicoloured	15	10 ☐ ☐
946	**428**	3p multicoloured	15	10 ☐ ☐
947	**429**	3p multicoloured	15	10 ☐ ☐
948	**430**	3½p multicoloured	15	10 ☐ ☐
		Set of 6	2·75	65 ☐ ☐
		First Day Cover		4·00 ☐
		Presentation Pack	3·50	☐

Collectors Pack 1973

1973 (28 NOV.) *Comprises Nos. 919/48*

| | | Collectors Pack .... | 30·00 | ☐ |

431 Horse Chestnut

British Trees (2nd issue)

1974 (27 FEB.) *'All-over' phosphor*

949	**431**	10p multicoloured	35	40 ☐ ☐
		First Day Cover		2·50 ☐
		Presentation Pack	2·50	☐
		PHQ Card	£110	80·00 ☐ ☐
		Gutter Pair	3·00	☐
		Traffic Light Gutter Pair	50·00	☐

432 First Motor Fire-engine, 1904

433 Prize-winning Fire-engine, 1863

434 First Steam Fire-engine, 1830

435 Fire-engine, 1766

Bicentenary of Public Fire Services

1974 (24 APR.) *'All-over' phosphor*

950	432	3½p multicoloured	. . . . .	10	10	□	□
951	433	5½p multicoloured	. . . . .	20	30	□	□
952	434	8p multicoloured	. . . . .	30	40	□	□
953	435	10p multicoloured	. . . . .	35	45	□	□
		Set of 4	. . . .	85	1·10	□	□
		First Day Cover	. . . .		4·00	□	
		Presentation Pack	. . . .	2·75		□	
		PHQ Card (No. 950)	. . . .	£120	70·00	□	□
		Set of 4 Gutter Pairs	. . . . . .	3·50		□	
		Set of 4 Traffic Light Gutter Pairs		50·00		□	

436 P & O Packet *Peninsular*, 1888

437 Farman H.F. III Biplane, 1911

438 Airmail-blue Van and Postbox, 1930

439 Imperial Airways Short S.21 Flying Boat *Maia*, 1937

Centenary of Universal Postal Union

1974 (12 JUNE) *'All-over' phosphor*

954	436	3½p multicoloured	. . . . .	10	10	□	□
955	437	5½p multicoloured	. . . . .	25	35	□	□
956	438	8p multicoloured	. . . . .	30	45	□	□
957	439	10p multicoloured	. . . . .	45	50	□	□
		Set of 4	. . . .	1·00	1·25	□	□
		First Day Cover	. . . . .		4·00	□	
		Presentation Pack	. . . . .	2·75		□	
		Set of 4 Gutter Pairs	. . . . . .	3·00		□	
		Set of 4 Traffic Light Gutter Pairs		40·00		□	

440 Robert the Bruce

441 Owain Glyndŵr

442 Henry V

443 The Black Prince

Medieval Warriors

1974 (10 JULY) *'All-over' phosphor*

958	440	4½p multicoloured	. . . . .	10	10	□	□
959	441	5½p multicoloured	. . . . .	15	30	□	□
960	442	8p multicoloured	. . . . .	45	50	□	□
961	443	10p multicoloured	. . . . .	50	50	□	□
		Set of 4	. . . .	1·10	1·25	□	□
		First Day Cover	. . . . .		4·00	□	
		Presentation Pack	. . . .	3·75		□	
		PHQ Cards (set of 4)	. . . . . .	32·00	30·00	□	□
		Set of 4 Gutter Pairs	. . . . . .	4·50		□	
		Set of 4 Traffic Light Gutter Pairs		55·00		□	

444 Churchill in Royal Yacht Squadron Uniform

445 Prime Minister, 1940

446 Secretary for War and Air, 1919

447 War Correspondent, South Africa, 1899

Birth Centenary of Sir Winston Churchill
1974 (9 Oct.) *Queen's head and inscription in silver. 'All-over' phosphor*

962	**444**	4½p green and blue	. . . .	20	10	□	□
963	**445**	5½p grey and black	. . . . .	35	30	□	□
964	**446**	8p rose and lake	. . . . .	65	50	□	□
965	**447**	10p stone and brown	. . .	70	50	□	□
	Set of 4	. . . .		1·75	1·25	□	□
	First Day Cover	. . . .			3·25		□
	Presentation Pack	. . . .		2·75			□
	Souvenir Book	. . . .		4·00			□
	PHQ Card (No. 963)	. . . . . .		6·00	14·00	□	□
	Set of 4 Gutter Pairs	. . . .		4·50			□
	Set of 4 Traffic Light Gutter Pairs			40·00			□

448 Adoration of the Magi (York Minster, *c* 1355)

449 The Nativity (St Helen's Church, Norwich, *c* 1480)

450 Virgin and Child (Ottery St Mary Church, *c* 1350)

451 Virgin and Child (Worcester Cathedral, *c* 1224)

Christmas
1974 (27 Nov.) *Designs show church roof bosses. One phosphor band (3½p) or 'all-over' phosphor (others)*

966	**448**	3½p multicoloured	. . . . .	10	10	□	□
967	**449**	4½p multicoloured	. . . . .	10	10	□	□

968	**450**	8p multicoloured	. . . . .	30	45	□	□
969	**451**	10p multicoloured	. . . . .	40	55	□	□
	Set of 4	. . . .		80	1·10	□	□
	First Day Cover				3·50		□
	Presentation Pack	. . . .		2·00			□
	Set of 4 Gutter Pairs	. . . .		2·50			□
	Set of 4 Traffic Light Gutter Pairs			40·00			□

Collectors Pack 1974
1974 (27 Nov.) *Comprises Nos. 949/69*

	Collectors Pack	. . . .	13·00	□

452 Invalid in Wheelchair

Health and Handicap Funds
1975 (22 Jan.) *'All-over' phosphor*

970	**452**	4½p + 1½p azure and blue	. .	15	30	□	□
	First Day Cover	. . . .			2·50		□
	Gutter Pair	. . . .		70			□
	Traffic Light Gutter Pair	. . . . .		1·25			□

453 'Peace – Burial at Sea'

454 'Snowstorm – Steamer off a Harbour's Mouth'

455 'The Arsenal, Venice'

456 'St Laurent'

Birth Bicentenary of J. M. W. Turner
1975 (19 Feb.) *'All-over' phosphor*

971	**453**	4½p multicoloured	. . . . .	10	10	□	□
972	**454**	5½p multicoloured	. . . . .	15	20	□	□

973	455	8p multicoloured	35	50	☐	☐
974	456	10p multicoloured	45	60	☐	☐
		Set of 4	95	1·25	☐	☐
		First Day Cover		3·00		☐
		Presentation Pack	2·75		☐	
		PHQ Card (No. 972)	40·00	15·00	☐	☐
		Set of 4 Gutter Pairs	2·50		☐	
		Set of 4 Traffic Light Gutter Pairs	6·50		☐	

457 Charlotte Square, Edinburgh   **458** The Rows, Chester

The above were printed horizontally *se-tenant* throughout the sheet.

459 Royal Observatory, Greenwich   **460** St George's Chapel, Windsor

461 National Theatre, London

European Architectural Heritage Year
1975 (23 APR.) *'All-over' phosphor*

975	457	7p multicoloured	50	55	☐	☐
		a. Pair. Nos. 975/6	1·00	1·25	☐	☐
976	458	7p multicoloured	50	55	☐	☐
977	459	8p multicoloured	20	25	☐	☐
978	460	10p multicoloured	20	25	☐	☐
979	461	12p multicoloured	20	35	☐	☐
		Set of 5	1·40	1·75	☐	☐
		First Day Cover		5·00		☐
		Presentation Pack	3·50		☐	
		PHQ Cards (Nos. 975/7)	11·00	15·00	☐	☐
		Set of 5 Gutter Pairs	3·50		☐	
		Set of 5 Traffic Light Gutter Pairs	28·00		☐	

462 Sailing Dinghies   **463** Racing Keel Boats

464 Cruising Yachts   **465** Multihulls

Sailing
1975 (11 JUNE) *'All-over' phosphor*

980	462	7p multicoloured	20	10	☐	☐
981	463	8p multicoloured	25	30	☐	☐
982	464	10p multicoloured	25	35	☐	☐
983	465	12p multicoloured	40	55	☐	☐
		Set of 4	1·00	1·10	☐	☐
		First Day Cover		3·00		☐
		Presentation Pack	2·00		☐	
		PHQ Card (No. 981)	6·50	13·00	☐	☐
		Set of 4 Gutter Pairs	2·75		☐	
		Set of 4 Traffic Light Gutter Pairs	20·00		☐	

466 Stephenson's Locomotion, 1825   **467** *Abbotsford*, 1876

468 *Caerphilly Castle*, 1923   **469** High Speed Train, 1975

150th Anniversary of Public Railways
1975 (13 AUG.) *'All-over' phosphor*

984	466	7p multicoloured	20	10	☐	☐
985	467	8p multicoloured	35	40	☐	☐

986	**468**	10p multicoloured	45	40 ☐ ☐
987	**469**	12p multicoloured	50	40 ☐ ☐
		Set of 4	1·40	1·10 ☐ ☐
		First Day Cover		4·00 ☐
		Presentation Pack	3·50	☐
		Souvenir Book	5·00	☐
		PHQ Cards (set of 4)	65·00	30·00 ☐ ☐
		Set of 4 Gutter Pairs	3·00	☐
		Set of 4 Traffic Light Gutter Pairs	10·00	☐

470 Palace of Westminster

62nd Inter-Parliamentary Union Conference
1975 (3 Sept.) *'All-over' phosphor*

988	**470**	12p multicoloured	25	30 ☐ ☐
		First Day Cover		2·00 ☐
		Presentation Pack	1·75	☐
		Gutter Pair	75	☐
		Traffic Light Gutter Pair	2·25	☐

471 Emma and Mr Woodhouse (*Emma*)

472 Catherine Morland (*Northanger Abbey*)

473 Mr Darcy (*Pride and Prejudice*)

474 Mary and Henry Crawford (*Mansfield Park*)

Birth Bicentenary of Jane Austen (novelist)
1975 (22 Oct.) *'All-over' phosphor*

989	**471**	8½p multicoloured	20	10 ☐ ☐
990	**472**	10p multicoloured	35	35 ☐ ☐

991	**473**	11p multicoloured	40	40 ☐ ☐
992	**474**	13p multicoloured	45	45 ☐ ☐
		Set of 4	1·25	1·10 ☐ ☐
		First Day Cover		4·25 ☐
		Presentation Pack	2·25	☐
		PHQ Cards (set of 4)	30·00	21·00 ☐ ☐
		Set of 4 Gutter Pairs	2·50	☐
		Set of 4 Traffic Light Gutter Pairs	6·00	☐

475 Angels with Harp and Lute

476 Angel with Mandolin

477 Angel with Horn

478 Angel with Trumpet

Christmas
1975 (26 Nov.) *One phosphor band (6½p). phosphor-inked (8½p)* (*background*) *or 'all-over' phosphor* (*others*)

993	**475**	6½p multicoloured	20	10 ☐ ☐
994	**476**	8½p multicoloured	30	30 ☐ ☐
995	**477**	11p multicoloured	40	45 ☐ ☐
996	**478**	13p multicoloured	45	45 ☐ ☐
		Set of 4	1·25	1·10 ☐ ☐
		First Day Cover		2·25 ☐
		Presentation Pack	2·50	☐
		Set of 4 Gutter Pairs	2·75	☐
		Set of 4 Traffic Light Gutter Pairs	6·50	☐

Collectors Pack 1975
1975 (26 Nov.) *Comprises Nos. 970/96*

		Collectors Pack	9·00 ☐

479 Housewife

480 Policeman

481 District Nurse   482 Industrialist

487 Benjamin Franklin (bust by Jean-Jacques Caffieri)

Telephone Centenary
1976 (10 MAR.) *'All-over' phosphor*

997	**479**	8½p multicoloured	15	10	☐	☐
998	**480**	10p multicoloured	35	35	☐	☐
999	**481**	11p multicoloured	40	40	☐	☐
1000	**482**	13p multicoloured	40	45	☐	☐
		Set of 4	1·10	1·10	☐	☐
		First Day Cover		3·00		☐
		Presentation Pack	2·50		☐	
		Set of 4 Gutter Pairs	2·75		☐	
		Set of 4 Traffic Light Gutter Pairs	6·50		☐	

Bicentenary of American Revolution
1976 (2 JUNE) *'All-over' phosphor*

1005	**487**	11p multicoloured	35	45	☐	☐
		First Day Cover		1·75		☐
		Presentation Pack	1·75		☐	
		PHQ Card	4·50	10·00	☐	☐
		Gutter Pair	85		☐	
		Traffic Light Gutter Pair	2·00		☐	

483 Hewing Coal (Thomas Hepburn)   484 Machinery (Robert Owen)

488 'Elizabeth of Glamis'   489 'Grandpa Dickson'

485 Chimney Cleaning (Lord Shaftesbury)   486 Hands clutching Prison Bars (Elizabeth Fry)

490 'Rosa Mundi'   491 'Sweet Briar'

Social Reformers
1976 (28 APR.) *'All-over' phosphor*

1001	**483**	8½p multicoloured	15	10	☐	☐
1002	**484**	10p multicoloured	35	35	☐	☐
1003	**485**	11p black, slate-grey and drab	40	40	☐	☐
1004	**486**	13p slate-grey, black and green	40	45	☐	☐
		Set of 4	1·10	1·10	☐	☐
		First Day Cover		3·00		☐
		Presentation Pack	2·50		☐	
		PHQ Card (No. 1001)	6·00	10·00	☐	☐
		Set of 4 Gutter Pairs	2·50		☐	
		Set of 4 Traffic Light Gutter Pairs	6·50		☐	

Centenary of Royal National Rose Society
1976 (30 JUNE) *'All-over' phosphor*

1006	**488**	8½p multicoloured	15	10	☐	☐
1007	**489**	10p multicoloured	30	35	☐	☐
1008	**490**	11p multicoloured	50	50	☐	☐
1009	**491**	13p multicoloured	60	60	☐	☐
		Set of 4	1·40	1·40	☐	☐
		First Day Cover		3·00		☐
		Presentation Pack	2·50		☐	
		PHQ Cards (set of 4)	32·00	13·00	☐	☐
		Set of 4 Gutter Pairs	3·25		☐	
		Set of 4 Traffic Light Gutter Pairs	8·50		☐	

8½P

1176   1176

Eisteddfod Genedlaethol Frenhinol Cymru
Royal National Eisteddfod of Wales

492   Archdruid

10P

Morris Dancing

493   Morris Dancing

William Caxton 1476   **11P**

498   *Game and Playe*
      of Chesse

William Caxton 1476   **13P**

499   Early Printing Press

500th Anniversary of British Printing

1976 (29 Sept.) *'All-over' phosphor*

1014	**496**	8½p black, blue and gold .	20	10	□	□
1015	**497**	10p black, olive-green and gold	35	30	□	□
1016	**498**	11p black, grey and gold .	40	40	□	□
1017	**499**	13p brown, ochre and gold	45	45	□	□
		Set of 4	1·25	1·10	□	□
		First Day Cover		3·75		□
		Presentation Pack	2·50		□	
		PHQ Cards (set of 4)	13·00	13·00	□	□
		Set of 4 Gutter Pairs	3·00		□	
		Set of 4 Traffic Light Gutter Pairs	8·50		□	

11P

Highland Gathering
Na Geamannan

494   Scots Piper

13P

1176   1176

Eisteddfod Genedlaethol Frenhinol Cymru
Royal National Eisteddfod of Wales

495   Welsh Harpist

British Cultural Traditions

1976 (4 Aug.) *'All-over' phosphor*

1010	**492**	8½p multicoloured	15	10	□	□
1011	**493**	10p multicoloured	30	30	□	□
1012	**494**	11p multicoloured	35	40	□	□
1013	**495**	13p multicoloured	40	45	□	□
		Set of 4	1·10	1·10	□	□
		First Day Cover		3·75		□
		Presentation Pack	2·50		□	
		PHQ Cards (set of 4)	17·00	13·00	□	□
		Set of 4 Gutter Pairs	2·50		□	
		Set of 4 Traffic Light Gutter Pairs	8·50		□	

English Embroidery c.1272   **6½₂**

500   Virgin and Child

English Embroidery c.1340   **8½₂**

501   Angel with Crown

William Caxton 1476   **8½₂**

496   *The Canterbury*
      Tales

William Caxton 1476   **10P**

497   *The Tretyse of Love*

English Embroidery c.1320   **11P**

502   Angel appearing to
      Shepherds

English Embroidery c.1330   **13P**

503   The Three Kings

Christmas

1976 (24 Nov.) *Designs show English medieval embroidery.*
One phosphor band (6½p) or 'all-over' phosphor (others)

1018	**500**	6½p multicoloured	15	10	□	□
1019	**501**	8½p multicoloured	30	10	□	□
1020	**502**	11p multicoloured	40	45	□	□

For full information on all future British issues, collectors
should write to Royal Mail, Freepost EH3647, 21 South Gyle
Crescent, Edinburgh EH12 9PE.

1021	**503**	13p multicoloured	40	50 □ □
		Set of 4	1·10	1·00 □ □
		First Day Cover		3·75 □
		Presentation Pack	2·75	□
		PHQ Cards (set of 4)	4·00	11·00 □ □
		Set of 4 Gutter Pairs	2·50	□
		Set of 4 Traffic Light Gutter Pairs	6·50	□

Collectors Pack 1976
1976 (24 Nov.) Comprises Nos. 997/1021

| | Collectors Pack . . . . | 12·00 | □ |

504 Lawn Tennis

505 Table Tennis

506 Squash

507 Badminton

Racket Sports
1977 (12 Jan.) Phosphorised paper

1022	**504**	8½p multicoloured	20	10 □ □
1023	**505**	10p multicoloured	35	35 □ □
1024	**506**	11p multicoloured	40	40 □ □
1025	**507**	13p multicoloured	45	40 □ □
		Set of 4	1·25	1·10 □ □
		First Day Cover		3·75 □
		Presentation Pack	2·75	□
		PHQ Cards (set of 4)	7·00	16·00 □ □
		Set of 4 Gutter Pairs	2·50	□
		Set of 4 Traffic Light Gutter Pairs	6·50	□

508

1977 (2 Feb.)–**87** Type **508** Ordinary paper

1026		£1 green and olive	2·75	15 □ □
1026b		£1·30 drab and deep greenish blue	4·75	5·00 □ □
1026c		£1·33 pale mauve and grey-black	7·50	7·50 □ □
1026d		£1·41 drab and deep greenish blue	8·00	8·00 □ □
1026e		£1·50 pale mauve and grey-black	6·00	6·00 □ □
1026f		£1·60 drab and deep greenish blue	7·50	7·50 □ □
1027		£2 green and brown	5·00	50 □ □
1028		£5 pink and blue	13·00	2·25 □ □
		Set of 8	50·00	32·00 □ □
		Presentation Pack (P.O. Pack No. 91 (small size)) (Nos. 1026, 1027/8)	22·00	□
		Presentation Pack (P.O. Pack No.13 (large size)) (Nos. 1026, 1027/8)	80·00	□
		Presentation Pack (P.O. Pack No. 14) (No. 1026f)	20·00	□
		Set of 8 Gutter Pairs	£110	□
		Set of 8 Traffic Light Gutter Pairs	£180	□

First Day Covers

2 Feb. 1977	Nos. 1026, 1027/8	7·50 □
3 Aug. 1983	No. 1026b	5·50 □
28 Aug. 1984	No. 1026c	7·50 □
17 Sept. 1985	No. 1026d	8·00 □
2 Sept. 1986	No. 1026e	6·00 □
15 Sept. 1987	No. 1026f	7·50 □

509 Steroids — Conformational Analysis

510 Vitamin C — Synthesis

511 Starch — Chromatography

512 Salt — Crystallography

Centenary of Royal Institute of Chemistry
1977 (2 Mar.) 'All-over' phosphor

1029	**509**	8½p multicoloured	15	10 □ □
1030	**510**	10p multicoloured	35	40 □ □
1031	**511**	11p multicoloured	35	40 □ □

1032	**512**	13p multicoloured	35	35	☐	☐
		Set of 4	1·10	1·10	☐	☐
		First Day Cover		3·00		☐
		Presentation Pack	2·75		☐	
		PHQ Cards (set of 4)	8·00	11·00	☐	☐
		Set of 4 Gutter Pairs	2·50		☐	
		Set of 4 Traffic Light Gutter Pairs	6·00		☐	

513

Silver Jubilee
1977 (11 May–15 June) *'All-over' phosphor*

1033	**513**	8½p multicoloured	15	10	☐	☐
1034		9p multicoloured (15 June)	25	10	☐	☐
1035		10p multicoloured	20	25	☐	☐
1036		11p multicoloured	30	35	☐	☐
1037		13p multicoloured	35	40	☐	☐
		Set of 5	1·10	1·10	☐	☐
		First Day Covers (2)		5·00		☐
		Presentation Pack (ex 9p)	1·75		☐	
		Souvenir Book (ex 9p)	4·50		☐	
		PHQ Cards (set of 5)	11·00	12·00	☐	☐
		Set of 5 Gutter Pairs	2·50		☐	
		Set of 5 Traffic Light Gutter Pairs	4·25		☐	

517 'Gathering of Nations'

Commonwealth Heads of Government Meeting, London
1977 (8 June) *'All-over' phosphor*

1038	**517**	13p black, deep green, rose and silver	35	40	☐	☐
		First Day Cover		1·50		☐
		Presentation Pack	1·25		☐	
		PHQ Card	3·00	5·00	☐	☐
		Gutter Pair	80		☐	
		Traffic Light Gutter Pair	1·25		☐	

518 Hedgehog   **519** Brown Hare

520 Red Squirrel   **521** Otter

522 Badger

T **518/22** were printed together, *se-tenant*, throughout the sheet.

British Wildlife
1977 (5 Oct.) *'All-over' phosphor*

1039	**518**	9p multicoloured	25	10	☐	☐
		a. Strip of 5. Nos. 1039/43	1·75	2·00	☐	☐
1040	**519**	9p multicoloured	25	10	☐	☐
1041	**520**	9p multicoloured	25	10	☐	☐
1042	**521**	9p multicoloured	25	10	☐	☐
1043	**522**	9p multicoloured	25	10	☐	☐
		Set of 5	1·75	50	☐	☐
		First Day Cover		4·00		☐
		Presentation Pack	2·75		☐	
		PHQ Cards (set of 5)	5·00	6·00	☐	☐
		Gutter Strip of 10	3·75		☐	
		Traffic Light Gutter Strip of 10 .	4·00		☐	

523 'Three French Hens,
Two Turtle Doves and a
Partridge in a Pear Tree'

524 'Six Geese a laying,
Five Gold Rings,
Four Colly Birds'

525 'Eight Maids a-milking,
Seven Swans a-
swimming'

526 'Ten Pipers piping,
Nine Drummers
drumming'

527 'Twelve Lords a-leaping,
Eleven Ladies dancing'

528 'A Partridge in a
Pear Tree'

T **523/8** depict the carol 'The Twelve Days of Christmas'.
T **523/7** were printed horizontally *se-tenant* throughout the sheet.

Christmas

1977 (23 Nov.) *One centre phosphor band* (7p) *or 'all-over'
phosphor* (9p)

1044	**523**	7p multicoloured	25	10	☐	☐	
		a. Strip of 5. Nos. 1044/8	1·25	1·50	☐	☐	
1045	**524**	7p multicoloured	25	10	☐	☐	
1046	**525**	7p multicoloured	25	10	☐	☐	
1047	**526**	7p multicoloured	25	10	☐	☐	
1048	**527**	7p multicoloured	25	10	☐	☐	
1049	**528**	9p multicoloured	25	10	☐	☐	
		Set of 6	1·25	50	☐	☐	
		First Day Cover		4·00	☐		
		Presentation Pack	2·25		☐		
		PHQ Cards (set of 6)	2·50	5·00	☐	☐	
		Set of 6 Gutter Pairs	2·50		☐		
		Set of 6 Traffic Light Gutter Pairs	4·50		☐		

Collectors Pack 1977

1977 (23 Nov.) *Comprises Nos.* 1022/5 1029/49

	Collectors Pack	7·00	☐

529 Oil — North Sea
Production Platform

530 Coal — Modern
Pithead

531 Natural Gas —
Flame Rising
from Sea

532 Electricity — Nuclear
Power Station and
Uranium Atom

Energy Resources

1978 (25 Jan.) *'All-over' phosphor*

1050	**529**	9p multicoloured	20	10	☐	☐	
1051	**530**	10½p multicoloured	20	25	☐	☐	
1052	**531**	11p multicoloured	20	25	☐	☐	
1053	**532**	13p multicoloured	20	25	☐	☐	
		Set of 4	70	75	☐	☐	
		First Day Cover		1·75		☐	
		Presentation Pack	2·25		☐		
		PHQ Cards (set of 4)	2·00	4·00	☐	☐	
		Set of 4 Gutter Pairs	2·00		☐		
		Set of 4 Traffic Light Gutter Pairs	4·00		☐		

533 Tower of London

534 Holyroodhouse

535 Caernarvon Castle

536 Hampton Court Palace

British Architecture (Historic Buildings)

1978 (1 Mar.) *'All-over' phosphor*

1054	**533**	9p multicoloured	20	10	☐	☐
1055	**534**	10½p multicoloured	20	25	☐	☐
1056	**535**	11p multicoloured	20	25	☐	☐
1057	**536**	13p multicoloured	25	20	☐	☐
		Set of 4	75	70	☐	☐
		First Day Cover		1·75	☐	
		Presentation Pack	2·25		☐	
		PHQ Cards (set of 4)	2·00	4·00	☐	☐
		Set of 4 Gutter Pairs	2·00		☐	
		Set of 4 Traffic Light Gutter Pairs	4·00		☐	
MS1058	121 × 90 mm. Nos. 1054/7 . .	1·25	1·50	☐	☐	
		First Day Cover		2·00	☐	

No. **MS**1058 was sold at 53½p, the premium being used for the London 1980 Stamp Exhibition.

537 State Coach

538 St Edward's Crown

539 The Sovereign's Orb

540 Imperial State Crown

25th Anniversary of Coronation

1978 (31 May) *'All-over' phosphor*

1059	**537**	9p gold and blue	20	10	☐	☐
1060	**538**	10½p gold and red	20	30	☐	☐
1061	**539**	11p gold and green	20	30	☐	☐
1062	**540**	13p gold and violet	25	35	☐	☐
		Set of 4	75	95	☐	☐
		First Day Cover		1·75	☐	
		Presentation Pack	2·00		☐	
		Souvenir Book	4·00		☐	
		PHQ Cards (set of 4)	2·00	3·75	☐	☐
		Set of 4 Gutter Pairs	2·00		☐	
		Set of 4 Traffic Light Gutter Pairs	4·00		☐	

541 Shire Horse

542 Shetland Pony

543 Welsh Pony

544 Thoroughbred

Horses

1978 (5 July) *'All-over' phosphor*

1063	**541**	9p multicoloured	15	10	☐	☐
1064	**542**	10½p multicoloured	30	30	☐	☐
1065	**543**	11p multicoloured	30	35	☐	☐
1066	**544**	13p multicoloured	35	35	☐	☐
		Set of 4	1·00	1·00	☐	☐
		First Day Cover		1·50		☐
		Presentation Pack	1·90		☐	
		PHQ Cards (set of 4)	2·25	5·00	☐	☐
		Set of 4 Gutter Pairs	2·50		☐	
		Set of 4 Traffic Light Gutter Pairs	4·00		☐	

545 Penny-farthing and 1884 Safety Bicycle

546 1920 Touring Bicycles

547 Modern Small-wheel Bicycles

548 1978 Road-racers

Centenaries of Cyclists Touring Club and British Cycling Federation

1978 (2 Aug.) *'All-over' phosphor*

1067	**545**	9p multicoloured	15	10	☐	☐
1068	**546**	10½p multicoloured	20	25	☐	☐
1069	**547**	11p multicoloured	20	35	☐	☐
1070	**548**	13p multicoloured	25	30	☐	☐
		Set of 4	70	90	☐	☐
		First Day Cover		2·25		☐
		Presentation Pack	2·00		☐	
		PHQ Cards (set of 4)	2·00	4·00	☐	☐
		Set of 4 Gutter Pairs	2·00		☐	
		Set of 4 Traffic Light Gutter Pairs	4·00		☐	

549 Singing Carols round the Christmas Tree

550 The Waits

551 18th-Century Carol Singers

552 'The Boar's Head Carol'

Christmas

1978 (22 Nov.) *One centre phosphor band* (7p) *or 'all-over' phosphor* (others)

1071	**549**	7p multicoloured	15	10	☐	☐
1072	**550**	9p multicoloured	20	10	☐	☐
1073	**551**	11p multicoloured	25	30	☐	☐
1074	**552**	13p multicoloured	25	35	☐	☐
		Set of 4	75	75	☐	☐
		First Day Cover		1·50		☐
		Presentation Pack	1·75		☐	
		PHQ Cards (set of 4)	1·50	4·00	☐	☐
		Set of 4 Gutter Pairs	2·00		☐	
		Set of 4 Traffic Light Gutter Pairs	3·00		☐	

Collectors Pack 1978

1978 (22 Nov.) *Comprises Nos.* 1050/7, 1059/74

	Collectors Pack	8·00		☐

553 Old English Sheepdog

554 Welsh Springer Spaniel

555 West Highland Terrier

556 Irish Setter

Dogs

1979 (7 Feb.) *'All-over' phosphor*

1075	**553**	9p multicoloured	15	10	☐	☐
1076	**554**	10½p multicoloured	25	30	☐	☐
1077	**555**	11p multicoloured	25	40	☐	☐
1078	**556**	13p multicoloured	25	40	☐	☐
		Set of 4	80	1·10	☐	☐
		First Day Cover		1·90		☐
		Presentation Pack	1·90		☐	
		PHQ Cards (set of 4)	2·25	5·00	☐	☐
		Set of 4 Gutter Pairs	2·00		☐	
		Set of 4 Traffic Light Gutter Pairs	3·75		☐	

557 Primrose

558 Daffodil

559 Bluebell

560 Snowdrop

Spring Wild Flowers

1979 (21 Mar.) *'All-over' phosphor*

1079	**557**	9p multicoloured	15	10	□	□
1080	**558**	10½p multicoloured	25	35	□	□
1081	**559**	11p multicoloured	25	35	□	□
1082	**560**	13p multicoloured	25	30	□	□
		Set of 4	80	1·00	□	□
		First Day Cover		1·50	□	
		Presentation Pack	1·75		□	
		PHQ Cards (set of 4)	1·25	3·75	□	□
		Set of 4 Gutter Pairs	2·00		□	
		Set of 4 Traffic Light Gutter Pairs	3·75		□	

561

562

563

564

T **561/4** show hands placing the flags of the member nations into ballot boxes.

First Direct Elections to European Assembly

1979 (9 May) *Phosphorised paper*

1083	**561**	9p multicoloured	15	10	□	□
1084	**562**	10½p multicoloured	25	25	□	□
1085	**563**	11p multicoloured	25	25	□	□
1086	**564**	13p multicoloured	30	25	□	□
		Set of 4	85	75	□	□
		First Day Cover		1·50	□	
		Presentation Pack	2·00		□	
		PHQ Cards (set of 4)	1·50	4·00	□	□
		Set of 4 Gutter Pairs	2·00		□	
		Set of 4 Traffic Light Gutter Pairs	3·75		□	

565 'Saddling "Mahmoud"
for the Derby, 1936'
(Sir Alfred Munnings)

566 'The Liverpool Great
National Steeple Chase,
1839' (aquatint by F. C.
Turner)

567 'The First Spring
Meeting, Newmarket,
1793' (J. N. Sartorius)

568 'Racing at Dorsett Ferry,
Windsor, 1684'
(Francis Barlow)

Horseracing Paintings and Bicentenary of The Derby (9p)

1979 (6 June) *'All-over' phosphor*

1087	**565**	9p multicoloured	15	10	□	□
1088	**566**	10½p multicoloured	20	25	□	□
1089	**567**	11p multicoloured	25	30	□	□
1090	**568**	13p multicoloured	25	25	□	□
		Set of 4	75	80	□	□
		First Day Cover		1·75	□	
		Presentation Pack	2·00		□	
		PHQ Cards (set of 4)	1·50	3·75	□	□
		Set of 4 Gutter Pairs	2·00		□	
		Set of 4 Traffic Light Gutter Pairs	3·75		□	

569 The Tale of
Peter Rabbit
(Beatrix Potter)

570 The Wind in the
Willows (Kenneth
Grahame)

571 Winnie-the-Pooh
(A. A. Milne)

572 Alice's Adventures in
in Wonderland
(Lewis Carroll)

T **569/72** depict original illustrations from the four books.

International Year of the Child

1979 (11 July) *'All-over' phosphor*

1091	**569**	9p multicoloured	25	20	☐	☐
1092	**570**	10½p multicoloured	30	35	☐	☐
1093	**571**	11p multicoloured	35	35	☐	☐
1094	**572**	13p multicoloured	65	65	☐	☐
		Set of 4	1·40	1·40	☐	
		First Day Cover		2·25		☐
		Presentation Pack	2·00		☐	
		PHQ Cards (set of 4)	2·50	4·00	☐	☐
		Set of 4 Gutter Pairs	3·00		☐	
		Set of 4 Traffic Light Gutter Pairs	5·00		☐	

573 Sir Rowland Hill, 1795–1879

574 General Post, *c* 1839

575 London Post, *c* 1839

576 Uniform Postage, 1840

Death Centenary of Sir Rowland Hill (postal reformer)

1979 (22 Aug.–24 Oct.) *'All-over' phosphor*

1095	**573**	10p multicoloured	20	10	☐	☐
1096	**574**	11½p multicoloured	20	25	☐	☐
1097	**575**	13p multicoloured	25	35	☐	☐
1098	**576**	15p multicoloured	40	35	☐	☐
		Set of 4	95	95	☐	☐
		First Day Cover		2·00		☐
		Presentation Pack	2·00		☐	
		PHQ Cards (set of 4)	1·25	3·50	☐	☐
		Set of 4 Gutter Pairs	2·25		☐	
		Set of 4 Traffic Light Gutter Pairs	3·75		☐	
MS1099	89 × 121 mm. Nos. 1095/8 .		1·25	1·40	☐	
		First Day Cover (24 Oct.)		1·75		☐

No. **MS**1099 was sold at 59½p, the premium being used for the London 1980 Stamp Exhibition.

577 Policeman on the Beat

578 Policeman directing Traffic

579 Mounted Policewoman

580 River Patrol Boat

150th Anniversary of Metropolitan Police

1979 (26 Sept.) *Phosphorised paper*

1100	**577**	10p multicoloured	20	10	☐	☐
1101	**578**	11½p multicoloured	25	35	☐	☐
1102	**579**	13p multicoloured	25	40	☐	☐
1103	**580**	15p multicoloured	40	40	☐	☐
		Set of 4	1·00	1·10	☐	☐
		First Day Cover		1·90		☐
		Presentation Pack	2·00		☐	
		PHQ Cards (set of 4)	1·25	3·50	☐	☐
		Set of 4 Gutter Pairs	2·50		☐	
		Set of 4 Traffic Light Gutter Pairs	4·00		☐	

581 The Three Kings

582 Angel appearing to the Shepherds

583 The Nativity

584 Mary and Joseph travelling to Bethlehem

585 The Annunciation

Christmas

1979 (21 Nov.) *One centre phosphor band (8p) or phosphorised paper (others)*

1104	**581**	8p multicoloured	15	10	□	□
1105	**582**	10p multicoloured	20	10	□	□
1106	**583**	11½p multicoloured	20	25	□	□
1107	**584**	13p multicoloured	30	35	□	□
1108	**585**	15p multicoloured	35	35	□	□
		Set of 5	1·10	1·00	□	□
		First Day Cover		1·75		□
		Presentation Pack	2·00		□	
		PHQ Cards (set of 5)	1·25	3·25	□	□
		Set of 5 Gutter Pairs	2·75		□	
		Set of 5 Traffic Light Gutter Pairs	3·75		□	

Collectors Pack 1979

1979 (21 Nov.) *Comprises Nos. 1075/98, 1100/8*

	Collectors Pack	10·00	□

586 Common Kingfisher

587 Dipper

588 Moorhen

589 Yellow Wagtails

Centenary of Wild Bird Protection Act

1980 (16 Jan.) *Phosphorised paper*

1109	**586**	10p multicoloured	20	10	□	□
1110	**587**	11½p multicoloured	35	35	□	□

1111	**588**	13p multicoloured	45	50	□	□
1112	**589**	15p multicoloured	45	50	□	□
		Set of 4	1·40	1·25	□	□
		First Day Cover		1·75		□
		Presentation Pack	2·00		□	
		PHQ Cards (set of 4)	1·25	4·00	□	□
		Set of 4 Gutter Pairs	3·50		□	

590 *Rocket* approaching Moorish Arch, Liverpool

591 First and Second Class Carriages passing through Olive Mount Cutting

592 Third Class Carriage and Sheep Truck crossing Chat Moss

593 Horsebox and Carriage Truck near Bridgewater Canal

594 Goods Truck and Mail-coach at Manchester

T **590/4** were printed together, *se-tenant,* in horizontal strips of 5 throughout the sheet.

150th Anniversary of Liverpool and Manchester Railway

1980 (12 Mar.) *Phosphorised paper*

1113	**590**	12p multicoloured	20	10	□	□
		a. Strip of 5. Nos. 1113/17	1·25	1·75	□	□
1114	**591**	12p multicoloured	20	10	□	□
1115	**592**	12p multicoloured	20	10	□	□
1116	**593**	12p multicoloured	20	10	□	□
1117	**594**	12p multicoloured	20	10	□	□
		Set of 5	1·25	50	□	□
		First Day Cover		1·75		□
		Presentation Pack	2·25		□	
		PHQ Cards (set of 5)	1·50	4·00	□	□
		Gutter block of 10	3·00		□	

INTERNATIONAL STAMP EXHIBITION

595 Montage of London Buildings

'London 1980' International Stamp Exhibition

1980 (9 APR.–7 MAY) *Phosphorised paper. Perf* $14\frac{1}{2} \times 14$

1118	595	50p agate	1·60	1·25	□	□
		First Day Cover		2·00		□
		Presentation Pack	2·00		□	
		PHQ Card	75	2·25	□	□
		Gutter Pair	3·00		□	
MS1119		90 × 123 mm. No. 1118 . . .	1·40	1·75	□	□
		First Day Cover (7 May)		2·00		□

No. **MS**1119 was sold at 75p, the premium being used for the exhibition.

596 Buckingham Palace

597 The Albert Memorial

598 Royal Opera House

599 Hampton Court

600 Kensington Palace

London Landmarks

1980 (7 MAY) *Phosphorised paper*

1120	596	10½p multicoloured	20	10	□	□
1121	597	12p multicoloured	20	10	□	□
1122	598	13½p multicoloured	25	40	□	□
1123	599	15p multicoloured	35	50	□	□
1124	600	17½p multicoloured	35	50	□	□
		Set of 5	1·25	1·40	□	□
		First Day Cover		1·75		□
		Presentation Pack	2·50		□	
		PHQ Cards (set of 5)	1·50	3·00	□	□
		Set of 5 Gutter Pairs	3·00		□	

601 Charlotte Brontë (*Jane Eyre*)

602 George Eliot (*The Mill on the Floss*)

603 Emily Brontë (*Wuthering Heights*)

604 Mrs Gaskell (*North and South*)

T **601/4** show authoresses and scenes from their novels. T **601/2** also include the 'Europa' C.E.P.T. emblem.

Famous Authoresses

1980 (9 JULY) *Phosphorised paper*

1125	601	12p multicoloured	25	10	□	□
1126	602	13½p multicoloured	25	35	□	□
1127	603	15p multicoloured	30	45	□	□
1128	604	17½p multicoloured	50	50	□	□
		Set of 4	1·10	1·25	□	□
		First Day Cover		1·75		□
		Presentation Pack	2·50		□	
		PHQ Cards (set of 4)	1·25	3·00	□	□
		Set of 4 Gutter Pairs	3·00		□	

605   Queen Elizabeth the Queen Mother

80th Birthday of Queen Elizabeth the Queen Mother

1980 (4 Aug.) *Phosphorised paper*

1129	**605**	12p multicoloured	1·00	1·00	☐	☐
		First Day Cover		2·25		☐
		PHQ Card	1·00	1·50	☐	☐
		Gutter Pair	2·00		☐	

606   Sir Henry Wood   607   Sir Thomas Beecham

608   Sir Malcolm Sargent   609   Sir John Barbirolli

British Conductors

1980 (10 Sept.) *Phosphorised paper*

1130	**606**	12p multicoloured	20	10	☐	☐
1131	**607**	13½p multicoloured	35	45	☐	☐
1132	**608**	15p multicoloured	40	45	☐	☐
1133	**609**	17½p multicoloured	50	45	☐	☐
		Set of 4	1·25	1·25	☐	☐
		First Day Cover		2·00		☐
		Presentation Pack	2·00		☐	
		PHQ Cards (set of 4)	1·25	3·50	☐	☐
		Set of 4 Gutter Pairs	3·00		☐	

For full information on all future British issues, collectors should write to Royal Mail, Freepost EH3647, 21 South Gyle Crescent, Edinburgh EH12 9PE.

610   Running   611   Rugby

612   Boxing   613   Cricket

Sports Centenaries

1980 (10 Oct.) *Phosphorised paper. Perf* 14 × 14½

1134	**610**	12p multicoloured	20	10	☐	☐
1135	**611**	13½p multicoloured	50	50	☐	☐
1136	**612**	15p multicoloured	25	40	☐	☐
1137	**613**	17½p multicoloured	45	45	☐	☐
		Set of 4	1·25	1·25	☐	☐
		First Day Cover		2·00		☐
		Presentation Pack	2·00		☐	
		PHQ Cards (set of 4)	1·25	3·50	☐	☐
		Set of 4 Gutter Pairs	3·50		☐	

Centenaries:—12p Amateur Athletics Association; 13½p Welsh Rugby Union; 15p Amateur Boxing Association; 17½p First England v Australia Test Match.

614   Christmas Tree   615   Candles

616   Apples and Mistletoe   617   Crown, Chains and Bell

618 Holly

Christmas

1980 (19 Nov.) *One centre phosphor band (10p) or phosphorised paper (others)*

1138	**614**	10p multicoloured	20	10	☐	☐
1139	**615**	12p multicoloured	20	10	☐	☐
1140	**616**	13½p multicoloured	25	35	☐	☐
1141	**617**	15p multicoloured	35	40	☐	☐
1142	**618**	17½p multicoloured	45	40	☐	☐
		Set of 5	1·25	1·25	☐	☐
		First Day Cover		1·75		☐
		Presentation Pack	2·00		☐	
		PHQ Cards (set of 5)	1·25	4·50	☐	☐
		Set of 5 Gutter Pairs	3·25		☐	

Collectors Pack 1980

1980 (19 Nov.) Comprises Nos. 1109/18, 1120/42

	Collectors Pack	14·00		☐

619 St Valentine's Day

620 Morris Dancers

621 Lammastide

622 Medieval Mummers

T **619/20** also include the 'Europa' C.E.P.T. emblem.

Folklore

1981 (6 Feb.) *Phosphorised paper*

1143	**619**	14p multicoloured	25	10	☐	☐
1144	**620**	18p multicoloured	30	50	☐	☐
1145	**621**	22p multicoloured	50	50	☐	☐
1146	**622**	25p multicoloured	60	60	☐	☐
		Set of 4	1·50	1·50	☐	☐
		First Day Cover		2·25		☐
		Presentation Pack	2·50		☐	
		PHQ Cards (set of 4)	1·50	3·00	☐	☐
		Set of 4 Gutter Pairs	4·00		☐	

623 Blind Man with Guide Dog

624 Hands spelling 'Deaf' in Sign Language

625 Disabled Man in Wheelchair

626 Disabled Artist painting with Foot

International Year of the Disabled

1981 (25 Mar.) *Phosphorised paper*

1147	**623**	14p multicoloured	25	10	☐	☐
1148	**624**	18p multicoloured	45	60	☐	☐
1149	**625**	22p multicoloured	50	75	☐	☐
1150	**626**	25p multicoloured	60	85	☐	☐
		Set of 4	1·60	2·10	☐	☐
		First Day Cover		2·25		☐
		Presentation Pack	2·25		☐	
		PHQ Cards (set of 4)	1·50	3·00	☐	☐
		Set of 4 Gutter Pairs	4·00		☐	

627 *Aglais urticae*

628 *Maculinea arion*

629 *Inachis io*

630 *Carterocephalus palaemon*

Butterflies

1981 (13 May) *Phosphorised paper*

1151	**627**	14p multicoloured	. . . . .	25	10	☐ ☐
1152	**628**	18p multicoloured	. . . . .	70	70	☐ ☐
1153	**629**	22p multicoloured	. . . . .	80	75	☐ ☐
1154	**630**	25p multicoloured	. . . . .	85	80	☐ ☐
		Set of 4	. . . .	2·40	2·10	☐ ☐
		First Day Cover	. . . .		3·00	☐
		Presentation Pack	. . . .	2·75		☐
		PHQ Cards (set of 4)		2·00	5·00	☐ ☐
		Set of 4 Gutter Pairs	. . . . .	5·50		☐

631 Glenfinnan, Scotland   **632** Derwentwater, England

633 Stackpole Head, Wales   **634** Giant's Causeway, N. Ireland

635 St Kilda, Scotland

50th Anniversary of National Trust for Scotland

1981 (24 June) *Phosphorised paper*

1155	**631**	14p multicoloured	. . . . .	25	10	☐ ☐
1156	**632**	18p multicoloured	. . . . .	35	40	☐ ☐
1157	**633**	20p multicoloured	. . . . .	60	70	☐ ☐
1158	**634**	22p multicoloured	. . . . .	60	85	☐ ☐
1159	**635**	25p multicoloured	. . . . .	70	90	☐ ☐
		Set of 5	. . . .	2·25	2·75	☐ ☐
		First Day Cover	. . . .		3·00	☐
		Presentation Pack	. . . .	2·75		☐
		PHQ Cards (set of 5)	. . . . .	2·00	5·00	☐ ☐
		Set of 5 Gutter Pairs	. . . . .	5·00		☐

636 Prince Charles and Lady Diana Spencer

Royal Wedding

1981 (22 July) *Phosphorised paper*

1160	**636**	14p multicoloured	. . . . .	1·00	20	☐ ☐
1161		25p multicoloured	. . . . .	2·00	2·40	☐ ☐
		Set of 2	. . . .	3·00	2·50	☐ ☐
		First Day Cover	. . . .		4·00	☐
		Presentation Pack	. . . .	4·00		☐
		Souvenir Book	. . . .	6·00		☐
		PHQ Cards (set of 2)	. . . . .	3·00	5·50	☐ ☐
		Set of 2 Gutter Pairs	. . . . .	6·50		☐

637 'Expeditions'   **638** 'Skills'

639 'Service'   **640** 'Recreation'

25th Anniversary of Duke of Edinburgh Award Scheme

1981 (12 Aug.) *Phosphorised paper. Perf 14*

1162	**637**	14p multicoloured	. . . . .	25	10	☐ ☐
1163	**638**	18p multicoloured	. . . . .	40	50	☐ ☐
1164	**639**	22p multicoloured	. . . . .	50	50	☐ ☐
1165	**640**	25p multicoloured	. . . . .	60	50	☐ ☐
		Set of 4	. . . .	1·60	1·40	☐ ☐
		First Day Cover	. . . .		2·25	☐
		Presentation Pack	. . . .	2·75		☐
		PHQ Cards (set of 4)	. . . . .	2·00	4·00	☐ ☐
		Set of 4 Gutter Pairs	. . . . .	3·50		☐

641 Cockle-dredging from *Linsey II*

642 Hauling Trawl Net

643 Lobster Potting

644 Hoisting Seine Net

Fishing Industry

1981 (23 SEPT.) *Phosphorised paper*

1166	**641**	14p multicoloured	25	10	□	□
1167	**642**	18p multicoloured	40	50	□	□
1168	**643**	22p multicoloured	45	50	□	□
1169	**644**	25p multicoloured	55	50	□	□
		Set of 4	1·50	1·40	□	□
		First Day Cover		1·90		□
		Presentation Pack	2·75		□	
		PHQ Cards (set of 4)	2·00	4·00	□	□
		Set of 4 Gutter Pairs	3·50		□	

Nos. 1166/9 were issued on the occasion of the centenary of Royal National Mission to Deep Sea Fishermen.

645 Father Christmas

646 Jesus Christ

647 Flying Angel

648 Joseph and Mary arriving at Bethlehem

649 Three Kings approaching Bethlehem

Christmas. Children's Pictures

1981 (18 NOV.) *One phosphor band (11½p) or phosphorised paper (others)*

1170	**645**	11½p multicoloured	20	10	□	□
1171	**646**	14p multicoloured	30	10	□	□
1172	**647**	18p multicoloured	45	45	□	□
1173	**648**	22p multicoloured	50	55	□	□
1174	**649**	25p multicoloured	60	50	□	□
		Set of 5	1·90	1·50	□	□
		First Day Cover		2·50		□
		Presentation Pack	2·75		□	
		PHQ Cards (set of 5)	2·00	5·00	□	□
		Set of 5 Gutter Pairs	4·25		□	

Collectors Pack 1981

1981 (18 NOV.) *Comprises Nos. 1143/74*

	Collectors Pack	18·00	□

650 Charles Darwin and Giant Tortoises

651 Darwin and Marine Iguanas

652 Darwin, Cactus Ground Finch and Large Ground Finch

653 Darwin and Prehistoric Skulls

Death Centenary of Charles Darwin

1982 (10 FEB.) *Phosphorised paper*

1175	**650**	15½p multicoloured	35	10	□	□
1176	**651**	19½p multicoloured	50	50	□	□
1177	**652**	26p multicoloured	70	70	□	□
1178	**653**	29p multicoloured	70	70	□	□
		Set of 4	2·00	1·75	□	□
		First Day Cover		2·75		□
		Presentation Pack	3·00		□	
		PHQ Cards (set of 4)	2·50	6·50	□	□
		Set of 4 Gutter Pairs	4·50		□	

654 Boys' Brigade

655 Girls' Brigade

656 Boy Scout Movement

657 Girl Guide Movement

660 Hamlet

661 Opera Singer

Europa. British Theatre
1982 (28 APR.) *Phosphorised paper*

1183	**658**	15½p multicoloured	25	10	☐	☐
1184	**659**	19½p multicoloured	50	60	☐	☐
1185	**660**	26p multicoloured	85	85	☐	☐
1186	**661**	29p multicoloured	95	1·10	☐	☐
		Set of 4	2·40	2·40	☐	☐
		First Day Cover		3·00		☐
		Presentation Pack	3·00		☐	
		PHQ Cards (set of 4)	2·50	6·50	☐	☐
		Set of 4 Gutter Pairs	5·50		☐	

Youth Organizations
1982 (24 MAR.) *Phosphorised paper*

1179	**654**	15½p multicoloured	25	10	☐	☐
1180	**655**	19½p multicoloured	55	70	☐	☐
1181	**656**	26p multicoloured	75	95	☐	☐
1182	**657**	29p multicoloured	90	1·00	☐	☐
		Set of 4	2·25	2·50	☐	☐
		First Day Cover		2·75		☐
		Presentation Pack	3·25		☐	
		PHQ Cards (set of 4)	2·25	6·50	☐	☐
		Set of 4 Gutter Pairs	5·00		☐	

Nos. 1179/82 were issued on the occasion of the 75th anniversary of the Boy Scout Movement, the 125th birth anniversary of Lord Baden-Powell and the centenary of the Boys' Brigade (1983).

662 Henry VIII and *Mary Rose*

663 Admiral Blake and *Triumph*

664 Lord Nelson and HMS *Victory*

665 Lord Fisher and HMS *Dreadnought*

658 Ballerina

659 Harlequin

666 Viscount Cunningham and HMS *Warspite*

Maritime Heritage

1982 (16 JUNE) *Phosphorised paper*

1187	662	15½p multicoloured	40	10	□	□
1188	663	19½p multicoloured	60	55	□	□
1189	664	24p multicoloured	80	80	□	□
1190	665	26p multicoloured	90	90	□	□
1191	666	29p multicoloured	1·00	1·00	□	□
		Set of 5	3·25	3·00	□	□
		First Day Cover		3·50		□
		Presentation Pack	3·75		□	
		PHQ Cards (set of 5)	3·00	7·50	□	□
		Set of 5 Gutter Pairs	7·00		□	

667 'Strawberry Thief'
(William Morris)

668 Untitled
(Steiner and Co)

669 'Cherry Orchard'
(Paul Nash)

670 'Chevron'
(Andrew Foster)

British Textiles

1982 (23 JULY) *Phosphorised paper*

1192	667	15½p multicoloured	30	10	□	□
1193	668	19½p multicoloured	60	70	□	□
1194	669	26p multicoloured	80	90	□	□
1195	670	29p multicoloured	90	1·10	□	□
		Set of 4	2·40	2·50	□	□
		First Day Cover		3·00		□
		Presentation Pack	3·00		□	
		PHQ Cards (set of 4)	3·00	6·50	□	□
		Set of 4 Gutter Pairs	5·50		□	

Nos 1192/5 were issued on the occasion of the 250th birth anniversary of Sir Richard Arkwright (inventor of spinning machine).

For full information on all future British issues, collectors should write to Royal Mail, Freepost EH3647, 21 South Gyle Crescent, Edinburgh EH12 9PE.

671 Development of Communications

672 Modern Technological Aids

Information Technology

1982 (8 SEPT.) *Phosphorised paper. Perf* 14 × 15

1196	671	15½p multicoloured	35	10	□	□
1197	672	26p multicoloured	60	90	□	□
		Set of 2	95	1·00	□	□
		First Day Cover		1·75		□
		Presentation Pack	1·75		□	
		PHQ Cards (set of 2)	1·50	4·50	□	□
		Set of 2 Gutter Pairs	2·00		□	

673 Austin 'Seven' and 'Metro'

674 Ford 'Model T' and 'Escort'

675 Jaguar 'SS1' and 'XJ6'

676 Rolls-Royce 'Silver Ghost' and 'Silver Spirit'

British Motor Industry

1982 (13 OCT.) *Phosphorised paper. Perf* 14½ × 14

1198	673	15½p multicoloured	35	10	□	□
1199	674	19½p multicoloured	60	60	□	□
1200	675	26p multicoloured	70	75	□	□
1201	676	29p multicoloured	1·10	1·00	□	□
		Set of 4	2·50	2·25	□	□
		First Day Cover		3·00		□
		Presentation Pack	3·00		□	
		PHQ Cards (set of 4)	2·75	6·75	□	□
		Set of 4 Gutter Pairs	5·50		□	

677 'While Shepherds Watched'

678 'The Holly and the Ivy'

679 'I Saw Three Ships'

680 'We Three Kings'

681 'Good King Wenceslas'

Christmas. Carols
1982 (17 Nov.) *One phosphor band* (12½p) *or phosphorised paper* (*others*).

1202	677	12½p multicoloured	25	10	☐	☐
1203	678	15½p multicoloured	35	10	☐	☐
1204	679	19½p multicoloured	75	80	☐	☐
1205	680	26p multicoloured	85	90	☐	☐
1206	681	29p multicoloured	90	1·00	☐	☐
		Set of 5	2·75	2·50	☐	☐
		First Day Cover		3·00		☐
		Presentation Pack	3·00		☐	
		PHQ Cards (*set of 5*)	3·00	7·00	☐	☐
		Set of 5 Gutter Pairs	6·00		☐	

Collectors Pack 1982
1982 (17 Nov.) *Comprises Nos.* 1175/1206

	Collectors Pack	22·00	☐

682 Atlantic Salmon

683 Northern Pike

684 Brown Trout

685 Eurasian Perch

British River Fishes
1983 (26 Jan.) *Phosphorised paper*

1207	682	15½p multicoloured	35	10	☐	☐
1208	683	19½p multicoloured	75	75	☐	☐
1209	684	26p multicoloured	90	90	☐	☐
1210	685	29p multicoloured	1·10	1·10	☐	☐
		Set of 4	2·75	2·50	☐	☐
		First Day Cover		3·00		☐
		Presentation Pack	3·00		☐	
		PHQ Cards (*set of 4*)	3·00	7·50	☐	☐
		Set of 4 Gutter Pairs	6·00		☐	

686 Tropical Island

687 Desert

688 Temperate Farmland

689 Mountain Range

Commonwealth Day. Geographical Regions
1983 (9 Mar.) *Phosphorised paper*

1211	686	15½p multicoloured	30	10	☐	☐
1212	687	19½p multicoloured	65	75	☐	☐
1213	688	26p multicoloured	85	90	☐	☐
1214	689	29p multicoloured	1·00	1·00	☐	☐
		Set of 4	2·50	2·50	☐	☐
		First Day Cover		3·00		☐
		Presentation Pack	3·25		☐	
		PHQ Cards (*set of 4*)	3·00	6·50	☐	☐
		Set of 4 Gutter Pairs	5·25		☐	

690   Humber Bridge

691   Thames Flood Barrier

692   *Iolair* (oilfield emergency support vessel)

Europa. Engineering Achievements

1983 (25 MAY) *Phosphorised paper*

1215	**690**	16p multicoloured	35	10	☐	☐
1216	**691**	20½p multicoloured	1·00	1·25	☐	☐
1217	**692**	28p multicoloured	1·10	1·25	☐	☐
		Set of 3	2·25	2·40	☐	☐
		First Day Cover		2·75		☐
		Presentation Pack	3·25			☐
		PHQ Cards (set of 3)	2·50	5·00	☐	☐
		Set of 3 Gutter Pairs	4·75			☐

693   Musketeer and Pikeman, The Royal Scots (1633)

694   Fusilier and Ensign, The Royal Welch Fusiliers (mid-18th century)

695   Riflemen, 95th Rifles (The Royal Green Jackets) (1805)

696   Sergeant (khaki service uniform) and Guardsman full dress), The Irish Guards (1900).

697   Paratroopers, The Parachute Regiment (1983)

British Army Uniforms

1983 (6 JULY) *Phosphorised paper*

1218	**693**	16p multicoloured	35	10	☐	☐
1219	**694**	20½p multicoloured	55	75	☐	☐
1220	**695**	26p multicoloured	85	1·10	☐	☐
1221	**696**	28p multicoloured	90	1·10	☐	☐
1222	**697**	31p multicoloured	95	1·00	☐	☐
		Set of 5	3·25	3·75	☐	☐
		First Day Cover		4·00		☐
		Presentation Pack	4·25			☐
		PHQ Cards (set of 5)	3·00	7·50	☐	☐
		Set of 5 Gutter Pairs	6·50			☐

Nos. 1218/22 were issued on the occasion of the 350th anniversary of The Royal Scots, the senior line regiment of the British Army.

698   20th-Century Garden, Sissinghurst

699   19th-Century Garden, Biddulph Grange

700   18th-Century Garden, Blenheim

701   17th-Century Garden, Pitmedden

British Gardens

1983 (24 Aug.) *Phosphorised paper. Perf* 14

1223	**698**	16p multicoloured	35	10	☐	☐
1224	**699**	20½p multicoloured	50	70	☐	☐
1225	**700**	28p multicoloured	95	1·10	☐	☐
1226	**701**	31p multicoloured	1·00	1·10	☐	☐
		Set of 4	2·50	2·75	☐	☐
		First Day Cover		3·00		☐
		Presentation Pack	3·75		☐	
		PHQ Cards (set of 4)	3·00	6·00	☐	☐
		Set of 4 Gutter Pairs	5·50		☐	

702 Merry-go-round

703 Big Wheel, Helter-skelter and Performing Animals

704 Side-shows

705 Early Produce Fair

British Fairs

1983 (5 Oct.) *Phosphorised paper*

1227	**702**	16p multicoloured	35	10	☐	☐
1228	**703**	20½p multicoloured	65	80	☐	☐
1229	**704**	28p multicoloured	80	90	☐	☐
1230	**705**	31p multicoloured	90	95	☐	☐
		Set of 4	2·40	2·50	☐	☐
		First Day Cover		2·75		☐
		Presentation Pack	3·75		☐	
		PHQ Cards (set of 4)	3·00	6·00	☐	☐
		Set of 4 Gutter Pairs	5·25		☐	

Nos. 1227/30 were issued to mark the 850th anniversary of St Bartholomew's Fair, Smithfield, London.

706 'Christmas Post' (pillar-box)

707 'The Three Kings' (chimney-pots)

708 'World at Peace' (Dove and Blackbird)

709 'Light of Christmas' (street lamp)

710 'Christmas Dove' (hedge sculpture)

Christmas

1983 (16 Nov.) *One phosphor band* (12½p) *or phosphorised paper* (*others*)

1231	**706**	12½p multicoloured	25	10	☐	☐
1232	**707**	16p multicoloured	30	10	☐	☐
1233	**708**	20½p multicoloured	65	95	☐	☐
1234	**709**	28p multicoloured	85	1·00	☐	☐
1235	**710**	31p multicoloured	1·00	1·25	☐	☐
		Set of 5	2·75	3·00	☐	☐
		First Day Cover		3·50		☐
		Presentation Pack	3·75		☐	
		PHQ Cards (set of 5)	3·00	6·00	☐	☐
		Set of 5 Gutter Pairs	6·00		☐	

Collectors Pack 1983

1983 (16 Nov.) *Comprises Nos.* 1207/35

	Collectors Pack	38·00	☐

711 Arms of the College of Arms

712 Arms of King Richard III (founder)

713 Arms of the Earl Marshal of England

714 Arms of the City of London

500th Anniversary of College of Arms

1984 (17 Jan.) *Phosphorised paper. Perf* 14½

1236	**711**	16p multicoloured	35	10	□	□
1237	**712**	20½p multicoloured	50	75	□	□
1238	**713**	28p multicoloured	95	1·10	□	□
1239	**714**	31p multicoloured	1·00	1·25	□	□
		Set of 4	2·50	3·00	□	□
		First Day Cover		3·50		□
		Presentation Pack	3·50		□	
		PHQ *Cards* (*set of 4*)	3·00	7·50	□	□
		Set of 4 Gutter Pairs	5·50		□	

715 Highland Cow

716 Chillingham Wild Bull

717 Hereford Bull

718 Welsh Black Bull

719 Irish Moiled Cow

British Cattle

1984 (6 Mar.) *Phosphorised paper*

1240	**715**	16p multicoloured	45	10	□	□
1241	**716**	20½p multicoloured	70	75	□	□
1242	**717**	26p multicoloured	90	90	□	□
1243	**718**	28p multicoloured	95	1·00	□	□
1244	**719**	31p multicoloured	1·25	1·10	□	□
		Set of 5	3·75	3·50	□	□
		First Day Cover		4·00		□
		Presentation Pack	4·00		□	
		PHQ *Cards* (*set of 5*)	3·00	7·50	□	□
		Set of 5 Gutter Pairs	7·50		□	

Nos. 1240/4 marked the centenary of the Highland Cattle Society and the bicentenary of the Royal Highland and Agricultural Society of Scotland.

720 Festival Hall, Liverpool   **721** Milburngate Shopping Centre, Durham

722 Bush House, Bristol   **723** Commercial Street Housing Scheme, Perth

Urban Renewal

1984 (10 Apr.) *Phosphorised paper*

1245	**720**	16p multicoloured	35	10	□	□
1246	**721**	20½p multicoloured	60	75	□	□
1247	**722**	28p multicoloured	1·10	1·25	□	□
1248	**723**	31p multicoloured	1·25	1·25	□	□
		Set of 4	3·00	3·00	□	□
		First Day Cover		3·50		□
		Presentation Pack	3·50		□	
		PHQ *Cards* (*set of 4*)	3·00	6·00	□	□
		Set of 4 Gutter Pairs	6·25		□	

Nos. 1245/8 marked the opening of the International Gardens Festival, Liverpool, and the 150th anniversaries of the Royal Institute of British Architects and the Chartered Institute of Building.

724 C.E.P.T. 25th Anniversary Logo   **725** Abduction of Europa

Nos. 1249/50 and 1251/2 were each printed together, *se-tenant,* in horizontal pairs throughout the sheets.

For full information on all future British issues, collectors should write to Royal Mail, Freepost EH3647, 21 South Gyle Crescent, Edinburgh EH12 9PE.

Europa. 25th Anniversary of C.E.P.T. and 2nd European Parliamentary Elections

1984 (15 MAY) *Phosphorised paper*

1249	**724**	16p greenish slate, deep blue and gold	70	15	☐	☐
		a. Horiz pair. Nos. 1249/50	1·50	1·50	☐	☐
1250	**725**	16p greenish slate, deep blue, black and gold .	70	15	☐	☐
1251	**724**	20½p Venetian red, deep magenta and gold . .	1·60	1·00	☐	☐
		a. Horiz pair. Nos. 1251/2	3·25	2·75	☐	☐
1252	**725**	20½p Venetian red, deep magenta, black and gold	1·60	1·00	☐	☐
		Set of 4	4·25	2·10	☐	☐
		First Day Cover		4·50		☐
		Presentation Pack	4·50		☐	
		PHQ Cards (set of 4)	3·00	6·00	☐	☐
		Set of 2 Gutter Blocks of 4 . . .	9·00		☐	

726 Lancaster House

London Economic Summit Conference

1984 (5 JUNE) *Phosphorised paper*

1253	**726**	31p multicoloured	1·00	1·00	☐	☐
		First Day Cover		2·25		☐
		PHQ Card	1·00	3·50	☐	☐
		Gutter Pair	2·00		☐	

727 View of Earth from 'Apollo 11'

728 Navigational Chart of English Channel

729 Greenwich Observatory

730 Sir George Airey's Transit Telescope

Centenary of Greenwich Meridian

1984 (26 JUNE) *Phosphorised paper. Perf* 14 × 14½

1254	**727**	16p multicoloured	45	10	☐	☐
1255	**728**	20½p multicoloured	70	75	☐	☐
1256	**729**	28p multicoloured	95	95	☐	☐
1257	**730**	31p multicoloured	1·25	1·25	☐	☐
		Set of 4	3·00	2·75	☐	☐
		First Day Cover		3·00		☐
		Presentation Pack	3·75		☐	
		PHQ Cards (set of 4)	3·00	6·00	☐	☐
		Set of 4 Gutter Pairs	6·25		☐	

731 Bath Mail Coach, 1784

732 Attack on Exeter Mail, 1816

733 Norwich Mail in Thunderstorm, 1827

734 Holyhead and Liverpool Mails leaving London, 1828

735 Edinburgh Mail Snowbound, 1831

T **731/5** were printed together, *se-tenant,* in horizontal strips of 5 throughout the sheet.

Bicentenary of First Mail Coach Run, Bath and Bristol to London

1984 (31 JULY) *Phosphorised paper*

1258	731	16p multicoloured	50	15	☐	☐
		a. Horiz strip of 5. Nos.				
		1258/62	2·75	3·25	☐	☐
1259	732	16p multicoloured	50	15	☐	☐
1260	733	16p multicoloured	50	15	☐	☐
1261	734	16p multicoloured	50	15	☐	☐
1262	735	16p multicoloured	50	15	☐	☐
		Set of 5	2·75	60	☐	☐
		First Day Cover		3·50		☐
		Presentation Pack	3·75			☐
		Souvenir Book	6·00			☐
		PHQ Cards (set of 5)	3·00	7·50	☐	☐
		Gutter Block of 10	6·00			☐

736 Nigerian Clinic

737 Violinist and Acropolis, Athens

738 Building Project, Sri Lanka

739 British Council Library

50th Anniversary of The British Council

1984 (25 SEPT.) *Phosphorised paper*

1263	736	17p multicoloured	45	10	☐	☐
1264	737	22p multicoloured	65	90	☐	☐
1265	738	31p multicoloured	80	1·25	☐	☐
1266	739	34p multicoloured	90	1·10	☐	☐
		Set of 4	2·50	3·00	☐	☐
		First Day Cover		3·25		☐
		Presentation Pack	3·25			☐
		PHQ Cards (set of 4)	3·00	6·00	☐	☐
		Set of 4 Gutter Pairs	5·00			☐

For full information on all future British issues, collectors should write to Royal Mail, Freepost EH3647, 21 South Gyle Crescent, Edinburgh EH12 9PE.

740 The Holy Family

741 Arrival in Bethlehem

742 Shepherd and Lamb

743 Virgin and Child

744 Offering of Frankincense

Christmas

1984 (20 NOV.) *One phosphor band (13p) or phosphorised paper (others)*

1267	740	13p multicoloured	25	10	☐	☐
1268	741	17p multicoloured	45	10	☐	☐
1269	742	22p multicoloured	50	80	☐	☐
1270	743	31p multicoloured	75	1·10	☐	☐
1271	744	34p multicoloured	1·00	1·25	☐	☐
		Set of 5	2·75	3·00	☐	☐
		First Day Cover		3·25		☐
		Presentation Pack	4·00			☐
		PHQ Cards (set of 5)	3·00	6·00	☐	☐
		Set of 5 Gutter Pairs	6·00			☐

Collectors Pack 1984

1984 (20 NOV.) *Comprises Nos. 1236/71*

Collectors Pack	38·00		☐

Post Office Yearbook

1984 *Comprises Nos. 1236/71 in hardbound book with slip case*

Yearbook	£100		☐

745 'Flying Scotsman'

746 'Golden Arrow'

747 'Cheltenham Flyer'

748 'Royal Scot'

749 'Cornish Riviera'

Wart-Biter Bush-Cricket

752 *Decticus verrucivorus*
(bush-cricket)

Stag Beetle

753 *Lucanus cervus*
(stag beetle)

Emperor Dragonfly

754 *Anax imperator* (dragonfly)

Famous Trains

1985 (22 JAN.) *Phosphorised paper*

1272	**745**	17p multicoloured	40	10	☐	☐
1273	**746**	22p multicoloured	75	95	☐	☐
1274	**747**	29p multicoloured	90	1·10	☐	☐
1275	**748**	31p multicoloured	1·10	1·40	☐	☐
1276	**749**	34p multicoloured	1·25	1·40	☐	☐
		Set of 5	4·00	4·50	☐	☐
		First Day Cover		5·00		☐
		Presentation Pack	4·75		☐	
		PHQ Cards (*set of* 5)	5·00	16·00	☐	☐
		Set of 5 *Gutter Pairs*	8·00		☐	

Nos. 1272/6 were issued on the occasion of the 150th anniversary of the Great Western Railway Company.

Insects

1985 (12 MAR.) *Phosphorised paper*

1277	**750**	17p multicoloured	45	10	☐	☐
1278	**751**	22p multicoloured	65	65	☐	☐
1279	**752**	29p multicoloured	95	1·00	☐	☐
1280	**753**	31p multicoloured	1·10	1·10	☐	☐
1281	**754**	34p multicoloured	1·10	1·00	☐	☐
		Set of 5	3·75	3·50	☐	☐
		First Day Cover		4·00		☐
		Presentation Pack	4·50		☐	
		PHQ Cards (*set of* 5)	3·00	8·00	☐	☐
		Set of 5 *Gutter Pairs*	7·50		☐	

Nos. 1277/81 were issued on the occasion of the centenaries of the Royal Entomological Society of London's Royal Charter and of the Selborne Society.

Buff Tailed Bumble Bee

750 *Bombus terrestris*
(bee)

Seven Spotted Ladybird

751 *Coccinella septempunctata*
(ladybird)

SEVENTEEN·PENCE

WATER·MUSIC
George Frideric Handel

755 'Water Music',
by Handel

TWENTY·TWO·PENCE

THE·PLANETS·SUITE
Gustav Holst

756 'The Planets',
by Holst

757 'The First Cuckoo', by Delius

758 'Sea Pictures', by Elgar

Europa. European Music Year

1985 (14 May) *Phosphorised paper. Perf 14½*

1282	**755**	17p multicoloured	65	10	☐	☐
1283	**756**	22p multicoloured	90	1·10	☐	☐
1284	**757**	31p multicoloured	1·40	1·50	☐	☐
1285	**758**	34p multicoloured	1·50	1·60	☐	☐
		Set of 4	4·00	4·00	☐	☐
		First Day Cover		4·00		☐
		Presentation Pack	4·50		☐	
		PHQ Cards (set of 4)	3·00	6·00	☐	☐
		Set of 4 Gutter Pairs	8·00		☐	

Nos. 1282/5 were issued on the occasion of the 300th birth anniversary of Handel.

759 R.N.L.I. Lifeboat and Signal Flags

760 Beachy Head Lighthouse and Chart

761 'Marecs A' Communications Satelite and Dish Aerials

762 Buoys

Safety at Sea

1985 (18 June) *Phosphorised paper. Perf 14*

1286	**759**	17p multicoloured	45	10	☐	☐
1287	**760**	22p multicoloured	65	85	☐	☐

1288	**761**	31p multicoloured	1·00	1·25	☐	☐
1289	**762**	34p multicoloured	1·10	1·25	☐	☐
		Set of 4	3·00	3·25	☐	☐
		First Day Cover		4·00		☐
		Presentation Pack	3·75		☐	
		PHQ Cards (set of 4)	3·00	6·00	☐	☐
		Set of 4 Gutter Pairs	6·00		☐	

Nos. 1286/9 were issued to mark the bicentenary of the unimmersible lifeboat and the 50th anniversary of Radar.

763 Datapost Motorcyclist, City of London

764 Rural Postbus

765 Parcel Delivery in Winter

766 Town Letter Delivery

350 Years of Royal Mail Public Postal Service

1985 (30 July) *Phosphorised paper*

1290	**763**	17p multicoloured	40	10	☐	☐
1291	**764**	22p multicoloured	60	85	☐	☐
1292	**765**	31p multicoloured	95	1·25	☐	☐
1293	**766**	34p multicoloured	1·10	1·25	☐	☐
		Set of 4	2·75	3·25	☐	☐
		First Day Cover		3·75		☐
		Presentation Pack	3·75		☐	
		PHQ Cards (set of 4)	3·00	6·00	☐	☐
		Set of 4 Gutter Pairs	5·50		☐	

767 King Arthur and Merlin

768 The Lady of the Lake

769 Queen Guinevere and Sir Lancelot   **770** Sir Galahad

Arthurian Legends

1985 (3 Sept.) *Phosphorised paper*

1294	**767**	17p multicoloured	40	10	☐	☐
1295	**768**	22p multicoloured	65	85	☐	☐
1296	**769**	31p multicoloured	1·10	1·40	☐	☐
1297	**770**	34p multicoloured	1·25	1·40	☐	☐
		Set of 4	3·00	3·50	☐	☐
		First Day Cover		4·50		☐
		Presentation Pack	5·00		☐	
		PHQ Cards (set of 4)	3·00	7·50	☐	☐
		Set of 4 Gutter Pairs	6·00		☐	

Nos. 1294/7 were issued to mark the 500th anniversary of the printing of Sir Thomas Malory's *Morte d'Arthur*.

771 Peter Sellers (from photo by Bill Brandt)

772 David Niven (from photo by Cornell Lucas)

773 Charlie Chaplin (from photo by Lord Snowdon)

774 Vivien Leigh (from photo by Angus McBean)

775 Alfred Hitchcock (from photo by Howard Coster)

British Film Year

1985 (8 Oct.) *Phosphorised paper. Perf 14½*

1298	**771**	17p multicoloured	50	10	☐	☐
1299	**772**	22p multicoloured	65	85	☐	☐
1300	**773**	29p multicoloured	1·10	1·40	☐	☐
1301	**774**	31p multicoloured	1·25	1·50	☐	☐
1302	**775**	34p multicoloured	1·50	1·60	☐	☐
		Set of 5	4·50	5·00	☐	☐
		First Day Cover		5·25		☐
		Presentation Pack	7·00		☐	
		Souvenir Book	8·00		☐	
		PHQ Cards (set of 5)	3·00	9·00	☐	☐
		Set of 5 Gutter Pairs	9·00		☐	

776 Principal Boy   **777** Genie

778 Dame   **779** Good Fairy

780 Pantomime Cat

Christmas. Pantomime Characters

1985 (19 Nov.) *One phosphor band (12p) or phosphorised paper (others)*

1303	**776**	12p multicoloured	30	10	☐	☐
1304	**777**	17p multicoloured	35	10	☐	☐
1305	**778**	22p multicoloured	60	85	☐	☐
1306	**779**	31p multicoloured	90	1·00	☐	☐
1307	**780**	34p multicoloured	1·00	1·10	☐	☐
		Set of 5	2·75	2·75	☐	☐
		First Day Cover		4·00		☐
		Presentation Pack	4·00		☐	
		PHQ Cards (Set of 5)	3·00	8·00	☐	☐
		Set of 5 Gutter Pairs	5·50		☐	

Collectors Pack 1985

1985 (19 Nov.) *Comprises Nos.* 1272/1307
    Collectors Pack . . . . 38·00 □

Post Office Yearbook

1985 *Comprises Nos.* 1272/1307 *in hardbound book with slip case*
    Yearbook . . . . 80·00 □

781 Light Bulb and North Sea Oil Drilling Rig (Energy)
782 Thermometer and Pharmaceutical Laboratory (Health)

783 Garden Hoe and Steel Works (Steel)
784 Loaf of Bread and and Cornfield (Agriculture)

Industry Year

1986 (14 Jan.) *Phosphorised paper. Perf* $14\frac{1}{2} \times 14$

1308	**781**	17p multicoloured	45		10	□ □
1309	**782**	22p multicoloured	70		85	□ □
1310	**783**	31p multicoloured	1·10		1·25	□ □
1311	**784**	34p multicoloured	1·40		1·40	□ □
		Set of 4	3·25		3·25	□ □
		First Day Cover			4·00	□
		Presentation Pack	4·00			□
		PHQ Cards (set of 4)	3·00		6·00	□ □
		Set of 4 Gutter Pairs	6·50			□

785 Dr Edmond Halley as Comet
786 *Giotto* Spacecraft approaching Comet

787 'Twice in a Lifetime'
788 Comet orbiting Sun and Planets

Appearance of Halley's Comet

1986 (18 Feb.) *Phosphorised paper*

1312	**785**	17p multicoloured	40		10	□ □
1313	**786**	22p multicoloured	70		95	□ □
1314	**787**	31p multicoloured	1·00		1·25	□ □
1315	**788**	34p multicoloured	1·10		1·25	□ □
		Set of 4	3·00		3·25	□ □
		First Day Cover			4·00	□
		Presentation Pack	4·00			□
		PHQ Cards (set of 4)	4·00		6·00	□ □
		Set of 4 Gutter Pairs	6·00			□

789 Queen Elizabeth II in 1928, 1942 and 1952
790 Queen Elizabeth II in 1958, 1973 and 1982

Nos. 1316/17 and 1318/19 were each printed together, *se-tenant*, in horizontal pairs throughout the sheets.

60th Birthday of Queen Elizabeth II

1986 (21 Apr.) *Phosphorised paper*

1316	**789**	17p multicoloured	50		15	□ □
		a. Horiz pair. Nos. 1316/17	1·25		1·40	□ □
1317	**790**	17p multicoloured	50		15	□ □
1318	**789**	34p multicoloured	1·25		1·75	□ □
		a. Horiz pair. Nos. 1318/19	2·75		3·75	□ □
1319	**790**	34p multicoloured	1·25		1·75	□ □
		Set of 4	4·00		3·50	□ □
		First Day Cover			5·00	□
		Presentation Pack	5·00			□
		Souvenir Book	8·00			□
		PHQ Cards (set of 4)	3·00		7·00	□ □
		Set of 2 Gutter Blocks of 4 . . .	8·00			□

For full information on all future British issues, collectors should write to Royal Mail, Freepost EH3647, 21 South Gyle Crescent, Edinburgh EH12 9PE.

791 Barn Owl

792 Pine Marten

793 Wild Cat

794 Natterjack Toad

Europa. Nature Conservation. Endangered Species

1986 (20 May) *Phosphorised paper. Perf* 14½ × 14

1320	**791**	17p multicoloured	. . . . .	50		10	☐ ☐
1321	**792**	22p multicoloured	. . . . .	1·00		1·25	☐ ☐
1322	**793**	31p multicoloured	. . . . .	1·50		1·60	☐ ☐
1323	**794**	34p multicoloured	. . . . .	1·75		1·75	☐ ☐
		Set of 4	. . . .	4·25		4·25	☐ ☐
		First Day Cover	. . . .			5·00	☐
		Presentation Pack	. . . .	5·00			☐
		PHQ Cards (set of 4)	. . . . . .	3·00		7·00	☐ ☐
		Set of 4 Gutter Pairs	. . . . . .	8·50			☐

795 Peasants Working in Fields

796 Freemen working at Town Trades

797 Knight and Retainers

798 Lord at Banquet

900th Anniversary of Domesday Book

1986 (17 June) *Phosphorised paper*

1324	**795**	17p multicoloured	. . . . .	35		10	☐ ☐
1325	**796**	22p multicoloured	. . . . .	65		85	☐ ☐
1326	**797**	31p multicoloured	. . . . .	1·00		1·40	☐ ☐
1327	**798**	34p multicoloured	. . . . .	1·10		1·40	☐ ☐
		Set of 4	. . . .	2·75		3·50	☐ ☐
		First Day Cover	. . . .			4·00	☐
		Presentation Pack	. . . .	3·75			☐
		PHQ Cards (set of 4)	. . . . . .	3·00		6·00	☐ ☐
		Set of 4 Gutter Pairs	. . . . . .	6·00			☐

799 Athletics

800 Rowing

801 Weightlifting

802 Rifle-shooting

803 Hockey

Thirteenth Commonwealth Games, Edinburgh (Nos. 1328/31) and World Men's Hockey Cup, London (No. 1332)

1986 (15 July) *Phosphorised paper*

1328	**799**	17p multicoloured	. . . . .	50		10	☐ ☐
1329	**800**	22p multicoloured	. . . . .	70		85	☐ ☐
1330	**801**	29p multicoloured	. . . . .	90		1·00	☐ ☐
1331	**802**	31p multicoloured	. . . . .	1·25		1·40	☐ ☐
1332	**803**	34p multicoloured	. . . . .	1·40		1·40	☐ ☐
		Set of 5	. . . .	4·25		4·25	☐ ☐
		First Day Cover	. . . .			5·00	☐
		Presentation Pack	. . . .	5·00			☐
		PHQ Cards (set of 5)	. . . . . .	4·00		8·00	☐ ☐
		Set of 5 Gutter Pairs	. . . . . .	8·50			☐

No. 1332 also marked the centenary of the Hockey Association.

804 Prince Andrew and Miss Sarah Ferguson 805

Royal Wedding

1986 (22 JULY) *One side band* (12p) *or phosphorised paper* (17p)

1333	**804**	12p multicoloured	50	15	□	□
1334	**805**	17p multicoloured	90	60	□	□
		Set of 2	1·40	75	□	□
		First Day Cover		2·75		□
		Presentation Pack	2·00		□	
		PHQ Cards (*set of 2*)	1·50	5·00	□	□
		Set of 2 Gutter Pairs	3·00		□	

806 Stylised Cross on Ballot Paper

2nd Commonwealth Parliamentary Conference, London

1986 (19 AUG.) *Phosphorised paper. Perf* 14 × 14½

1335	**806**	34p multicoloured	1·10	1·10	□	□
		First Day Cover		1·75		□
		PHQ Card	1·00	2·50	□	□
		Gutter Pair	2·25		□	

807 Lord Dowding and
    Hawker Hurricane Mk. I

808 Lord Tedder and
    Hawker Typhoon 1B

809 Lord Trenchard and
    De Havilland D.H.9A

810 Sir Arthur Harris and
    Avro Type 683 Lancaster

811 Lord Portal and De
    Havilland D.H.98 Mosquito

History of the Royal Air Force

1986 (16th SEPT.) *Phosphorised paper. Perf* 14½ × 14

1336	**807**	17p multicoloured	65	10	□	□
1337	**808**	22p multicoloured	85	95	□	□
1338	**809**	29p multicoloured	1·10	1·10	□	□
1339	**810**	31p multicoloured	1·40	1·40	□	□
1340	**811**	34p multicoloured	1·60	1·50	□	□
		Set of 5	5·00	4·50	□	□
		First Day Cover		7·00		□
		Presentation Pack	5·25		□	
		PHQ Cards (*set of 5*)	4·00	10·00	□	□
		Set of 5 Gutter Pairs	10·00		□	

Nos. 1336/40 were issued to celebrate the 50th anniversary of the first R.A.F. Commands.

812 The Glastonbury Thorn

813 The Tanad Valley Plygain

814 The Hebrides Tribute

815 The Dewsbury Church
    Knell

816 The Hereford Boy Bishop

Christmas. Folk Customs

1986 (18 Nov.–2 Dec.) *One phosphor band* (12p, 13p) *or phosphorised paper* (others)

1341	812	12p multicoloured (2 Dec.)	50	20	□	□
1342		13p multicoloured	25	10	□	□
1343	813	18p multicoloured	40	10	□	□
1344	814	22p multicoloured	70	90	□	□
1345	815	31p multicoloured	80	95	□	□
1346	816	34p multicoloured	95	1·00	□	□
		Set of 6	3·25	3·00	□	□
		First Day Covers (2)		6·00		□
		Presentation Pack (*Nos.* 1342/6)	5·00		□	
		PHQ Cards (set of 5) (*Nos.* 1342/6)	3·00	7·00	□	□
		Set of 6 Gutter Pairs	6·50		□	

Collectors Pack 1986

1986 (18 Nov.) Comprises Nos. 1308/40, 1342/6
Collectors Pack . . . . 38·00 □

Post Office Yearbook

1986 Comprises Nos. 1308/40, 1342/6 *in hardbound book with slip case*
Yearbook . . . . 75·00 □

817 North American Blanket Flower

818 Globe Thistle

819 Echeveria

820 Autumn Crocus

Flower Photographs by Alfred Lammer

1987 (20 Jan.) *Phosphorised paper. Perf* $14\frac{1}{2} \times 14$

1347	817	18p multicoloured	45	10	□	□
1348	818	22p multicoloured	75	85	□	□
1349	819	31p multicoloured	1·10	1·40	□	□
1350	820	34p multicoloured	1·25	1·40	□	□
		Set of 4	3·25	3·50	□	□
		First Day Cover		4·00		□
		Presentation Pack	4·75		□	
		PHQ Cards (set of 4)	3·00	7·50	□	□
		Set of 4 Gutter Pairs	6·50		□	

821 The Principia Mathematica

822 Motion of Bodies in Ellipses

823 Optick Treatise

824 The System of the World

300th Anniversary of The Principia Mathematica by Sir Isaac Newton

1987 (24 Mar.) *Phosphorised paper*

1351	821	18p multicoloured	65	10	□	□
1352	822	22p multicoloured	90	95	□	□
1353	823	31p multicoloured	1·50	1·60	□	□
1354	824	34p multicoloured	1·60	1·50	□	□
		Set of 4	4·25	3·75	□	□
		First Day Cover		4·00		□
		Presentation Pack	4·50		□	
		PHQ Cards (set of 4)	3·00	6·00	□	□
		Set of 4 Gutter Pairs	8·50		□	

For full information on all future British issues, collectors should write to Royal Mail, Freepost EH3647, 21 South Gyle Crescent, Edinburgh EH12 9PE.

825 Willis Faber and Dumas Building, Ipswich **826** Pompidou Centre, Paris

827 Staatsgalerie, Stuttgart **828** European Investment Bank, Luxembourg

Europa. British Architects in Europe

1987 (12 MAY) *Phosphorised paper*

1355	**825**	18p multicoloured	50		10	☐	☐
1356	**826**	22p multicoloured	75		85	☐	☐
1357	**827**	31p multicoloured	1·25		1·40	☐	☐
1358	**828**	34p multicoloured	1·40		1·40	☐	☐
		Set of 4	3·50		3·50	☐	☐
		First Day Cover			3·50		☐
		Presentation Pack	4·50			☐	
		PHQ Cards (set of 4)	3·00		6·00	☐	☐
		Set of 4 Gutter Pairs	7·00			☐	

829 Brigade Members with Ashford Litter, 1887 **830** Bandaging Blitz Victim, 1940

831 Volunteer with fainting Girl, 1965 **832** Transport of Transplant Organ by Air Wing, 1987

Centenary of St John Ambulance Brigade

1987 (16 JUNE) *Phosphorised paper. Perf* 14 × 14½

1359	**829**	18p multicoloured	50		10	☐	☐
1360	**830**	22p multicoloured	75		85	☐	☐
1361	**831**	31p multicoloured	1·10		1·25	☐	☐
1362	**832**	34p multicoloured	1·25		1·40	☐	☐
		Set of 4	3·25		3·25	☐	☐
		First Day Cover			3·25		☐
		Presentation Pack	4·50			☐	
		PHQ Cards (set of 4)	3·00		6·00	☐	☐
		Set of 4 Gutter Pairs	6·50			☐	

833 Arms of the Lord Lyon King of Arms **834** Scottish Heraldic Banner of Prince Charles

835 Arms of Royal Scottish Academy of Painting, Sculpture and Architecture **836** Arms of Royal Society of Edinburgh

300th Anniversary of Revival of Order of the Thistle

1987 (21 JULY) *Phosphorised paper. Perf* 14½

1363	**833**	18p multicoloured	50		10	☐	☐
1364	**834**	22p multicoloured	75		90	☐	☐
1365	**835**	31p multicoloured	1·25		1·40	☐	☐
1366	**836**	34p multicoloured	1·40		1·40	☐	☐
		Set of 4	3·50		3·50	☐	☐
		First Day Cover			4·00		☐
		Presentation Pack	4·50			☐	
		PHQ Cards (set of 4)	3·00		7·50	☐	☐
		Set of 4 Gutter Pairs	7·00			☐	

For full information on all future British issues, collectors should write to Royal Mail, Freepost EH3647, 21 South Gyle Crescent, Edinburgh EH12 9PE.

837 Crystal Palace, 'Monarch of the Glen' (Landseer) and Grace Darling

838 Great Eastern, Beeton's Book of Household Management and Prince Albert

839 Albert Memorial, Ballot Box and Disraeli

840 Diamond Jubilee Emblem, Morse Key and Newspaper Placard for Relief of Mafeking

150th Anniversary of Queen Victoria's Accession

1987 (8 SEPT.) *Phosphorised paper*

1367	**837**	18p multicoloured	50	10	□	□
1368	**838**	22p multicoloured	75	90	□	□
1369	**839**	31p multicoloured	1·25	1·40	□	□
1370	**840**	34p multicoloured	1·40	1·40	□	□
		Set of 4	3·50	3·50	□	□
		First Day Cover		4·00		□
		Presentation Pack	5·00		□	
		PHQ Cards (set of 4)	3·00	7·00	□	□
		Set of 4 Gutter Pairs	7·00		□	

841 Pot by Bernard Leach

842 Pot by Elizabeth Fritsch

843 Pot by Lucie Rie

844 Pot by Hans Coper

Studio Pottery

1987 (13 OCT.) *Phosphorised paper. Perf* $14\frac{1}{2} \times 14$

1371	**841**	18p multicoloured	60	10	□	□
1372	**842**	26p multicoloured	90	90	□	□
1373	**843**	31p multicoloured	1·40	1·25	□	□
1374	**844**	34p multicoloured	1·50	1·50	□	□
		Set of 4	4·00	3·50	□	□
		First Day Cover		3·50		□
		Presentation Pack	4·50		□	
		PHQ Cards (set of 4)	3·00	6·00	□	□
		Set of 4 Gutter Pairs	8·00		□	

Nos. 1371/4 also mark the birth centenary of Bernard Leach, the potter.

845 Decorating the Christmas Tree

846 Waiting for Father Christmas

847 Sleeping Child and Father Christmas in Sleigh

848 Child reading

849 Child playing Flute and Snowman

Christmas

1987 (17 NOV.) *One phosphor band* (13p) *or phosphorised paper* (*others*)

1375	**845**	13p multicoloured	25	10	□	□
1376	**846**	18p multicoloured	35	10	□	□
1377	**847**	26p multicoloured	70	95	□	□
1378	**848**	31p multicoloured	1·00	1·40	□	□
1379	**849**	34p multicoloured	1·10	1·40	□	□
		Set of 5	3·00	3·50	□	□
		First Day Cover		4·00		□
		Presentation Pack	4·50		□	
		PHQ Cards (set of 5)	3·00	6·00	□	□
		Set of 5 Gutter Pairs	6·00		□	

Collectors Pack 1987

1987 (17 Nov.) *Comprises Nos. 1347/79*
Collectors Pack . . . . 45·00 ☐

Post Office Yearbook

1987 *Comprises Nos. 1347/79 in hardbound book with slip case*
Yearbook . . . . 45·00 ☐

850 Short-spined
Seascorpion ('Bull-rout')
(Jonathan Couch)

851 Yellow Waterlily
(Major Joshua Swatkin)

852 Whistling ('Bewick's')
Swan (Edward Lear)

853 *Morchella esculenta*
(James Sowerby)

Bicentenary of Linnean Society. Archive Illustrations

1988 (19 Jan.) *Phosphorised paper*

1380	850	18p multicoloured	60	10	☐	☐
1381	851	26p multicoloured	95	1·10	☐	☐
1382	852	31p multicoloured	1·25	1·40	☐	☐
1383	853	34p multicoloured	1·40	1·50	☐	☐
		Set of 4	3·75	3·75	☐	☐
		First Day Cover		3·75		☐
		Presentation Pack	4·50		☐	
		PHQ Cards (set of 4)	3·00	6·00	☐	☐
		Set of 4 Gutter Pairs	7·50		☐	

854 Revd William
Morgan (Bible
translator, 1588)

855 William Salesbury
(New Testament
translator, 1567)

856 Bishop Richard
Davies (New
Testament translator,
1567)

857 Bishop Richard Parry
(editor of Revised
Welsh Bible, 1620)

400th Anniversary of Welsh Bible

1988 (1 Mar.) *Phosphorised paper. Perf 14½ × 14*

1384	854	18p multicoloured	40	10	☐	☐
1385	855	26p multicoloured	70	95	☐	☐
1386	856	31p multicoloured	1·00	1·25	☐	☐
1387	857	34p multicoloured	1·10	1·25	☐	☐
		Set of 4	3·00	3·25	☐	☐
		First Day Cover		3·25		☐
		Presentation Pack	4·25		☐	
		PHQ Cards (set of 4)	3·00	6·00	☐	☐
		Set of 4 Gutter Pairs	6·00		☐	

858 Gymnastics
(Centenary of British
Amateur Gymnastics
Association)

859 Downhill Skiing
(Ski Club of
Great Britain)

860 Tennis (Centenary
of Lawn Tennis
Association)

861 Football (Centenary
of Football League)

Sports Organizations

1988 (22 Mar.) *Phosphorised paper. Perf* 14½

1388	858	18p multicoloured	45	15	□	□
1389	859	26p multicoloured	80	90	□	□
1390	860	31p multicoloured	1·25	1·40	□	□
1391	861	34p multicoloured	1·40	1·40	□	□
		Set of 4	3·50	3·50	□	□
		First Day Cover		3·50		□
		Presentation Pack	4·50		□	
		PHQ Cards (set of 4)	2·50	6·00	□	□
		Set of 4 Gutter Pairs	7·00		□	

862 *Mallard* and Mailbags on Pick-up Arms

863 Loading Transatlantic Mail on Liner *Queen Elizabeth*

864 Glasgow Tram No. 1173 and Pillar Box

865 Imperial Airways Handley Page H.P.45 *Horatius* and Airmail Van

Europa. Transport and Mail Services in 1930's

1988 (10 May) *Phosphorised paper*

1392	862	18p multicoloured	40	15	□	□
1393	863	26p multicoloured	80	95	□	□
1394	864	31p multicoloured	1·00	1·40	□	□
1395	865	34p multicoloured	1·25	1·40	□	□
		Set of 4	3·00	3·50	□	□
		First Day Cover		3·50		□
		Presentation Pack	4·50		□	
		PHQ Cards (set of 4)	2·00	5·00	□	□
		Set of 4 Gutter Pairs	6·00		□	

866 Early Settler and Sailing Clipper

867 Queen Elizabeth II with British and Australian Parliament Buildings

868 W. G. Grace (cricketer) and Tennis Racquet

869 Shakespeare, John Lennon (entertainer) and Sydney Landmarks

Nos. 1396/7 and 1398/9 were each printed together, *se-tenant,* in horizontal pairs throughout the sheets, each pair showing a background design of the Australian flag.

Bicentenary of Australian Settlement

1988 (21 June) *Phosphorised paper. Perf* 14½

1396	866	18p multicoloured	60	15	□	□
		a. Horiz pair. Nos. 1396/7	1·50	1·50	□	□
1397	867	18p multicoloured	60	15	□	□
1398	868	34p multicoloured	1·25	75	□	□
		a. Horiz pair. Nos. 1398/9	2·75	2·75	□	□
1399	869	34p multicoloured	1·25	75	□	□
		Set of 4	4·25	1·50	□	□
		First Day Cover		4·00		□
		Presentation Pack	4·50		□	
		Souvenir Book	8·50		□	
		PHQ Cards (set of 4)	2·00	6·50	□	□
		Set of 2 Gutter Blocks of 4 . . .	8·50		□	

Stamps in similar designs were also issued by Australia. These are included in the Souvenir Book.

870 Spanish Galeasse off The Lizard

871 English Fleet leaving Plymouth

872 Engagement off Isle of Wight

873 Attack of English Fire-ships, Calais

874 Armada in Storm, North Sea

Nos. 1400/4 were printed together, *se-tenant*, in horizontal strips of 5 throughout the sheet, forming a composite design.

400th Anniversary of Spanish Armada

1988 (19 JULY) *Phosphorised paper*

1400	870	18p multicoloured	85	20	□	□
		a. Horiz strip of 5. *Nos.* .				
		1400/4	4·25	4·25	□	□
1401	871	18p multicoloured	85	20	□	□
1402	872	18p multicoloured	85	20	□	□
1403	873	18p multicoloured	85	20	□	□
1404	874	18p multicoloured	85	20	□	□
		Set of 5	4·25	1·00	□	□
		First Day Cover		5·00		□
		Presentation Pack	4·75		□	
		PHQ Cards (*set of 5*)	2·50	8·00	□	□
		Gutter Block of 10	8·50		□	

875 'The Owl and the Pussy-cat'

876 'Edward Lear as a Bird' (self-portrait)

877 'Cat' (from alphabet book)

878 'There was a Young Lady whose Bonnet . . .' (limerick)

Death Centenary of Edward Lear (artist and author)

1988 (6–27 SEPT.) *Phosphorised paper*

1405	875	19p black, pale cream and				
		carmine	65	15	□	□
1406	876	27p black, pale cream and				
		yellow	1·00	1·00	□	□
1407	877	32p black, pale cream and				
		emerald	1·25	1·25	□	□
1408	878	35p black, pale cream and				
		blue	1·40	1·25	□	□
		Set of 4	4·00	3·25	□	□
		First Day Cover		3·75		□
		Presentation Pack	4·75		□	
		PHQ Cards (*set of 4*)	2·00	6·50	□	□
		Set of 4 Gutter Pairs	8·00		□	
MS1409		122 × 90 mm. Nos. 1405/8 .	6·50	7·50	□	□
		First Day Cover (27 Sept.) . . .		8·00		□

No. **MS**1409 was sold at £1·35, the premium being used for the 'Stamp World London 90' International Stamp Exhibition.

879 Carrickfergus Castle

880 Caernarvon Castle

881 Edinburgh Castle

882 Windsor Castle

1988 (18 OCT.) *Ordinary paper*

1410	879	£1 deep green	5·00	50	□	□
1411	880	£1·50 maroon	7·25	50	□	□
1412	881	£2 indigo	10·00	75	□	□
1413	882	£5 deep brown	23·00	3·00	□	□
		Set of 4	40·00	4·25	□	□
		First Day Cover		35·00		□
		Presentation Pack	42·00		□	
		Set of 4 Gutter pairs	80·00		□	

For similar designs, but with silhouette of Queen's head see Nos. 1611/14 and 1993/6.

883 Journey to Bethlehem   **884** Shepherds and Star

885 Three Wise Men   **886** Nativity

887 The Annunciation

Christmas

1988 (15 Nov.) *One phosphor band (14p) or phosphorised paper (others)*

1414	**883**	14p multicoloured	50	10	☐	☐
1415	**884**	19p multicoloured	60	10	☐	☐
1416	**885**	27p multicoloured	95	1·10	☐	☐
1417	**886**	32p multicoloured	1·25	1·25	☐	☐
1418	**887**	35p multicoloured	1·50	1·25	☐	☐
		Set of 5	4·50	3·50	☐	☐
		First Day Cover		3·75		☐
		Presentation Pack	5·25		☐	
		PHQ Cards (set of 5)	2·50	6·50	☐	☐
		Set of 5 Gutter Pairs	9·00		☐	

Collectors Pack 1988

1988 (15 Nov.) *Comprises Nos. 1380/1408, 1414/18*

	Collectors Pack	40·00	☐

Post Office Yearbook

1988 *Comprises Nos. 1380/1404,* **MS**1409, *1414/18 in hardbound book with slip case*

	Yearbook	45·00	☐

888 Atlantic Puffin   **889** Avocet

890 Oystercatcher   **891** Northern Gannet

Centenary of Royal Society for the Protection of Birds

1989 (17 Jan.) *Phosphorised paper*

1419	**888**	19p multicoloured	50	15	☐	☐
1420	**889**	27p multicoloured	1·40	1·40	☐	☐
1421	**890**	32p multicoloured	1·40	1·40	☐	☐
1422	**891**	35p multicoloured	1·50	1·50	☐	☐
		Set of 4	4·25	4·00	☐	☐
		First Day Cover		4·75		☐
		Presentation Pack	4·75		☐	
		PHQ Cards (set of 4)	2·50	8·00	☐	☐
		Set of 4 Gutter Pairs	9·00		☐	

892 Rose   **893** Cupid

894 Yachts   **895** Fruit

896 Teddy Bear

Nos. 1423/7 were printed together, *se-tenant*, in horizontal strips of five, two such strips forming the booklet pane with twelve half stamp-size labels.

Greetings Booklet Stamps

1989 (31 Jan.) *Phosphorised paper*

1423	892	19p multicoloured	6·25	4·50	☐	☐
		a. Booklet pane. Nos.				
		1423/7 × 2	55·00		☐	
1424	893	19p multicoloured	6·25	4·50	☐	☐
1425	894	19p multicoloured	6·25	4·50	☐	☐
1426	895	19p multicoloured	6·25	4·50	☐	☐
1427	896	19p multicoloured	6·25	4·50	☐	☐
		Set of 5	28·00	20·00	☐	☐
		First Day Cover		20·00		☐

897 Fruit and Vegetables   898 Meat Products

899 Dairy Produce   900 Cereal Products

Food and Farming Year

1989 (7 Mar.) *Phosphorised paper. Perf* 14 × 14½

1428	897	19p multicoloured	40	15	☐	☐
1429	898	27p multicoloured	75	85	☐	☐
1430	899	32p multicoloured	1·10	1·40	☐	☐
1431	900	35p multicoloured	1·10	1·50	☐	☐
		Set of 4	3·00	3·50	☐	☐
		First Day Cover		3·75		☐
		Presentation Pack	4·50		☐	
		PHQ *Cards* (*set of* 4)	2·00	6·00	☐	☐
		Set of 4 *Gutter Pairs*	6·00		☐	

901 Mortar Board   902 Cross on Ballot Paper
     (150th Anniv of   (3rd Direct Elections
     Public Education   to European Parliament)
     in England)

903 Posthorn (26th   904 Globe (Inter-
     Postal, Telegraph and   Parliamentary Union
     Telephone International   Centenary Conference,
     Congress, Brighton)   London)

Nos. 1432/3 and 1434/5 were each printed together, *se-tenant*, in horizontal pairs throughout the sheets.

Anniversaries

1989 (11 Apr.) *Phosphorised paper. Perf* 14 × 14½

1432	901	19p multicoloured	1·25	40	☐	☐
		a. Horiz pair. Nos. 1432/3	2·50	2·00	☐	☐
1433	902	19p multicoloured	1·25	40	☐	☐
1434	903	35p multicoloured	1·75	2·00	☐	☐
		a. Horiz pair. Nos. 1434/5	3·50	4·00	☐	☐
1435	904	35p multicoloured	1·75	2·00	☐	☐
		Set of 4	5·50	4·50	☐	☐
		First Day Cover		4·50		☐
		Presentation Pack	6·50		☐	
		PHQ *Cards* (*set of* 4)	2·00	7·00	☐	☐
		Set of 2 *Gutter Strips of* 4 . . .	11·00		☐	

905 Toy Train and Airplane   906 Building Bricks
     Airplane

907 Dice and Board Games

908 Toy Robot, Boat and Doll's House

Europa. Games and Toys

1989 (16 May) *Phosphorised paper*

1436	**905**	19p multicoloured	65	15	□	□
1437	**906**	27p multicoloured	95	95	□	□
1438	**907**	32p multicoloured	1·40	1·50	□	□
1439	**908**	35p multicoloured	1·50	1·40	□	□
		Set of 4	4·00	3·50	□	□
		First Day Cover		4·00		□
		Presentation Pack	4·50		□	
		PHQ Cards (set of 4)	2·00	6·00	□	□
		Set of 4 Gutter Pairs	8·00		□	

909 Ironbridge, Shropshire

910 Tin Mine. St Agnes Head, Cornwall

911 Cotton Mills, New Lanark, Strathclyde

912 Pontcysylite Aqueduct, Clwyd

912a

Industrial Archaeology

1989 (4–25 July) *Phosphorised paper*

1440	**909**	19p multicoloured	60	15	□	□
1441	**910**	27p multicoloured	1·00	1·10	□	□
1442	**911**	32p multicoloured	1·10	1·25	□	□
1443	**912**	35p multicoloured	1·25	1·50	□	□
		Set of 4	3·50	3·50	□	□
		First Day Cover		4·00		□
		Presentation Pack	4·50		□	
		PHQ Cards (set of 4)	2·00	6·25	□	□
		Set of 4 Gutter Pairs	7·00		□	

MS1444 122 × 90 mm. **912a** As Nos.
1440/3 but designs horizontal . 5·00 6·00 □ □
First Day Cover (25 July) . . . . 6·00 □

No. **MS**1444 was sold at £1·40, the premium being used for the 'Stamp World London 90' International Stamp Exhibition.

913

914

Booklet Stamps

1989 (22 Aug.)–92 (a) *Printed in photogravure by Harrison and Sons. Perf* 15 × 14

1445	**913**	(2nd) bright blue (1 centre band)	1·00	1·00	□	□
1446		(2nd) bright blue (1 side band) (20.3.90)	2·25	2·25	□	□
1447	**914**	(1st) black (phosphorised paper)	1·75	1·50	□	□
1448		(1st) brownish black (2 bands (20.3.90)	2·50	2·50	□	□

(b) *Printed in lithography by Walsall. Perf* 14

1449	**913**	(2nd) bright blue (1 centre band)	1·00	75	□	□
1450	**914**	(1st) black (2 bands) . . .	2·50	2·00	□	□

(c) Printed in lithography by Questa. Perf 15 × 14

1451	913	(2nd) bright blue (1 centre band) (19.9.89)	1·00	1·00	□ □
1451a		(2nd) bright blue (1 side band) (25.2.92)	1·75	2·50	□ □
1452	914	(1st) black (phosphorised paper) (19.9.89)	2·75	2·50	□ □
		First Day Cover (Nos. 1445, 1447)		4·00	□

For similar stamps showing changed colours see Nos. 1511/16, for those with elliptical perforations Nos. 1663a/6 and 1979 and for self-adhesive versions Nos. 2039/40.

No. 1451a exists with the phosphor band at the left or right of the stamp.

915 Snowflake (×10)

916 *Calliphora erythrocephala* (fly) (×5)

917 Blood Cells (×500)

918 Microchip (×600)

150th Anniversary of Royal Microscopical Society

1989 (5 SEPT.) *Phosphorised paper. Perf 14½ × 14*

1453	915	19p multicoloured	45	15	□ □
1454	916	27p multicoloured	95	1·10	□ □
1455	917	32p multicoloured	1·10	1·40	□ □
1456	918	35p multicoloured	1·25	1·40	□ □
		Set of 4	3·50	3·75	□ □
		First Day Cover		4·25	□
		Presentation Pack	4·50		□
		PHQ Cards (set of 4)	2·00	6·00	□ □
		Set of 4 Gutter Pairs	7·50		□

919 Royal Mail Coach

920 Escort of Blues and Royals

921 Lord Mayor's Coach

922 Coach Team passing St Paul's

923 Blues and Royals Drum Horse

Nos. 1457/61 were printed together, *se-tenant*, in horizontal strips of 5 throughout the sheet, forming a composite design.

Lord Mayor's Show, London

1989 (17 OCT.) *Phosphorised paper*

1457	919	20p multicoloured	70	25	□ □
		a. Horiz strip of 5. Nos. 1457/61	3·50	3·50	□ □
1458	920	20p multicoloured	70	25	□ □
1459	921	20p multicoloured	70	25	□ □
1460	922	20p multicoloured	70	25	□ □
1461	923	20p multicoloured	70	25	□ □
		Set of 5	3·50	1·25	□ □
		First Day Cover		4·00	□
		Presentation Pack	4·00		□
		PHQ Cards (set of 5)	2·50	7·00	□ □
		Gutter Strip of 10	7·00		□

Nos. 1457/61 commemorate the 800th anniversary of the installation of the first Lord Mayor of London.

924 14th-century Peasants from Stained-glass Window

925 Arches and Roundels, West Front

926 Octagon Tower

927 Arcade from West Transept

928 Triple Arch from West Front

Christmas. 800th Anniversary of Ely Cathedral

1989 (14 Nov.) *One phosphor band (Nos. 1462/3) or phosphorised paper (others)*

1462	**924**	15p gold, silver and blue .	45	10	□	□
1463	**925**	15p + 1p gold, silver and blue	55	35	□	□
1464	**926**	20p + 1p gold, silver and rosine	70	75	□	□
1465	**927**	34p + 1p gold, silver and emerald	1·50	1·60	□	□
1466	**928**	37p + 1p gold, silver and yellow-olive	1·60	1·75	□	□
		Set of 5	4·50	4·00	□	□
		First Day Cover		4·50		□
		Presentation Pack	5·00		□	
		PHQ Cards (set of 5) . . .	2·50	7·00	□	□
		Set of 5 Gutter Pairs . . .	9·00		□	

Collectors Pack 1989

1989 (14 Nov.) *Comprises Nos. 1419/22, 1428/43 and 1453/66*

	Collectors Pack	45·00	□

Post Office Yearbook

1989 (14 Nov.) *Comprises Nos. 1419/22, 1428/44 and 1453/66 in hardback book with slip case*

	Yearbook	45·00	□

929 Queen Victoria and Queen Elizabeth II

150th Anniversary of the Penny Black

1990 (10 JAN.–17 APR.) (*a*) *Printed in photogravure by Harrison and Sons (Nos. 1468, 1470, 1472 from booklets only). Perf 15 × 14*

1467	**929**	15p bright blue (1 centre band)	50	50	□	□
1468		15p bright blue (1 side band) (30 Jan.)	2·25	2·75	□	□
1469		20p brownish black and cream (phosphorised paper)	50	50	□	□
1470		20p brownish black and cream (2 bands) (30 Jan.)	2·25	2·50	□	□
1471		29p deep mauve (phosphorised paper)	1·75	1·50	□	□
1472		29p deep mauve (2 bands) (20 Mar.)	7·00	7·50	□	□
1473		34p deep bluish grey (phosphorised paper)	1·90	1·75	□	□
1474		37p rosine (phosphorised paper)	2·00	1·75	□	□
		Set of 5 (Nos. 1467, 1469, 1471, 1473/4)	6·00	5·50	□	□
		First Day Cover (Nos. 1467, 1469, 1471, 1473/4)		6·00		□
		Presentation Pack (Nos. 1467, 1469, 1471, 1473/4)	8·00		□	

(*b*) *Litho Walsall (booklets). Perf 14 (30 Jan.)*

1475	**929**	15p bright blue (1 centre band)	1·25	1·00	□	□
1476		20p brownish black and cream (phosphorised paper)	1·25	1·50	□	□

(*c*) *Litho Questa (booklets). Perf 15 × 14 (17 Apr.)*

1477	**929**	15p bright blue (1 centre band)	2·00	2·00	□	□
1478		20p brownish black (phosphorised paper)	2·00	2·00	□	□

No. 1468 exists with the phosphor band at the left or right of the stamp.

For Type **929** redrawn with "1st" face value see No. 2133.

> **Minimum Price.** The minimum price quoted is 10p. This represents a handling charge rather than a basis for valuing common stamps. Where the actual value of a stamp is less than 10p this may be apparent when set prices are shown, particularly for sets including a number of 10p stamps. It therefore follows that in valuing common stamps the 10p catalogue price should not be reckoned automatically since it covers a variation in real scarcity.

930 Kitten

931 Rabbit

932 Duckling

933 Puppy

150th Anniversary of Royal Society for Prevention of Cruelty to Animals

1990 (23 JAN.) *Phosphorised paper. Perf 14 × 14½*

1479	**930**	20p multicoloured	75	15	☐	☐
1480	**931**	29p multicoloured	1·40	1·40	☐	☐
1481	**932**	34p multicoloured	1·60	1·60	☐	☐
1482	**933**	37p multicoloured	1·75	1·75	☐	☐
		Set of 4	5·00	4·50	☐	☐
		First Day Cover		5·00		☐
		Presentation Pack	5·25		☐	
		PHQ Cards (set of 4)	2·50	8·00	☐	☐
		Set of 4 Gutter Pairs	10·00		☐	

934 Teddy Bear

935 Dennis the Menace

936 Punch

937 Cheshire Cat

938 The Man in the Moon

939 The Laughing Policeman

940 Clown

941 Mona Lisa

942 Queen of Hearts

943 Stan Laurel (comedian)

T **934/43** were printed together, *se-tenant,* in booklet panes of 10.

Greetings Booklet Stamps. 'Smiles'

1990 (6 FEB.) *Two phosphor bands*

1483	**934**	20p multicoloured	3·50	2·50	☐	☐
		a. Booklet pane. Nos.				
		1483/92	30·00		☐	
1484	**935**	20p multicoloured	3·50	2·50	☐	☐
1485	**936**	20p multicoloured	3·50	2·50	☐	☐
1486	**937**	20p multicoloured	3·50	2·50	☐	☐
1487	**938**	20p multicoloured	3·50	2·50	☐	☐
1488	**939**	20p multicoloured	3·50	2·50	☐	☐
1489	**940**	20p multicoloured	3·50	2·50	☐	☐
1490	**941**	20p multicoloured	3·50	2·50	☐	☐
1491	**942**	20p multicoloured	3·50	2·50	☐	☐
1492	**943**	20p gold and grey-black . . .	3·50	2·50	☐	☐
		Set of 10	30·00	22·00	☐	☐
		First Day Cover		25·00		☐

For these designs with the face value expressed as '1st' see Nos. 1550/9.

For full information on all future British issues, collectors should write to Royal Mail, Freepost EH3647, 21 South Gyle Crescent, Edinburgh EH12 9PE.

"AT HOME" AUCTIONS
Every Week!
The WORLD'S LARGEST
MAIL-BID
AUCTION COMPANY

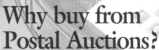

If you need it we have it!

From delightful topical stamp collections to serious specialist studies. From multi-volume world collections to cigarette cards. From huge boxes with hidden gems to silk flags dropped over Java during World War II!

Why buy from Postal Auctions?

Even the richest and most enthusiastic collector would find it impossible to attend a mere fraction of the stamp auctions that take place throughout the world.

Thousands of overseas buyers choose us *(in fact most of our clients live outside the UK)* because we offer the widest choice of material from all over the world at the most competitive estimates.

Buy in comfort from your Home, Office, Aircraft or Train

Snatch a minute to buy from the World's largest weekly source of interesting and unusual lots -it just couldn't be easier, safer or more enjoyable.

The Ultimate Source of World Stamps

Our weekly auction catalogue has been designed to fit into your pocket, ensure you carry it with you wherever you go. You never quite know when you may decide to participate in one of the greatest stamp auctions, in the World!

Welcome to the MOST interesting stamp site in the world!

sandafayre.com

Everything you need to know about buying and selling stamps from the experts...

Browse our gallery of rare and famous stamps. Learn the history and geography behind your stamps with Sandafayre's World Stamp Atlas. View and bid on our auctions with over £1 million worth of lots at any one time including many interesting collections of Great Britain and Commonwealth. It's fast, it's fun...it's free!

If you'd prefer a FREE printed catalogue, please complete the coupon on the reverse and return to us today by mail or Fax.

Sandafayre Auctions, GBS, Knutsford, Cheshire, UK, WA16 8XN. Tel:+44 (0)1565 653214 Fax: +44 (0)1565 651637
E-mail: stamp@sandafayre.com   Website: www.sandafayre.com

Sandafayre Auctions (GBS)
Knutsford
Cheshire
WA16 8XN
UK

AFFIX
POSTAGE
HERE

944 Alexandra Palace ('Stamp World London 90' Exhibition)

945 Glasgow School of Art

946 British Philatelic Bureau, Edinburgh

947 Templeton Carpet Factory, Glasgow

Europa (*Nos. 1493 and 1495*) and '*Glasgow*' 1990 *European City of Culture*' (*Nos. 1494 and 1496*)

1990 (6 Mar.) *Phosphorised paper*

1493	**944**	20p multicoloured	60	20	☐	☐
1494	**945**	20p multicoloured	60	20	☐	☐
1495	**946**	29p multicoloured	1·40	1·60	☐	☐
1496	**947**	37p multicoloured	1·50	1·60	☐	☐
		Set of 4	3·75	3·25	☐	☐
		First Day Cover		4·25		☐
		Presentation Pack	4·25		☐	
		PHQ Cards (set of 4)	2·50	6·50	☐	☐
		Set of 4 Gutter Pairs	7·50		☐	

948 Export Achievement Award

949 Technological Achievement Award

Nos. 1497/8 and 1499/500 were each printed together, *se-tenant*, in horizontal pairs throughout the sheets.

25th Anniversary of Queen's Awards for Export and Technology

1990 (10 Apr.) *Phosphorised paper. Perf* 14 × 14½

1497	**948**	20p multicoloured	1·00	25	☐	☐
		a. Horiz pair. Nos. 1497/8	2·00	1·50	☐	☐
1498	**949**	20p multicoloured	1·00	25	☐	☐
1499	**948**	37p multicoloured	1·50	1·60	☐	☐
		a. Horiz pair. Nos. 1499/1500	3·00	3·25	☐	☐
1500	**949**	37p multicoloured	1·50	1·60	☐	☐
		Set of 4	4·50	3·50	☐	☐
		First Day Cover		4·00		☐
		Presentation Pack	5·00		☐	
		PHQ Cards (set of 4)	2·50	6·50	☐	☐
		Set of 2 Gutter Strips of 4 . . .	9·00		☐	

949a

'Stamp World 90' International Stamp Exhibition, London

1990 (3 May) *Sheet* 122 × 90 *mm. Phosphorised paper*

MS1501	**949a**	20p brownish black and cream	4·50	4·50	☐ ☐
		First Day Cover		5·50	☐
		Souvenir Book (Nos. 1467, 1469, 1471, 1473/4 and **MS**1501 . .	20·00		☐

No. **MS**1501 was sold at £1, the premium being used for the exhibition.

950 Cycad and Sir Joseph Banks Building

951 Stone Pine and Princess of Wales Conservatory

952 Willow Tree and Palm House

953 Cedar Tree and Pagoda

957 Elizabeth, Duchess of York

958 Lady Elizabeth Bowes-Lyon

150th Anniversary of Kew Gardens

1990 (5 JUNE) *Phosphorised paper*

1502	**950**	20p multicoloured	55	15	□	□
1503	**951**	29p multicoloured	90	1·00	□	□
1504	**952**	34p multicoloured	1·40	1·60	□	□
1505	**953**	37p multicoloured	1·60	1·50	□	□
		Set of 4	4·00	3·75	□	□
		First Day Cover		4·25	□	
		Presentation Pack	4·50		□	
		PHQ Cards (set of 4)	2·50	6·50	□	□
		Set of 4 Gutter Pairs	8·00		□	

90th Birthday of Queen Elizabeth the Queen Mother

1990 (2 AUG.) *Phosphorised paper*

1507	**955**	20p multicoloured	95	20	□	□
1508	**956**	29p silver, indigo and grey-blue	1·40	1·25	□	□
1509	**957**	34p multicoloured	2·00	1·90	□	□
1510	**958**	37p silver, sepia and stone	2·25	2·00	□	□
		Set of 4	6·00	5·00	□	□
		First Day Cover		6·50	□	
		Presentation Pack	6·50		□	
		PHQ Cards (set of 4)	2·75	7·50	□	□
		Set of 4 Gutter Pairs	12·00		□	

954 Thomas Hardy and Clyffe Clump, Dorset

150th Birth Anniversary of Thomas Hardy (author)

1990 (10 JULY) *Phosphorised paper*

1506	**954**	20p multicoloured	80	40	□	□
		First Day Cover		1·50	□	
		Presentation Pack	1·50		□	
		PHQ Card	1·00	2·00	□	□
		Gutter Pair	1·60		□	

Booklet Stamps

1990 (7 AUG.)–**92** *As Types* **913/14**, *but colours changed*

(a) *Photo Harrison. Perf* 15 × 14

1511	**913**	(2nd) deep blue (1 centre band)	1·25	1·00	□	□
1512	**914**	(1st) bright orange-red (phosphorised paper)	1·25	1·25	□	□

(b) *Litho Questa. Perf* 15 × 14

1513	**913**	(2nd) deep blue (1 centre band)	2·75	2·50	□	□
1514	**914**	(1st) bright orange-red (phosphorised paper)	75	80	□	□
1514a		(1st) bright orange-red (2 bands) (25.2.92) . . .	2·75	2·25	□	□

(c) *Litho Walsall. Perf* 14

1515	**913**	(2nd) deep blue (1 centre band)	75	75	□	□
1516	**914**	(1st) bright orange-red (phosphorised paper)	70	75	□	□
		c. Perf 13	3·00	2·75	□	□
		First Day Cover (Nos. 1515/16) .		4·00	□	

For similar stamps with elliptical perforations see Nos. 1663*a*/6.

955 Queen Elizabeth the Queen Mother

956 Queen Elizabeth

For full information on all future British issues, collectors should write to Royal Mail, Freepost EH3647, 21 South Gyle Crescent, Edinburgh EH12 9PE.

959 Victoria Cross

960 George Cross

961 Distinguished Service
Cross and Distinguished
Service Medal

962 Military Cross and
Military Medal

963 Distinguished Flying Cross
and Distinguished Flying
Medal

Gallantry Awards

1990 (11 SEPT.) *Phosphorised paper*

1517	**959**	20p multicoloured	. . . . .	80	40	□	□
1518	**960**	20p multicoloured	. . . . .	80	40	□	□
1519	**961**	20p multicoloured	. . . . .	80	40	□	□
1520	**962**	20p multicoloured	. . . . .	80	40	□	□
1521	**963**	20p multicoloured	. . . . .	80	40	□	□
		Set of 5	. . . .	3·75	2·00	□	□
		First Day Cover	. . . .		3·25		□
		Presentation Pack	. . . .	4·50		□	
		PHQ Cards (set of 5)	. . . . . .	3·00	7·50	□	□
		Set of 5 Gutter Pairs	. . . . . .	7·50		□	

964 Armagh Observatory,
Jodrell Bank Radio
Telescope and La Palma
Telescope

965 Newton's Moon and Tides
Diagram with Early
Telescopes

966 Greenwich Old
Observatory and Early
Astronomical Equipment

967 Stonehenge, Gyroscope
and Navigating by Stars

Astronomy

1990 (16 OCT.) *Phosphorised paper. Perf* 14 × 14½

1522	**964**	22p multicoloured	. . . . .	65	20	□	□
1523	**965**	26p multicoloured	. . . . .	1·00	1·10	□	□
1524	**966**	31p multicoloured	. . . . .	1·25	1·40	□	□
1525	**967**	37p multicoloured	. . . . .	1·50	1·40	□	□
		Set of 4	. . . .	4·00	3·75	□	□
		First Day Cover	. . . .		4·25		□
		Presentation Pack	. . . .	4·50		□	
		PHQ Cards (set of 4)	. . . . . .	2·50	7·00	□	□
		Set of 4 Gutter Pairs	. . . . . .	8·00		□	

Nos. 1522/5 commemorate the centenary of the British
Astronomical Association and the bicentenary of the Armagh
Observatory.

968 Building a Snowman

969 Fetching the Christmas Tree

970 Carol Singing

971 Tobogganing

972 Ice-skating

Christmas

1990 (13 Nov.) *One phosphor band* (17p) *or phosphorised paper* (others)

1526	968	17p multicoloured	50	10	☐	☐
1527	969	22p multicoloured	70	15	☐	☐
1528	970	26p multicoloured	95	1·00	☐	☐
1529	971	31p multicoloured	1·25	1·40	☐	☐
1530	972	37p multicoloured	1·40	1·40	☐	☐
		Set of 5	4·50	3·75	☐	☐
		First Day Cover		4·25		☐
		Presentation Pack	5·00		☐	
		PHQ Cards (set of 5)	3·25	7·00	☐	☐
		Set of 5 Gutter Pairs	9·00		☐	

Collectors Pack 1990

1990 (13 Nov.) *Comprises Nos.* 1479/82, 1493/1510 *and* 1517/30

	Collectors Pack	60·00	☐

Post Office Yearbook

1990 *Comprises Nos.* 1479/82, 1493/1500, 1502/10 *and* 1517/30 *in hardback book with slip case*

	Yearbook	60·00	☐

973 'King Charles Spaniel'   **974** 'A Pointer'

975 'Two Hounds in a Landscape'   **976** 'A Rough Dog'

977 'Fino and Tiny'

Dogs. Paintings by George Stubbs

1991 (8 JAN.) *Phosphorised paper. Perf* 14 × 14½

1531	973	22p multicoloured	85	15	☐	☐
1532	974	26p multicoloured	1·10	1·25	☐	☐

1533	975	31p multicoloured	1·25	1·25	☐	☐
1534	976	33p multicoloured	1·40	1·40	☐	☐
1535	977	37p multicoloured	1·50	1·40	☐	☐
		Set of 5	5·50	5·00	☐	☐
		First Day Cover		5·25		☐
		Presentation Pack	6·00		☐	
		PHQ Cards (set of 5)	3·25	7·00	☐	☐
		Set of 5 Gutter Pairs	11·00		☐	

978 Thrush's Nest   **979** Shooting Star and Rainbow

980 Magpies and Charm Bracelet   **981** Black Cat

982 Common Kingfisher with Key   **983** Mallard and Frog

984 Four-leaf Clover in Boot and Match Box   **985** Pot of Gold at End of Rainbow

986 Heart-shaped Butterflies   **987** Wishing Well and Sixpence

T **978/87** were printed together, *se-tenant,* in booklet panes of 10 stamps and 12 half stamp-size labels, the backgrounds of the stamps forming a composite design.

Greetings Booklet Stamps. 'Good Luck'

1991 (5 FEB.) *Two phosphor bands*

1536	**978**	(1st) multicoloured	1·90	1·90	☐	☐
		a. Booklet pane. Nos.				
		1536/45	17·00		☐	
1537	**979**	(1st) multicoloured	1·90	1·90	☐	☐
1538	**980**	(1st) multicoloured	1·90	1·90	☐	☐
1539	**981**	(1st) multicoloured	1·90	1·90	☐	☐
1540	**982**	(1st) multicoloured	1·90	1·90	☐	☐
1541	**983**	(1st) multicoloured	1·90	1·90	☐	☐
1542	**984**	(1st) multicoloured	1·90	1·90	☐	☐
1543	**985**	(1st) multicoloured	1·90	1·90	☐	☐
1544	**986**	(1st) multicoloured	1·90	1·90	☐	☐
1545	**987**	(1st) multicoloured	1·90	1·90	☐	☐
		Set of 10	17·00	17·00	☐	☐
		First Day Cover		19·00		☐

988 Michael Faraday (inventor of electric motor) (Birth Bicentenary)

989 Charles Babbage (computer science pioneer) (Birth Bicentenary)

990 Radar Sweep of East Anglia (50th Anniv of Discovery by Sir Robert Watson-Watt)

991 Gloster Whittle E28/39 Aircraft over East Anglia (50th Anniv of First Flight of Sir Frank Whittle's Jet Engine

Scientific Achievements

1991 (5 MAR.) *Phosphorised paper*

1546	**988**	22p multicoloured	45	15	☐	☐
1547	**989**	22p multicoloured	45	15	☐	☐
1548	**990**	31p multicoloured	85	1·00	☐	☐
1549	**991**	37p multicoloured	1·00	1·25	☐	☐
		Set of 4	2·50	2·25	☐	☐
		First Day Cover		3·00		☐
		Presentation Pack	3·75		☐	
		PHQ Cards (set of 4)	3·00	6·50	☐	☐
		Set of 4 Gutter Pairs	5·00		☐	

992 Teddy Bear

Nos. 1550/9 were originally printed together, *se-tenant,* in booklet panes of 10 stamps and 12 half stamp-size labels.

Greetings Booklet Stamps. 'Smiles'

1991 (26 MAR.) *As Nos. 1483/92, but inscribed '1st' as T 992. Two phosphor bands*

1550	**992**	(1st) multicoloured	1·25	1·25	☐	☐
		a. Booklet pane. Nos.				
		1550/9	11·00		☐	
1551	**935**	(1st) multicoloured	1·25	1·25	☐	☐
1552	**936**	(1st) multicoloured	1·25	1·25	☐	☐
1553	**937**	(1st) multicoloured	1·25	1·25	☐	☐
1554	**938**	(1st) multicoloured	1·25	1·25	☐	☐
1555	**939**	(1st) multicoloured	1·25	1·25	☐	☐
1556	**940**	(1st) multicoloured	1·25	1·25	☐	☐
1557	**941**	(1st) multicoloured	1·25	1·25	☐	☐
1558	**942**	(1st) multicoloured	1·25	1·25	☐	☐
1559	**943**	(1st) multicoloured	1·25	1·25	☐	☐
		Set of 10	11·00	11·00	☐	☐
		First Day Cover		12·00		☐

The stamps were re-issued in sheets of 10 each with *se-tenant* label on 22 May 2000 in connection with 'customised' stamps available at 'Stamp Show 2000'. The labels show either a pattern of ribbons or a personal photograph.

A similar sheet, but in lithography instead of photogravure, appeared on 3 July 2001 with the labels showing either greetings or a personal photograph.

993 Man looking at Space **994**

995   Space looking at Man   **996**

Nos. 1560/1 and 1562/3 were each printed together, *se-tenant,* in horizontal pairs throughout the sheets, each pair forming a composite design.

Europa. Europe in Space

1991 (23 APR.) *Phosphorised paper*

1560	**993**	22p multicoloured	75	40	☐	☐
		a. Horiz pair. Nos. 1560/1	1·50	1·10	☐	☐
1561	**994**	22p multicoloured	75	40	☐	☐
1562	**995**	37p multicoloured	2·00	1·25	☐	☐
		a. Horiz pair. Nos. 1562/3	4·00	2·50	☐	☐
1563	**996**	37p multicoloured	2·00	1·25	☐	☐
		Set of 4	5·00	3·00	☐	☐
		First Day Cover		3·50		☐
		Presentation Pack	5·50		☐	
		PHQ Cards (set of 4)	3·00	6·50	☐	☐
		Set of 2 Gutter Strips of 4 . . .	10·00		☐	

997   Fencing   **998**   Hurdling

999   Diving   **1000**   Rugby

World Student Games, Sheffield (Nos. 1564/6) and World Cup Rugby Championship, London (No. 1567)

1991 (11 JUNE) *Phosphorised paper. Perf 14½ × 14*

1564	**997**	22p multicoloured	60	20	☐	☐
1565	**998**	26p multicoloured	95	1·00	☐	☐
1566	**999**	31p multicoloured	1·10	1·10	☐	☐
1567	**1000**	37p multicoloured	1·25	1·25	☐	☐
		Set of 4	3·50	3·00	☐	☐
		First Day Cover		3·50		☐
		Presentation Pack	4·25		☐	
		PHQ Cards (set of 4)	3·00	6·50	☐	☐
		Set of 4 Gutter Pairs	7·00		☐	

1001   'Silver Jubilee'   **1002**   'Mme Alfred Carrière'

1003   Rosa moyesii   **1004**   'Harvest Fayre'

1005   'Mutabilis'

9th World Congress of Roses, Belfast

1991 (16 JULY) *Phosphorised paper. Perf 14½ × 14*

1568	**1001**	22p multicoloured	95	20	☐	☐
1569	**1002**	26p multicoloured	1·10	1·25	☐	☐
1570	**1003**	31p multicoloured	1·25	1·25	☐	☐
1571	**1004**	33p multicoloured	1·50	1·50	☐	☐
1572	**1005**	37p multicoloured	1·60	1·50	☐	☐
		Set of 5	5·75	5·00	☐	☐
		First Day Cover		6·25		☐
		Presentation Pack	6·00		☐	
		PHQ Cards (set of 5)	3·25	8·50	☐	☐
		Set of 5 Gutter Pairs	11·50		☐	

1006 Iguanodon

1007 Stegosaurus

1008 Tyrannosaurus

1009 Protoceratops

1010 Triceratops

150th Anniversary of Dinosaurs' Identification by Owen

1991 (20 Aug.) *Phosphorised paper. Perf* 14½ × 14

1573	**1006**	22p multicoloured	90	20	☐	☐
1574	**1007**	26p multicoloured	1·10	1·25	☐	☐
1575	**1008**	31p multicoloured	1·25	1·25	☐	☐
1576	**1009**	33p multicoloured	1·50	1·50	☐	☐
1577	**1010**	37p multicoloured	1·60	1·50	☐	☐
		Set of 5	5·75	5·00	☐	☐
		First Day Cover		6·25		☐
		Presentation Pack	6·00		☐	
		PHQ Cards (set of 5)	3·25	8·50	☐	☐
		Set of 5 Gutter Pairs	11·50		☐	

1011 Map of 1816

1012 Map of 1906

1013 Map of 1959

1014 Map of 1991

Bicentenary of Ordnance Survey. Maps of Hamstreet, Kent

1991 (17 Sept.) *Phosphorised paper. Perf* 14½ × 14

1578	**1011**	24p multicoloured	60	20	☐	☐
1579	**1012**	28p multicoloured	90	95	☐	☐
1580	**1013**	33p multicoloured	1·10	1·25	☐	☐
1581	**1014**	39p multicoloured	1·40	1·25	☐	☐
		Set of 4	3·50	3·25	☐	☐
		First Day Cover		4·00		☐
		Presentation Pack	4·00		☐	
		PHQ Cards (set of 4)	3·00	6·00	☐	☐
		Set of 4 Gutter Pairs	7·00		☐	

1015 Adoration of the Magi

1016 Mary and Baby Jesus in Stable

1017 Holy Family and Angel

1018 The Annunciation

1019 The Flight into Egypt

Christmas. Illuminated Manuscripts from the Bodleian Library, Oxford

1991 (12 Nov.) *One phosphor band* (18p) *or phosphorised paper* (*others*)

1582	**1015**	18p multicoloured	70		10	□	□
1583	**1016**	24p multicoloured	80		10	□	□
1584	**1017**	28p multicoloured	85		1·25	□	□
1585	**1018**	33p multicoloured	95		1·40	□	□
1586	**1019**	39p multicoloured	1·10		1·60	□	□
		Set of 5	4·00		4·00	□	□
		First Day Cover			5·00		□
		Presentation Pack	4·75			□	
		PHQ Cards (*set of* 5)	3·00		7·50	□	□
		Set of 5 *Gutter Pairs*	8·00			□	

Collectors Pack 1991

1991 (12 Nov.) *Comprises Nos.* 1531/5, 1546/9 *and* 1560/86

Collectors Pack . . . . 60·00 □

Post Office Yearbook

1991 *Comprises Nos.* 1531/5, 1546/9 *and* 1560/86 *in hardback book with slip case*

Yearbook . . . . 65·00 □

1020 Fallow Deer in Scottish Forest

1021 Hare on North Yorkshire Moors

1022 Fox in the Fens

1023 Redwing and Home Counties Village

1024 Welsh Mountain Sheep in Snowdonia

The Four Seasons. Wintertime

1992 (14 Jan.) *One phosphor band* (18p) *or phosphorised paper* (*others*)

1587	**1020**	18p multicoloured	50		15	□	□
1588	**1021**	24p multicoloured	70		20	□	□
1589	**1022**	28p multicoloured	90		1·10	□	□
1590	**1023**	33p multicoloured	1·10		1·40	□	□
1591	**1024**	39p multicoloured	1·25		1·60	□	□
		Set of 5	4·00		4·00	□	□
		First Day Cover			4·50		□
		Presentation Pack	4·50			□	
		PHQ Cards (*set of* 5)	3·00		8·00	□	□
		Set of 5 *Gutter Pairs*	8·00			□	

1025 Flower Spray

1026 Double Locket

1027 Key

1028 Model Car and Cigarette Cards

1029 Compass and Map

1030 Pocket Watch

1031 1854 1d. Red Stamp and Pen

1032 Pearl Necklace

1033	Marbles
1034	Bucket, Spade and Starfish

1039	Queen Elizabeth and Commonwealth Emblem

T **1025/34** were printed together, *se-tenant*, in booklet panes of 10 stamps and 12 half stamp-size labels, the backgrounds of the stamps forming a composite design.

Nos. 1602/6 were printed together, *se-tenant*, in horizontal strips of 5 throughout the sheet.

Greetings Stamps. 'Memories'

1992 (28 Jan.) *Two phosphor bands*

1592	**1025**	(1st) multicoloured	1·10	1·10	☐	☐
		a. Booklet pane. Nos.				
		1592/1601	10·00		☐	
1593	**1026**	(1st) multicoloured	1·10	1·10	☐	☐
1594	**1027**	(1st) multicoloured	1·10	1·10	☐	☐
1595	**1028**	(1st) multicoloured	1·10	1·10	☐	☐
1596	**1029**	(1st) multicoloured	1·10	1·10	☐	☐
1597	**1030**	(1st) multicoloured	1·10	1·10	☐	☐
1598	**1031**	(1st) multicoloured	1·10	1·10	☐	☐
1599	**1032**	(1st) multicoloured	1·10	1·10	☐	☐
1600	**1033**	(1st) multicoloured	1·10	1·10	☐	☐
1601	**1034**	(1st) multicoloured	1·10	1·10	☐	☐
		Set of 10	10·00	10·00	☐	☐
		First Day Cover		12·00		☐
		Presentation Pack	14·00		☐	

40th Anniversary of Accession

1992 (6 Feb.) *Two phosphor bands. Perf* $14\frac{1}{2} \times 14$

1602	**1035**	24p multicoloured	1·00	70	☐	☐
		a. Horiz strip of 5. Nos.				
		1602/6	5·50	6·25	☐	☐
1603	**1036**	24p multicoloured	1·00	70	☐	☐
1604	**1037**	24p multicoloured	1·00	70	☐	☐
1605	**1038**	24p multicoloured	1·00	70	☐	☐
1606	**1039**	24p multicoloured	1·00	70	☐	☐
		Set of 5	5·50	3·25	☐	☐
		First Day Cover		7·00		☐
		Presentation Pack	6·75		☐	
		PHQ Cards (set of 5)	3·50	7·50	☐	☐
		Gutter Block of 10	11·00			☐

1035	Queen Elizabeth in Coronation Robes and Parliamentary Emblem
1036	Queen Elizabeth in Garter Robes and Archiepiscopal Arms

1040	Tennyson in 1888 and 'The Beguiling of Merlin' (Sir Edward Burne-Jones)
1041	Tennyson in 1856 and 'April Love' (Arthur Hughes)

1037	Queen Elizabeth with Baby Prince Andrew and Royal Arms
1038	Queen Elizabeth at Trooping the Colour and Service Emblems

1042	Tennyson in 1864 and 'I am Sick of the Shadows' (John Waterhouse)
1043	Tennyson as a Young Man and 'Mariana' (Dante Gabriel Rossetti)

Death Centenary of Alfred, Lord Tennyson (poet)

1992 (10 Mar.) *Phosphorised paper. Perf* 14½ × 14

1607	**1040**	24p multicoloured	60	20	□	□
1608	**1041**	28p multicoloured	85	85	□	□
1609	**1042**	33p multicoloured	1·40	1·60	□	□
1610	**1043**	39p multicoloured	1·50	1·60	□	□
		Set of 4	4·00	3·75	□	□
		First Day Cover		4·25		□
		Presentation Pack	4·50		□	
		PHQ Cards (set of 4)	2·50	6·50	□	□
		Set of 4 Gutter Pairs	8·00		□	

1044   Carrickfergus Castle

1992 (24 Mar.)–**95.** *Designs as Nos. 1410/13, but showing Queen's head in silhouette as T* **1044.** *Perf* 15 × 14 (*with one elliptical hole on each vertical side*)

1611	**1044**	£1 bottle green and gold†	5·50	50	□	□
1612	**880**	£1·50 maroon and gold†	5·00	1·00	□	□
1613	**881**	£2 indigo and gold† . . .	6·75	1·00	□	□
1613a	**1044**	£3 reddish violet and gold†	18·00	3·00	□	□
1614	**882**	£5 deep brown and gold†	17·00	2·50	□	□
		Set of 5	48·00	7·25	□	□
		First Day Cover (Nos. 1611/13, 1614)		35·00		□
		First Day Cover (22 Aug. 1995) (No. 1613a)		10·00		□
		Presentation Pack (P.O. Pack No. 27) (Nos. 1611/13, 1614) . . .	38·00		□	
		Presentation Pack (P.O. Pack No. 33) (No. 1613a)	20·00		□	
		PHQ Cards (Nos. 1611/14) . . .	2·50		□	
		PHQ Card (No. 1613a)	1·00	9·00	□	□
		Set of 5 Gutter Pairs	95·00		□	

†The Queen's head on these stamps is printed in optically variable ink which changes colour from gold to green when viewed from different angles.

PHQ cards for Nos. 1611/13 and 1614 were not issued until 16 February 1993.

Nos. 1611/14 were printed by Harrison. For stamps with different lettering by Enschedé see Nos. 1993/6.

For full information on all future British issues, collectors should write to Royal Mail, Freepost EH3647, 21 South Gyle Crescent, Edinburgh EH12 9PE.

1045   British Olympic Association Logo (Olympic Games, Barcelona)

1046   British Paralympic Association Symbol (Paralympics '92, Barcelona)

1047   *Santa Maria* (500th Anniv of Discovery of America by Columbus)

1048   *Kaisei* (Japanese cadet brigantine) (Grand Regatta Columbus, 1992)

1049   British Pavilion, 'EXPO 92', Seville

Nos. 1615/16 were printed together, *se-tenant,* in horizontal pairs throughout the sheet.

Europa. International Events

1992 (7 Apr.) *Phosphorised paper. Perf* 14 × 14½

1615	**1045**	24p multicoloured	1·00	75	□	□
		a. Horiz pair. Nos. 1615/16	2·25	2·00	□	□
1616	**1046**	24p multicoloured	1·00	75	□	□
1617	**1047**	24p multicoloured	1·00	50	□	□
1618	**1048**	39p multicoloured	1·25	1·25	□	□
1619	**1049**	39p multicoloured	1·40	1·25	□	□
		Set of 5	5·25	4·00	□	□
		First Day Cover		5·00		□
		Presentation Pack	5·75		□	
		PHQ Cards (set of 5)	3·00	6·50	□	□
		Set of 3 Gutter Pairs and a Gutter Strip of 4	10·50		□	

1050 Pikeman

1051 Drummer

1052 Musketeer

1053 Standard Bearer

350th Anniversary of the Civil War

1992 (16 JUNE) *Phosphorised paper. Perf* 14½ × 14

1620	**1050**	24p multicoloured	50	20	☐	☐
1621	**1051**	28p multicoloured	75	85	☐	☐
1622	**1052**	33p multicoloured	1·40	1·40	☐	☐
1623	**1053**	39p multicoloured	1·50	1·50	☐	☐
		Set of 4	3·75	3·50	☐	☐
		First Day Cover		4·25		☐
		Presentation Pack	4·50		☐	
		PHQ Cards (set of 4)	2·00	6·00	☐	☐
		Set of 4 Gutter Pairs	7·50		☐	

1054 The Yeomen of the Guard

1055 The Gondoliers

1056 The Mikado

1057 The Pirates of Penzance

1058 Iolanthe

150th Birth Anniversary of Sir Arthur Sullivan (composer). Gilbert and Sullivan Operas

1992 (21 JULY) *One phosphor band* (18p) *or phosphorised paper* (others). *Perf* 14½ × 14

1624	**1054**	18p multicoloured	50	20	☐	☐
1625	**1055**	24p multicoloured	80	20	☐	☐
1626	**1056**	28p multicoloured	95	1·00	☐	☐
1627	**1057**	33p multicoloured	1·50	1·60	☐	☐
1628	**1058**	39p multicoloured	1·60	1·60	☐	☐
		Set of 5	4·75	4·25	☐	☐
		First Day Cover		5·00		☐
		Presentation Pack	5·25		☐	
		PHQ Cards (set of 5)	2·25	6·00	☐	☐
		Set of 5 Gutter Pairs	9·50		☐	

1059 'Acid Rain Kills'

1060 'Ozone Layer'

1061 'Greenhouse Effect'

1062 'Bird of Hope'

Protection of the Environment. Children's Paintings

1992 (15 SEPT.) *Phosphorised paper. Perf* 14 × 14½

1629	**1059**	24p multicoloured	70	20	☐	☐
1630	**1060**	28p multicoloured	1·00	1·10	☐	☐
1631	**1061**	33p multicoloured	1·10	1·25	☐	☐
1632	**1062**	39p multicoloured	1·25	1·25	☐	☐
		Set of 4	3·75	3·50	☐	☐
		First Day Cover		4·25		☐
		Presentation Pack	4·50		☐	
		PHQ Cards (set of 4)	2·00	5·50	☐	☐
		Set of 4 Gutter Pairs	7·50		☐	

1063   European Star

Single European Market
1992 (13 Oct.) *Phosphorised paper*

1633	**1063**	24p multicoloured	1·00		70 ☐	☐
		First Day Cover		1·75		☐
		Presentation Pack	1·75		☐	
		PHQ Card	75	3·50 ☐	☐	
		Gutter Pair	2·00		☐	

1064 'Angel Gabriel',
      St James's, Pangbourne

1065 'Madonna and Child',
      St. Mary's, Bibury

1066 'King with Gold', Our Lady
      and St Peter, Leatherhead

1067 'Shepherds', All Saints,
      Porthcawl

1068 'Kings with Frankincense
      and Myrrh', Our Lady and
      St Peter, Leatherhead

Christmas. Stained Glass Windows
1992 (10 Nov.) *One phosphor band* (18p) *or phosphorised paper* (*others*)

1634	**1064**	18p multicoloured	45	15 ☐	☐
1635	**1065**	24p multicoloured	75	15 ☐	☐
1636	**1066**	28p multicoloured	90	1·10 ☐	☐
1637	**1067**	33p multicoloured	1·10	1·50 ☐	☐
1638	**1068**	39p multicoloured	1·25	1·40 ☐	☐
		Set of 5	4·00	4·00 ☐	☐
		First Day Cover		5·00	☐
		Presentation Pack	4·75		☐
		PHQ Cards (set of 5)	2·25	7·50 ☐	☐
		Set of 5 Gutter Pairs	8·00		☐

Collectors Pack 1992
1992 (10 Nov.) *Comprises Nos.* 1587/91, 1602/10 *and* 1615/38

Collectors Pack . . . . 60·00   ☐

Post Office Yearbook
1992 (11 Nov.) *Comprises Nos.* 1587/91, 1602/10 *and* 1615/38 *in hardback book with slip case*

Yearbook . . . . 65·00   ☐

1069 Mute Swan Cob
      and St Catherine's,
      Abbotsbury

1070 Cygnet and Decoy

1071 Swans and Cygnet

1072 Eggs in Nest and Tithe
      Barn, Abbotsbury

1073 Young Swan and the Fleet

600th Anniversary of Abbotsbury Swannery

1993 (19 JAN.) *One phosphor band* (18p) *or phosphorised paper* (*others*)

1639	**1069**	18p multicoloured	. . . .	1·50	25 ☐	☐
1640	**1070**	24p multicoloured	. . . .	1·40	25 ☐	☐
1641	**1071**	28p multicoloured	. . . .	1·60	1·75 ☐	☐
1642	**1072**	33p multicoloured	. . . .	2·25	2·40 ☐	☐
1643	**1073**	39p multicoloured	. . . .	2·40	2·40 ☐	☐
		Set of 5		8·25	6·25 ☐	☐
		First Day Cover			7·50	☐
		Presentation Pack		9·00		☐
		PHQ Cards (set of 5)		2·50	8·50 ☐	☐
		Set of 5 Gutter Pairs		17·00		☐

1074 Long John Silver and Parrot (*Treasure Island*)

1075 Tweedledum and Tweedledee (*Alice Through the Looking-Glass*)

1076 William (*William* books)

1077 Mole and Toad (*The Wind in the Willows*)

1078 Teacher and Wilfrid ('The Bash Street Kids')

1079 Peter Rabbit and Mrs Rabbit (*The Tale of Peter Rabbit*)

1080 Snowman (*The Snowman*) and Father Christmas (*Father Christmas*)

1081 The Big Friendly Giant and Sophie (*The BFG*)

1082 Bill Badger and Rupert Bear

1083 Aladdin and the Genie

T 1074/83 were printed together, *se-tenant*, in booklet panes of 10 stamps and 20 half stamp-size labels.

Greetings Stamps. 'Gift Giving'

1993 (2 FEB.) *Two phosphor bands. Perf* 15 × 14 (*with one elliptical hole on each vertical side*)

1644	**1074**	(1st) multicoloured		1·10	1·10 ☐	☐
		a. Booklet pane. Nos.				
		1644/53		10·00		☐
1645	**1075**	(1st) gold, cream and				
		black		1·10	1·10 ☐	☐
1646	**1076**	(1st) multicoloured		1·10	1·10 ☐	☐
1647	**1077**	(1st) multicoloured		1·10	1·10 ☐	☐
1648	**1078**	(1st) multicoloured		1·10	1·10 ☐	☐
1649	**1079**	(1st) multicoloured		1·10	1·10 ☐	☐
1650	**1080**	(1st) multicoloured		1·10	1·10 ☐	☐
1651	**1081**	(1st) multicoloured		1·10	1·10 ☐	☐
1652	**1082**	(1st) multicoloured		1·10	1·10 ☐	☐
1653	**1083**	(1st) multicoloured		1·10	1·10 ☐	☐
		Set of 10		10·00	10·00 ☐	☐
		First Day Cover			12·00	☐
		Presentation Pack		14·00		☐
		PHQ Cards (set of 10)		3·00	12·00 ☐	☐

1084 Decorated Enamel Dial

1085 Escapement, Remontoire and Fusee

1086 Balance, Spring and Temperature Compensator

1087 Back of Movement

300th Birth Anniversary of John Harrison (inventor of the marine chronometer). Details of 'H4' Clock

1993 (16 FEB.) *Phosphorised paper. Perf* 14½ × 14

1654	**1084**	24p multicoloured	60	20	☐	☐
1655	**1085**	28p multicoloured	95	1·00	☐	☐
1656	**1086**	33p multicoloured	1·25	1·25	☐	☐
1657	**1087**	39p multicoloured	1·40	1·40	☐	☐
		Set of 4	3·75	3·25	☐	☐
		First Day Cover		4·00		☐
		Presentation Pack	4·25		☐	
		PHQ Cards (set of 4)	2·50	7·50	☐	☐
		Set of 4 Gutter Pairs	7·50		☐	

1088 Britannia

1993 (2 MAR.) *Granite paper. Perf* 14 × 14½ (*with two elliptical holes on each horizontal side*)

1658	**1088**	£10 multicoloured	20·00	8·00	☐	☐
		First Day Cover		22·00		☐
		Presentation Pack	22·00		☐	
		PHQ Card	50	28·00	☐	☐

1089 Dendrobium hellwigianum

1090 Paphiopedilum Maudiae 'Magnifcum'

1091 Cymbidium lowianum

1092 Vanda Rothschildiana

1093 Dendrobium vexillarius var albiviride   **1093a**

14th World Orchid Conference, Glasgow

1993 (16 MAR.) *One phosphor band* (18p) *or phosphorised paper* (*others*)

1659	**1089**	18p multicoloured	45	20	☐	☐
1660	**1090**	24p multicoloured	75	20	☐	☐
1661	**1091**	28p multicoloured	1·00	1·10	☐	☐
1662	**1092**	33p multicoloured	1·25	1·50	☐	☐
1663	**1093**	39p multicoloured	1·60	1·40	☐	☐
		Set of 5	4·50	4·00	☐	☐
		First Day Cover		5·00		☐
		Presentation Pack	5·00		☐	
		PHQ Cards (set of 5)	3·00	7·50	☐	☐
		Set of 5 Gutter Pairs	9·00		☐	

Booklet Stamps

1993 (6 APR.)–**99** *As T* **913/14** *and* **1093a**, *but Perf* 14 (*No.* 1663b) *or* 15 × 14 (*others*) (*both with one elliptical hole on each vertical side*)

(*a*) *Photo Harrison* (No. 1664); *Questa* (Nos. 1663ab, 1664ab); *Walsall* (No. 1663b); *Harrison* (later De La Rue) *or Walsall* (No. 1664b); *Harrison* (later De La Rue), *Questa or Walsall* (Nos. 1663a, 1664a)

1663a	**913**	(2nd) bright blue (1 centre band)	30	35	☐	☐
		ab. Perf 14	30	35	☐	☐
1663b		(2nd) bright blue (1 side band)	75	75	☐	☐
1664	**914**	(1st) bright orange-red (phosphorised paper)	1·75	1·25	☐	☐
1664a		(1st) bright orange-red (2 phosphor bands) ..	40	45	☐	☐
		ab. Perf 14	1·10	90	☐	☐
1664b	**1093a**	(E) deep blue (2 phosphor bands)	55	60	☐	☐

(*b*) *Litho Questa or Walsall* (No. 1666 *also Enschedé*)

1665	**913**	(2nd) bright blue (1 centre band)	75	75	☐	☐
1666	**914**	(1st) bright orange-red (2 phosphor bands) ..	40	50	☐	☐
		First Day Cover (No. 1664b) (19.1.99)		2·00		☐

Nos. 1663a, 1664a, 1664b and 1665/6 also come from sheets.

No. 1663b exists with the phosphor band at the left or right of the stamp and was only issued in booklets.

No. 1664b was valid for the basic European airmail rate, initially 30p.

For 1st in gold see No. 1979.

For self-adhesive versions in these colours see Nos. 2039/40.

1993–2000 As Nos. X841 etc, but perf 14 (No. Y1676) or 15 × 14 (others) (both with one elliptical hole on each vertical side)

(a) Photo

Enschedé:— 20p (Y1677), 29p, 35p (Y1688), 36p, 38p (Y1692), 41p (Y1696), 43p (Y1699)

Harrison (later De La Rue):— 7p, 8p, 20p (Y1679/80), 25p (Y1681), 33p, 35p (Y1689), 41p (Y1697/8), 43p (Y1700), 44p, 45p

Walsall:— 10p (Y1674a), 19p (Y1676), 38p (Y1693a), 43p (Y1700a)

Enschedé or Harrison (later De La Rue):— 4p, 5p, 6p, 10p (Y1674), 25p (Y1682), 31p, 39p, 50p, £1

Enschedé, Harrison (later De La Rue) or Questa:— 1p, 2p

Enschedé, Harrison (later De La Rue) or Walsall:—30p, 37p, 63p

Harrison (later De La Rue) or Questa:— 19p (Y1675), 20p (Y1678), 26p

De La Rue or Walsall:— 38p (Y1693), 40p, 64p, 65p

Y1667	367	1p crimson (2 bands)	10	10	□	□
Y1668		2p deep green (2 bands)	10	10	□	□
Y1669		4p new blue (2 bands)	10	10	□	□
Y1670		5p dull red-brown (2 bands)	10	10	□	□
Y1671		6p yellow-olive (2 bands)	20	15	□	□
Y1672		7p grey (2 bands)	20	20	□	□
Y1673		8p yellow (2 bands)	10	15	□	□
Y1674		10p dull orange (2 bands)	15	10	□	□
		a. Perf 14	1·25	1·25	□	□
Y1675		19p bistre (1 centre band)	30	35	□	□
Y1676		19p bistre (1 side band)	75	75	□	□
Y1677		20p turquoise-green (2 bands)	80	80	□	□
Y1678		20p bright green (1 centre band)	45	35	□	□
Y1679		20p bright green (1 side band)	1·25	1·25	□	□
Y1680		20p bright green (2 bands)	30	35	□	□
Y1681		25p rose-red (phosphorised paper)	1·00	1·00	□	□
Y1682		25p rose-red (2 bands)	1·00	1·00	□	□
Y1683		26p red-brown (2 bands)	1·00	1·00	□	□
Y1684		29p grey (2 bands)	1·25	1·25	□	□
Y1685		30p deep olive-grey (2 bands)	1·00	80	□	□
Y1686		31p deep mauve (2 bands)	1·10	1·10	□	□
Y1687		33p grey-green (2 bands)	50	55	□	□
Y1688		35p yellow (2 bands)	1·40	1·40	□	□
Y1689		35p yellow (phosphorised paper)	4·00	4·00	□	□
Y1690	367	36p bright ultramarine (2 bands)	1·40	1·40	□	□
Y1691		37p bright mauve (2 bands)	1·25	1·25	□	□
Y1692		38p rosine (2 bands)	1·50	1·50	□	□
Y1693		38p ultramarine (2 bands)	1·40	1·40	□	□
		a. Perf 14	3·00	3·00	□	□
Y1694		39p bright magenta (2 bands)	1·25	1·25	□	□
Y1695		40p deep azure (2 bands)	60	65	□	□
Y1696		41p grey-brown (2 bands)	1·40	1·25	□	□
Y1697		41p drab (phosphorised paper)	4·75	4·75	□	□
Y1698		41p rosine (2 bands)	65	70	□	□
Y1699		43p deep olive-brown (2 bands)	2·00	2·00	□	□
Y1700		43p sepia (2 bands)	1·25	1·25	□	□
		a. Perf 14	2·00	1·75	□	□
Y1701		44p grey-brown (2 bands)	1·50	1·10	□	□
Y1702		45p bright mauve (2 bands)	70	75	□	□
Y1703		50p ochre (2 bands)	75	80	□	□
Y1704		63p light emerald (2 bands)	1·90	1·60	□	□
Y1705		64p turquoise-green (2 bands)	1·90	1·75	□	□
Y1706		65p greenish blue (2 bands)	1·00	1·10	□	□
Y1707		£1 bluish violet (2 bands)	1·50	1·60	□	□

(b) Litho Walsall (37p, 60p, 63p), Questa or Walsall (25p, 35p, 41p), Questa (others)

Y1743	367	1p lake (2 bands)	50	50	□	□
Y1748		6p yellow-olive (2 bands)	10·00	10·00	□	□
Y1749		10p dull orange (2 bands)	4·50	4·50	□	□
Y1750		19p bistre (1 side band)	1·40	1·40	□	□
Y1751		20p bright yellow-green (1 centre band)	1·25	1·00	□	□
Y1752		25p red (2 bands)	1·00	1·00	□	□
Y1753		26p chestnut (2 bands)	1·25	1·00	□	□
Y1754		30p olive-grey (2 bands)	2·50	2·50	□	□
Y1755		35p yellow (2 bands)	1·50	1·50	□	□
Y1756		37p bright mauve (2 bands)	2·00	1·50	□	□
Y1757		41p drab (2 bands)	1·75	1·50	□	□
Y1758		60p dull blue-grey (2 bands)	3·00	2·75	□	□
Y1759		63p light emerald (2 bands)	3·00	2·75	□	□

Y1800	**367**	£1·50 red	2·25	2·00	□	□
Y1801		£2 dull blue	3·00	2·25	□	□
Y1802		£3 dull violet	4·50	3·00	□	□
Y1803		£5 brown	7·50	5·00	□	□
		PHQ Card (No. Y1707)	40	2·75	□	□

Presentation Pack (P.O. Pack No.
30) (*contains* 19p (Y1675), 25p
(Y1681), 29p (Y1684), 36p (Y1690),
38p (Y1692), 41p (Y1696)) ..   8·00   □

Presentation Pack (P.O. Pack No.
34) (*contains* 1p (Y1667), 2p
(Y1668), 4p (Y1669), 5p (Y1670),
6p (Y1671), 10p (Y1674), 19p
(Y1675), 20p (Y1677), 25p (Y1682),
29p (Y1684), 30p (Y1685), 35p
(Y1688), 36p (Y1690), 38p (Y1692),
41p (Y1696), 50p (Y1703), 60p
(Y1758), £1 (Y1707)) ....   16·00   □

Presentation Pack (P.O. Pack No.
35) (*contains* 20p (Y1678), 26p
(Y1683), 31p (Y1686), 37p (Y1691),
39p (Y1694), 43p (Y1699), 63p
(Y1704)) ....   7·50   □

Presentation Pack (P.O. Pack No.
41) (*contains* 2nd (1663a), 1st
(1664a), 1p (Y1667), 2p (Y1668),
4p (Y1669), 5p (Y1670), 6p (Y1671),
10p (Y1674), 20p (Y1678), 26p
(Y1683), 30p (Y1685), 31p (Y1686),
37p (Y1691), 39p (Y1694), 43p
(Y1700), 50p (Y1703), 63p (Y1704),
£1 (Y1707)) ....   8·25   □

Presentation Pack (P.O. Pack No.
43) (*contains* £1·50 (Y1800), £2
(Y1801), £3 (Y1802), £5 (Y1803))   18·00   □

Presentation Pack (P.O. Pack No.
44) *contains* 7p (Y1672), 19p
(Y1675), 38p (Y1693), 44p
(Y1701), 64p (Y1705)) ....   3·25   □

Presentation Pack (P.O. Pack No.
49) (*contains* 8p (Y1673), 33p
(Y1687), 40p (Y1695), 41p
(Y1698), 45p (Y1702), 65p
(Y1706)) ....   4·00   □

First Day Covers

26 Oct. 1993	19p, 25p, 29p, 36p, 38p, 41p (Nos. Y1675, Y1681, Y1684, Y1690, Y1692, Y1696)	6·00	□	
9 Aug. 1994	60p (No. Y1758)	4·00	□	
22 Aug. 1995	£1 (No. Y1707)	3·50	□	
25 June 1996	20p, 26p, 31p, 37p, 39p, 43p, 63p (Nos. Y1678, Y1683, Y1686, Y1691, Y1694, Y1699, Y1704)	8·00	□	
9 Mar. 1999	£1·50, £2, £3, £5 (Nos. Y1800/3)	25·00	□	
20 Apr. 1999	7p, 38p, 44p, 64p (Nos. Y1672, Y1693, Y1701, Y1705)	5·00	□	
25 Apr. 2000	8p, 33p, 40p, 41p, 45p, 65p (Nos. Y1673, Y1687, Y1695, Y1698, Y1702, Y1706)	4·75	□	

No. Y1707 is printed in Iriodin ink which gives a shiny effect to the solid part of the background behind the Queen's head.

Nos. Y1689 and Y1697 were only issued in coils and Nos. Y1674a, Y1676, Y1679, Y1693a, Y1700a, Y1743 and Y1748/59 only in booklets.

No. Y1750 exists with the phosphor band at the left or right of the stamp, but Nos. Y1676 and Y1679 exist with band at right only.

For 26p in gold see No. 1978.

1094 'Family Group'
(bronze sculpture)
(Henry Moore)

1095 'Kew Gardens'
(lithograph)
(Edward Bawden)

1096 'St Francis and the
Birds' (Stanley Spencer)

1097 'Still Life: Odyssey I'
(Ben Nicholson)

Europa. Contemporary Art

1993 (11 MAY) *Phosphorised paper. Perf* 14 × 14½

1767	**1094**	24p multicoloured	60	20	☐	☐
1768	**1095**	28p multicoloured	90	95	☐	☐
1769	**1096**	33p multicoloured	1·25	1·25	☐	☐
1770	**1097**	39p multicoloured	1·40	1·25	☐	☐
		Set of 4	3·75	3·25	☐	☐
		First Day Cover		3·75		☐
		Presentation Pack	4·50		☐	
		PHQ Cards (set of 4)	2·50	6·50	☐	☐
		Set of 4 Gutter Pairs	7·50		☐	

1098 Emperor Claudius
(from gold coin)

1099 Emperor Hadrian
(bronze head)

1100 Goddess Roma
(from gemstone)

1101 Christ (Hinton
St Mary mosaic)

Roman Britain

1993 (15 JUNE) *Phosphorised paper with two phosphor bands.
Perf* 14 × 14½

1771	**1098**	24p multicoloured	40	20	☐	☐
1772	**1099**	28p multicoloured	70	90	☐	☐
1773	**1100**	33p multicoloured	1·00	1·25	☐	☐
1774	**1101**	39p multicoloured	1·10	1·40	☐	☐
		Set of 4	3·00	3·50	☐	☐
		First Day Cover		4·50		☐
		Presentation Pack	4·25		☐	
		PHQ Cards (set of 4)	2·50	6·50	☐	☐
		Set of 4 Gutter Pairs	6·00		☐	

1102 *Midland Maid* and
other Narrow Boats,
Grand Junction Canal

1103 *Yorkshire Maid* and
other Humber Keels,
Stainforth and Keadby
Canal

1104 *Valley Princess* and
other Horse-drawn
Barges, Brecknock and
Abergavenny Canal

1105 Steam Barges including
Pride of Scotland and
and Fishing Boats,
Crinan Canal

Inland Waterways

1993 (20 JULY) *Two phosphor bands. Perf* 14½ × 14

1775	**1102**	24p multicoloured	60	20	☐	☐
1776	**1103**	28p multicoloured	95	1·00	☐	☐
1777	**1104**	33p multicoloured	1·25	1·25	☐	☐
1778	**1105**	39p multicoloured	1·50	1·40	☐	☐
		Set of 4	4·00	3·50	☐	☐
		First Day Cover		4·25		☐
		Presentation Pack	4·25		☐	
		PHQ Cards (set of 4)	2·50	6·00	☐	☐
		Set of 4 Gutter Pairs	8·00		☐	

Nos. 1775/8 commemorate the bicentenaries of the Acts of
Parliament authorising the canals depicted.

1106 Horse Chestnut

1107 Blackberry

1108 Hazel

1109 Rowan

1110 Pear

SHERLOCK HOLMES & MORIARTY
"THE FINAL PROBLEM"

1115 *The Final Problem*

T **1111/15** were printed together, *se-tenant,* in horizontal strips of 5 throughout the sheet.

The Four Seasons. Autumn. Fruits and Leaves

1993 (14 SEPT.) *One phosphor band* (18p) *or phosphorised paper* (others)

1779	**1106**	18p multicoloured	50	20	☐	☐
1780	**1107**	24p multicoloured	75	20	☐	☐
1781	**1108**	28p multicoloured	1·10	1·25	☐	☐
1782	**1109**	33p multicoloured	1·40	1·50	☐	☐
1783	**1110**	39p multicoloured	1·50	1·50	☐	☐
		Set of 5	4·75	4·25	☐	☐
		First Day Cover		4·75	☐	
		Presentation Pack	5·00		☐	
		PHQ Cards (set of 5)	2·50	7·50	☐	☐
		Set of 5 Gutter Pairs	9·50		☐	

Sherlock Holmes. Centenary of the Publication of **The Final Problem**

1993 (12 OCT.) *Phosphorised paper. Perf* 14 × 14½

1784	**1111**	24p multicoloured	1·10	1·10	☐	☐
		a. Horiz strip of 5. Nos.				
		1784/8	5·50	5·50	☐	☐
1785	**1112**	24p multicoloured	1·10	1·10	☐	☐
1786	**1113**	24p multicoloured	1·10	1·10	☐	☐
1787	**1114**	24p multicoloured	1·10	1·10	☐	☐
1788	**1115**	24p multicoloured	1·10	1·10	☐	☐
		Set of 5	5·50	5·00	☐	☐
		First Day Cover		6·50	☐	
		Presentation Pack	6·00		☐	
		PHQ Cards (set of 5)	3·00	10·00	☐	☐
		Gutter Strip of 10	11·00		☐	

1116

SHERLOCK HOLMES & DR WATSON
"THE REIGATE SQUIRE"

1111 *The Reigate Squire*

SHERLOCK HOLMES & SIR HENRY
"THE HOUND OF THE BASKERVILLES"

1112 *The Hound of the Baskervilles*

Self-adhesive Booklet Stamp

1993 (19 OCT.) *Litho Walsall. Two phosphor bands. Die-cut perf* 14 × 15 (*with one elliptical hole on each vertical side*)

1789	**1116**	(1st) orange-red	1·25	1·40	☐	☐
		First Day Cover		4·50		☐
		Presentation Pack (booklet pane				
		of 20)	17·00		☐	
		PHQ Card	50	5·00	☐	☐

For similar 2nd and 1st designs printed in photogravure by Enschedé see Nos. 1976/7.

SHERLOCK HOLMES & LESTRADE
"THE SIX NAPOLEONS"

1113 *The Six Napoleons*

SHERLOCK HOLMES & MYCROFT
"THE GREEK INTERPRETER"

1114 *The Greek Interpreter*

1117 Bob Cratchit and Tiny Tim

1118 Mr and Mrs Fezziwig

1119 Scrooge

1124 Class 4 No. 43000
on Turntable at Blyth
North

1125 Class 4 No. 42455
near Wigan Central

1120 The Prize Turkey

1126 Class Castle No. 7002
Devizes Castle on Bridge
crossing Worcester and
Birmingham Canal

1121 Mr Scrooge's Nephew

Christmas. 150th Anniversary of Publication of A Christmas
Carol

1993 (9 Nov.) *One phosphor band* (19p) *or phosphorised paper*
(*others*)

1790	**1117**	19p multicoloured	60	15	□	□
1791	**1118**	25p multicoloured	90	15	□	□
1792	**1119**	30p multicoloured	1·25	1·40	□	□
1793	**1120**	35p multicoloured	1·40	1·50	□	□
1794	**1121**	41p multicoloured	1·50	1·50	□	□
		Set of 5	5·00	4·25	□	□
		First Day Cover		5·00		□
		Presentation Pack	5·25		□	
		PHQ Cards (set of 5)	3·00	7·50	□	□
		Set of 5 Gutter Pairs	10·00		□	

Collectors Pack 1993

1993 (9 Nov.) *Comprises Nos. 1639/43, 1654/7, 1659/63, 1767/88
and 1790/4*

	Collectors Pack	60·00	□

Post Office Yearbook

1993 (9 Nov.) *Comprises Nos. 1639/43, 1654/7, 1659/63, 1767/88
and 1790/4 in hardback book with slip case*

	Yearbook	65·00	□

The Age of Steam. Railway Photographs by Colin Gifford

1994 (18 Jan.) *One phosphor band* (19p) *or phosphorised paper
with two bands* (*others*). *Perf* 14½

1795	**1122**	19p deep blue-green, grey-black and black	55	20	□	□
1796	**1123**	25p slate-lilac, grey-black and black	85	90	□	□
1797	**1124**	30p lake-brown, grey-black and black . . .	1·25	1·25	□	□
1798	**1125**	35p deep claret, grey-black and black . . .	1·40	1·50	□	□
1799	**1126**	41p indigo, grey-black and black	1·50	1·40	□	□
		Set of 5	5·00	4·75	□	□
		First Day Cover		5·50		□
		Presentation Pack	6·00		□	
		PHQ Cards (set of 5)	3·00	8·00	□	□
		Set of 5 Gutter Pairs	10·00		□	

1127 Dan Dare and the Mekon

1129 Rupert Bear

1122 Class 5 No. 44957
and Class B1 No.
61342 on West
Highland Line

1123 Class A1 No. 60149
Amadis at Kings Cross

1128 The Three Bears

1130 Alice (*Alice in
Wonderland*)

1131 Noggin and the Ice Dragon

1132 Peter Rabbit posting Letter

1133 Red Riding Hood and Wolf

1134 Orlando the Marmalade Cat

1135 Biggles

1136 Paddington Bear on Station

T **1127/36** were printed together, *se-tenant*, in booklet panes of 10 stamps and 20 half stamp-size labels.

Greeting Stamps. 'Messages'

1994 (1 Feb.) *Two phosphor bands. Perf* 15 × 14 (*with one elliptical hole on each vertical side*)

1800	**1127**	(1st) multicoloured	1·00	90	☐	☐
		a. Booklet pane. Nos.				
		1800/9	11·00		☐	
1801	**1128**	(1st) multicoloured	1·00	90	☐	☐
1802	**1129**	(1st) multicoloured	1·00	90	☐	☐
1803	**1130**	(1st) gold, bistre-yellow				
		and black	1·00	90	☐	☐
1804	**1131**	(1st) multicoloured	1·00	90	☐	☐
1805	**1132**	(1st) multicoloured	1·00	90	☐	☐
1806	**1133**	(1st) multicoloured	1·00	90	☐	☐
1807	**1134**	(1st) multicoloured	1·00	90	☐	☐
1808	**1135**	(1st) multicoloured	1·00	90	☐	☐
1809	**1136**	(1st) multicoloured	1·00	90	☐	☐
		Set of 10	11·00	8·00	☐	☐
		First Day Cover		10·00		☐
		Presentation Pack	24·00		☐	
		PHQ Cards (set of 10)	6·00	12·00	☐	☐

1137 Castell Y Waun (Chirk Castle), Clwyd, Wales

1138 Ben Arkle, Sutherland, Scotland

1139 Mourne Mountains, County Down, Northern Ireland

1140 Dersingham, Norfolk, England

1141 Dolwyddelan, Gwynedd, Wales

25th Anniversary of Investiture of the Prince of Wales. Paintings by Prince Charles

1994 (1 Mar.) *One phosphor band* (19p) *or phosphorised paper* (*others*)

1810	**1137**	19p multicoloured	55	20	☐	☐
1811	**1138**	25p multicoloured	1·00	20	☐	☐
1812	**1139**	30p multicoloured	1·10	1·40	☐	☐
1813	**1140**	35p multicoloured	1·40	1·50	☐	☐
1814	**1141**	41p multicoloured	1·50	1·50	☐	☐
		Set of 5	5·00	4·50	☐	☐
		First Day Cover		4·75		☐
		Presentation Pack	5·25		☐	
		PHQ Cards (set of 5)	3·00	7·50	☐	☐
		Set of 5 Gutter Pairs	10·00		☐	

1142 Bather at Blackpool

1143 'Where's my Little Lad?'

1144 'Wish You were Here!'

1145 Punch and Judy Show

1146 'The Tower Crane' Machine

Centenary of Picture Postcards

1994 (12 APR.) *One side band* (19p) *or two phosphor bands* (others). *Perf* 14 × 14½

1815	**1142**	19p multicoloured	. . . .	60	20	□	□
1816	**1143**	25p multicoloured	. . . .	90	20	□	□
1817	**1144**	30p multicoloured	. . . .	1·10	1·25	□	□
1818	**1145**	35p multicoloured	. . . .	1·40	1·50	□	□
1819	**1146**	41p multicoloured	. . . .	1·50	1·50	□	□
		Set of 5	. . . .	5·00	4·25	□	□
		First Day Cover	. . . .		4·75		□
		Presentation Pack	. . . .	5·50		□	
		PHQ Cards (set of 5)	. . . . . .	3·00	7·50	□	□
		Set of 5 Gutter Pairs	. . . . .	10·00		□	

1147 British Lion and French Cockerel over Tunnel

Minimum Price. The minimum price quoted is 10p. This represents a handling charge rather than a basis for valuing common stamps. Where the actual value of a stamp is less than 10p this may be apparent when set prices are shown, particularly for sets including a number of 10p stamps. It therefore follows that in valuing common stamps the 10p catalogue price should not be reckoned automatically since it covers a variation in real scarcity.

1148 Symbolic Hands over Train

Nos. 1820/1 and 1822/3 were printed together, *se-tenant*, in horizontal pairs throughout the sheets.

Opening of Channel Tunnel

1994 (3 MAY) *Phosphorised paper. Perf* 14 × 14½

1820	**1147**	25p multicoloured	. . . .	80	70	□	□
		a. Horiz pair. Nos. 1820/1		1·75	1·60	□	□
1821	**1148**	25p multicoloured	. . . .	80	70	□	□
1822	**1147**	41p multicoloured	. . . .	1·50	1·50	□	□
		a. Horiz pair. Nos. 1822/3		3·25	3·25	□	□
1823	**1148**	41p multicoloured	. . . .	1·50	1·50	□	□
		Set of 4	. . . .	4·50	4·00	□	□
		First Day Cover	. . . .		5·50		□
		Presentation Pack	. . . .	5·50		□	
		Souvenir Book	. . . .	25·00		□	
		PHQ Cards (set of 4)	. . . . . .	3·00	7·50	□	□

Stamps in similar designs were also issued by France and these are included in the Souvenir Book.

1149 Groundcrew replacing Smoke Canisters on Douglas Boston of 88 Sqn

1150 H.M.S. *Warspite* (battleship) shelling Enemy Positions

1151 Commandos landing on Gold Beach

1152 Infantry regrouping on Sword Beach

1153　Tank and Infantry advancing, Ouistreham

Nos. 1824/8 were printed together, *se-tenant,* in horizontal strips of 5 throughout the sheet.

50th Anniversary of D-Day

1994 (6 JUNE) *Two phosphor bands. Perf* 14½ × 14

1824	**1149**	25p multicoloured	1·10	1·10	☐	☐
		a. Horiz strip of 5. Nos.				
		1824/8	5·00	5·50	☐	☐
1825	**1150**	25p multicoloured	1·10	1·10	☐	☐
1826	**1151**	25p multicoloured	1·10	1·10	☐	☐
1827	**1152**	25p multicoloured	1·10	1·10	☐	☐
1828	**1153**	25p multicoloured	1·10	1·10	☐	☐
		Set of 5	5·00	5·00	☐	☐
		First Day Cover		5·50		☐
		Presentation Pack	5·75		☐	
		PHQ Cards (*set of* 5)	3·00	7·50	☐	☐
		Gutter Block of 10	11·00		☐	

1158　The 9th Hole, Turnberry

Scottish Golf Courses

1994 (5 JULY) *One phosphor band* (19p) *or phosphorised paper* (*others*). *Perf* 14½ × 14

1829	**1154**	19p multicoloured	60	20	☐	☐
1830	**1155**	25p multicoloured	85	20	☐	☐
1831	**1156**	30p multicoloured	1·10	1·40	☐	☐
1832	**1157**	35p multicoloured	1·40	1·40	☐	☐
1833	**1158**	41p multicoloured	1·50	1·40	☐	☐
		Set of 5	5·00	4·25	☐	☐
		First Day Cover		5·00		☐
		Presentation Pack	5·50		☐	
		PHQ Cards (*set of* 5)	3·00	7·50	☐	☐
		Set of 5 *Gutter Pairs*	10·00			☐

Nos. 1829/33 commemorate the 250th anniversary of golf's first set of rules produced by the Honourable Company of Edinburgh Golfers.

1154　The Old Course, St Andrews

1155　The 18th Hole, Muirfield

1159　Royal Welsh Show, Llanelwedd

1160　All England Tennis Championships, Wimbledon

1156　The 15th Hole ('Luckyslap'), Carnoustie

1157　The 8th Hole ('The Postage Stamp'), Royal Troon

1161　Cowes Week

1162　Test Match, Lord's

1163   Braemar Gathering

The Four Seasons. Summertime. Events

1994 (2 Aug.) *One phosphor band* (19p) *or phosphorised paper* (*others*)

1834	**1159**	19p multicoloured	50	20	☐	☐
1835	**1160**	25p multicoloured	75	20	☐	☐
1836	**1161**	30p multicoloured	1·10	1·25	☐	☐
1837	**1162**	35p multicoloured	1·25	1·60	☐	☐
1838	**1163**	41p multicoloured	1·40	1·60	☐	☐
		Set of 5	4·50	4·25	☐	☐
		First Day Cover		5·00		☐
		Presentation Pack	5·00		☐	
		PHQ *Cards* (*set of* 5)	3·00	7·50	☐	☐
		Set of 5 *Gutter Pairs*	9·00		☐	

1164   Ultrasonic Imaging

 (Europa 30 — Scanning Electron Microscopy stamp placeholder)

1165   Scanning Electron Microscopy

1166   Magnetic Resonance Imaging

1167   Computed Tomography

Europa. Medical Discoveries

1994 (27 Sept.) *Phosphorised paper. Perf* 14 $\times$ 14$\frac{1}{2}$

1839	**1164**	25p multicoloured	75	20	☐	☐
1840	**1165**	30p multicoloured	1·10	1·10	☐	☐
1841	**1166**	35p multicoloured	1·10	1·25	☐	☐
1842	**1167**	41p multicoloured	1·25	1·25	☐	☐
		Set of 4	3·75	3·50	☐	☐
		First Day Cover		4·50		☐
		Presentation Pack	4·75		☐	
		PHQ *Cards* (*set of* 4)	2·50	7·50	☐	☐
		Set of 4 *Gutter Pairs*	7·50		☐	

1168   Virgin Mary and Joseph

1169   Three Wise Men

1170   Virgin and Child

1171   Shepherds

1172   Angels

Christmas. Children's Nativity Plays

1994 (1 Nov.) *One phosphor band* (19p) *or phosphorised paper* (*others*)

1843	**1168**	19p multicoloured	75	15	☐	☐
1844	**1169**	25p multicoloured	1·00	15	☐	☐
1845	**1170**	30p multicoloured	1·25	1·50	☐	☐
1846	**1171**	35p multicoloured	1·40	1·50	☐	☐
1847	**1172**	41p multicoloured	1·60	1·50	☐	☐
		Set of 5	5·50	4·50	☐	☐
		First Day Cover		5·00		☐
		Presentation Pack	6·00		☐	
		PHQ *Cards* (*set of* 5)	3·00	7·50	☐	☐
		Set of 5 *Gutter Pairs*	11·00		☐	

Collectors Pack 1994

1994 (14 Nov.) *Comprises Nos.* 1795/1847

	Collectors Pack	55·00	☐

Post Office Yearbook

1994 (14 Nov.) *Comprises Nos.* 1795/9 *and* 1810/47 *in hardback book with slip case*

	Yearbook	60·00	☐

1173 Sophie (black cat)

1174 Puskas (Siamese) and Tigger (tabby)

1175 Chloe (ginger cat)

1176 Kikko (tortoiseshell) and Rosie (Abyssinian)

1177 Fred (black and white cat)

Cats

1995 (17 JAN.) *One phosphor band (19p) or two phosphor bands (others). Perf* 14½ × 14

1848	**1173**	19p multicoloured	. . . .	80	20	☐ ☐
1849	**1174**	25p multicoloured	. . . .	95	20	☐ ☐
1850	**1175**	30p multicoloured	. . . .	1·10	1·25	☐ ☐
1851	**1176**	35p multicoloured	. . . .	1·25	1·40	☐ ☐
1852	**1177**	41p multicoloured	. . . .	1·60	1·50	☐ ☐
		Set of 5	. . . .	5·00	4·00	☐ ☐
		First Day Cover	. . . .		4·50	☐
		Presentation Pack	. . . .	5·50		☐
		PHQ Cards (set of 5)	. . . . . .	3·50	9·00	☐ ☐
		Set of 5 *Gutter Pairs*	. . . . . .	10·00		☐

1178 Dandelions

1179 Sweet Chestnut Leaves

1180 Garlic Leaves

1181 Hazel Leaves

1182 Spring Grass

The Four Seasons. Springtime. Plant Sculptures by Andy Goldsworthy

1995 (14 MAR.) *One phosphor band (19p) or two phosphor bands (others)*

1853	**1178**	19p multicoloured	. . . .	80	15	☐ ☐
1854	**1179**	25p multicoloured	. . . .	95	15	☐ ☐
1855	**1180**	30p multicoloured	. . . .	1·25	1·40	☐ ☐
1856	**1181**	35p multicoloured	. . . .	1·25	1·40	☐ ☐
1857	**1182**	41p multicoloured	. . . .	1·60	1·60	☐ ☐
		Set of 5	. . . .	5·25	4·25	☐ ☐
		First Day Cover	. . . .		4·75	☐
		Presentation Pack	. . . .	5·50		☐
		PHQ Cards (set of 5)	. . . . . .	3·00	6·50	☐ ☐
		Set of 5 *Gutter Pairs*	. . . . . .	10·50		☐

1183 'La Danse a la Campagne' (Renoir)

1184 'Troilus and Criseyde' (Peter Brookes)

1185 'The Kiss' (Rodin)

1186 'Girls on the Town' (Beryl Cook)

1187 'Jazz'
(Andrew Mockett)

1188 'Girls performing a
Kathal Dance'
(Aurangzeb period)

1189 'Alice Keppel with
her Daughter'
(Alice Hughes)

1190 'Children Playing'
(L. S. Lowry)

1191 'Circus Clowns'
(Emily Firmin and
Justin Mitchell)

1192 Decoration from
'All the Love Poems of
Shakespeare' (Eric Gill)

T **1183/92** were printed together, *se-tenant,* in booklet panes of 10 stamps and 20 half stamp-size labels.

Greetings Stamp. 'Greetings in Art'

1995 (21 Mar.) *Two phosphor bands. Perf* 14½ × 14 (*with one elliptical hole on each vertical side*)

1858	**1183**	(1st) multicoloured	70	70 □ □
		a. Booklet pane. Nos.		
		1858/67	6·25	□
1859	**1184**	(1st) multicoloured	70	70 □ □
1860	**1185**	(1st) multicoloured	70	70 □ □
1861	**1186**	(1st) multicoloured	70	70 □ □
1862	**1187**	(1st) multicoloured	70	70 □ □
1863	**1188**	(1st) multicoloured	70	70 □ □
1864	**1189**	(1st) purple-brown and		
		silver	70	70 □ □
1865	**1190**	(1st) multicoloured	70	70 □ □
1866	**1191**	(1st) multicoloured	70	70 □ □
1867	**1192**	(1st) black, greenish		
		yellow and silver . .	70	70 □ □
	Set of 10		6·25	6·25 □ □
	First Day Cover			8·00 □
	Presentation Pack		8·00	□
	PHQ Cards (set of 10)		6·00	10·00 □ □

The National Trust
Celebrating 100 Years **19**

1193 Fireplace Decoration,
Attingham Park,
Shropshire

The National Trust
Protecting Land **25**

1194 Oak Seedling

The National Trust
Conserving Art **30**

1195 Carved Table Leg,
Attingham Park

The National Trust
Saving Coast **35**

1196 St David's Head,
Dyfed, Wales

The National Trust
Repairing Buildings **41**

1197 Elizabethan Window,
Little Moreton Hall,
Cheshire

Centenary of The National Trust

1995 (11 Apr.) *One phosphor band* (19p), *two phosphor bands* (25p, 35p) *or phosphorised paper* (30p, 41p)

1868	**1193**	19p multicoloured	70	20 □ □
1869	**1194**	25p multicoloured	95	20 □ □
1870	**1195**	30p multicoloured	1·10	1·25 □ □
1871	**1196**	35p multicoloured	1·40	1·50 □ □
1872	**1197**	41p multicoloured	1·50	1·50 □ □
	Set of 5		5·00	4·25 □ □
	First Day Cover			4·75 □
	Presentation Pack		5·50	□
	PHQ Cards (set of 5)		3·00	7·50 □ □
	Set of 5 Gutter Pairs		10·00	□

1198 British Troops and French Civilians celebrating

1199 Symbolic Hands and Red Cross

1203 *The Time Machine*

1204 *The First Men in the Moon*

1200 St Paul's Cathedral and Searchlights

1201 Symbolic Hand releasing Peace Dove

1205 *The War of the Worlds*

1206 *The Shape of Things to Come*

Science Fiction. Novels by H. G. Wells

1995 (6 JUNE) *Two phosphor bands. Perf* $14\frac{1}{2} \times 14$

1878	**1203**	25p multicoloured	95	20	☐	☐
1879	**1204**	30p multicoloured	1·40	1·50	☐	☐
1880	**1205**	35p multicoloured	1·50	1·60	☐	☐
1881	**1206**	41p multicoloured	1·60	1·60	☐	☐
		Set of 4	5·00	4·50	☐	☐
		First Day Cover		5·50		☐
		Presentation Pack	5·75		☐	
		PHQ Cards (set of 4)	2·50	10·00	☐	
		Set of 4 Gutter Pairs	10·00		☐	

Nos. 1878/81 commemorate the centenary of publication of Wells's *The Time Machine*.

1202 Symbolic Hands

Europa. Peace and Freedom

1995 (2 MAY) *One phosphor band (Nos.* 1873/4) *or two phosphor bands (others). Perf* $14\frac{1}{2} \times 14$

1873	**1198**	19p silver, bistre-brown and grey-black . . .	75	25	☐	☐
1874	**1199**	19p multicoloured	75	25	☐	☐
1875	**1200**	25p silver, blue and grey-black	1·10	30	☐	☐
1876	**1201**	25p multicoloured	1·10	30	☐	☐
1877	**1202**	30p multicoloured	1·50	1·90	☐	☐
		Set of 5	4·75	2·75	☐	☐
		First Day Cover		3·50		☐
		Presentation Pack	5·25		☐	
		PHQ Cards (set of 5)	3·00	8·00	☐	☐
		Set of 5 Gutter Pairs	9·50		☐	

Nos. 1873 and 1875 commemorate the 50th anniversary of the end of the Second World War, No. 1874 the 125th anniversary of the British Red Cross Society and Nos. 1876/7 the 50th anniversary of the United Nations.

Nos. 1876/7 include the 'EUROPA' emblem.

1207 The Swan, 1595

1208 The Rose, 1592

For full information on all future British issues, collectors should write to Royal Mail, Freepost EH3647, 21 South Gyle Crescent, Edinburgh EH12 9PE.

1209 The Globe, 1599

1210 The Hope, 1613

1211 The Globe, 1614

T **1207/11** were printed together, *se-tenant,* in horizontal strips of 5 throughout the sheet, the backgrounds forming a composite design.

Reconstruction of Shakespeare's Globe Theatre

1995 (8 AUG.) *Two phosphor bands. Perf* 14½

1882	**1207**	25p multicoloured	90	85	□	□
		a. Horiz strip of 5. *Nos.*				
		1882/6	4·25	4·00	□	□
1883	**1208**	25p multicoloured	90	85	□	□
1884	**1209**	25p multicoloured	90	85	□	□
1885	**1210**	25p multicoloured	90	85	□	□
1886	**1211**	25p multicoloured	90	85	□	□
		Set of 5	4·25	3·75	□	□
		First Day Cover		5·25		□
		Presentation Pack	5·00		□	
		PHQ Cards (*set of* 5)	3·00	7·50	□	□
		Gutter Strip of 10	8·50		□	

1212 Sir Rowland Hill and Uniform Penny Postage Petition

1213 Hill and Penny Black

1214 Guglielmo Marconi and Early Wirelesss

1215 Marconi and Sinking of *Titanic* (liner)

Pioneers of Communications

1995 (5 SEPT.) *One phosphor band* (19p) *or phosphorised paper* (*others*). *Perf* 14½ × 14

1887	**1212**	19p silver, red and black	60	25	□	□
1888	**1213**	25p silver, brown and				
		black	85	30	□	□
1889	**1214**	41p silver, grey-green and				
		black	1·40	1·50	□	□
1890	**1215**	60p silver, deep ultra-				
		marine and black . .	1·60	1·75	□	□
		Set of 4	4·00	3·50	□	□
		First Day Cover		4·25		□
		Presentation Pack	4·50		□	
		PHQ Cards (*set of* 4)	2·50	7·50	□	□
		Set of 4 *Gutter Pairs*	8·00		□	

Nos. 1887/8 mark the birth bicentenary of Sir Rowland Hill and Nos. 1889/90 the centenary of the first radio transmissions.

1216 Harold Wagstaff

1217 Gus Risman

1218 Jim Sullivan

1219 Billy Batten

1220 Brian Bevan

Centenary of Rugby League

1995 (3 OCT.) *One phosphor band* (19p) *or two phosphor bands* (*others*). *Perf* 14 × 14½

1891	1216	19p multicoloured	. . . .	85	20	☐	☐
1892	1217	25p multicoloured	. . . .	1·00	20	☐	☐
1893	1218	30p multicoloured	. . . .	1·25	1·40	☐	☐
1894	1219	35p multicoloured	. . . .	1·25	1·50	☐	☐
1895	1220	41p multicoloured	. . . .	1·60	1·60	☐	☐
		Set of 5	. . . .	5·25	4·50	☐	☐
		First Day Cover	. . . .		5·25		☐
		Presentation Pack	. . . .	5·50		☐	
		PHQ Cards (set of 5)	. . . . . .	3·00	7·00	☐	☐
		Set of 5 Gutter Pairs	. . . . .	10·50		☐	

1221 European Robin in Mouth of Pillar Box

1222 European Robin on Railings and Holly

1223 European Robin on Snow-covered Milk Bottles

1224 European Robin on Road Sign

1225 European Robin on Door Knob and Christmas Wreath

Christmas. Christmas Robins

1995 (30 OCT.) *One phosphor band* (19p) *or two phosphor bands* (*others*)

1896	1221	19p multicoloured	. . . .	55	20	☐	☐
1897	1222	25p multicoloured	. . . .	75	20	☐	☐
1898	1223	30p multicoloured	. . . .	1·10	1·25	☐	☐
1899	1224	41p multicoloured	. . . .	1·50	1·50	☐	☐
1900	1225	60p multicoloured	. . . .	1·60	1·75	☐	☐
		Set of 5	. . . .	5·00	4·50	☐	☐
		First Day Cover	. . . .		5·00		☐
		Presentation Pack	. . . .	5·50		☐	
		PHQ Cards (set of 5)	. . . . . .	3·00	7·50	☐	☐
		Set of 5 Gutter Pairs	. . . . .	10·00		☐	

The 19p value was re-issued on 3 October 2000 in sheets of 20 each with *se-tenant* label, in connection with 'customised' stamps available from the Philatelic Bureau. The labels show either Christmas greetings or a personal photograph.

Collectors Pack 1995

1995 (30 OCT.) *Comprises Nos.* 1848/1900

		Collectors Pack	. . . .	60·00		☐

Post Office Yearbook

1995 (30 OCT.) *Comprises Nos.* 1848/57 *and* 1868/1900 *in hardback book with slip case*

		Yearbook	. . . .	65·00		☐

1226 Opening Lines of 'To a Mouse' and Fieldmouse

1227 'O my Luve's like a red, red rose' and Wild Rose

1228 'Scots, wha hae wi Wallace bled' and Sir William Wallace

1229 'Auld Lang Syne' and Highland Dancers

Death Bicentenary of Robert Burns (*Scottish poet*)

1996 (25 Jan.) *One phosphor band* (19p) *or two phosphor bands* (others). Perf 14½

1901	**1226**	19p cream, bistre-brown and black	55	20 □ □	
1902	**1227**	25p multicoloured	80	20 □ □	
1903	**1228**	41p multicoloured	1·25	1·25 □ □	
1904	**1229**	60p multicoloured	1·60	1·60 □ □	
		Set of 4	3·75	3·00 □ □	
		First Day Cover		4·50 □	
		Presentation Pack	4·50	□	
		PHQ Cards (set of 4)	3·00	6·00 □ □	
		Set of 4 Gutter Pairs	7·50	□	

1230 'MORE! LOVE' (Mel Calman)

1231 'Sincerely' (Charles Barsotti)

1232 'Do you have something for the HUMAN CONDITION?' (Mel Calman)

1233 'MENTAL FLOSS (Leo Cullum)

1234 '4.55 P.M.' (Charles Barsotti)

1235 'Dear lottery prize winner (Larry)

1236 'I'm writing to you because...' (Mel Calman)

1237 'FETCH THIS, FETCH THAT' (Charles Barsotti)

1238 'My day starts before I'm ready for it' (Mel Calman)

1239 'THE CHEQUE IN THE POST' (Jack Ziegler)

T **1230/9** were printed together, *se-tenant*, in booklet panes of 10 stamps and 20 half stamp-size labels.

Greetings Stamps. Cartoons

1996 (26 Feb.–11 Nov.) *'All-over' phosphor. Perf* 14½ × 14 (*with one elliptical hole on each vertical side*)

1905	**1230**	(1st) black and bright mauve	70	55 □ □	
		a. Booklet pane. Nos. 1905/14	6·25	□	
		p. Two phosphor bands	70	80 □ □	
		pa. Booklet pane. Nos. 1905p/14p (11 Nov.)	6·25	□	
1906	**1231**	(1st) black and blue-green	70	55 □ □	
		p. Two phosphor bands	70	80 □ □	
1907	**1232**	(1st) black and new blue .	70	55 □ □	
		p. Two phosphor bands	70	80 □ □	
1908	**1233**	(1st) black and bright violet	70	55 □ □	
		p. Two phosphor bands	70	80 □ □	
1909	**1234**	(1st) black and vermilion .	70	55 □ □	
		p. Two phosphor bands	70	80 □ □	
1910	**1235**	(1st) black and new blue .	70	55 □ □	
		p. Two phosphor bands	70	80 □ □	
1911	**1236**	(1st) black and vermilion .	70	55 □ □	
		p. Two phosphor bands	70	80 □ □	
1912	**1237**	(1st) black and bright violet	70	55 □ □	
		p. Two phosphor bands	70	80 □ □	
1913	**1238**	(1st) black and blue-green	70	55 □ □	
		p. Two phosphor bands	70	80 □ □	
1914	**1239**	(1st) black and bright mauve	70	55 □ □	
		p. Two phosphor bands	70	80 □ □	
		Set of 10 (Nos. 1905/14)	6·25	5·00 □ □	
		Set of 10 (Nos. 1905p/14p) . . .	6·25	7·25 □ □	
		First Day Cover (Nos. 1905/14) .		7·00 □	
		Presentation Pack (Nos. 1905/14)	8·00	□	
		PHQ Cards (set of 10)	6·00	12·00 □ □	

For full information on all future British issues, collectors should write to Royal Mail, Freepost EH3647, 21 South Gyle Crescent, Edinburgh EH12 9PE.

1240 'Muscovy Duck'

1241 'Lapwing'

1242 'White-fronted Goose'

1243 'Bittern'

1244 'Whooper Swan'

50th Anniversary of the Wildfowl and Wetlands Trust. Bird Paintings by C. F. Tunnicliffe

1996 (12 Mar.) *One phosphor band (19p) or phosphorised paper (others). Perf 14 × 14½*

1915	**1240**	19p multicoloured	75	20	☐	☐
1916	**1241**	25p multicoloured	1·00	20	☐	☐
1917	**1242**	30p multicoloured	1·10	1·25	☐	☐
1918	**1243**	35p multicoloured	1·25	1·50	☐	☐
1919	**1244**	41p multicoloured	1·60	1·60	☐	☐
		Set of 5	5·25	4·25	☐	☐
		First Day Cover		4·75		☐
		Presentation Pack	5·50		☐	
		PHQ Cards (set of 5)	3·00	7·50	☐	☐
		Set of 5 Gutter Pairs	10·50		☐	

1245 The Odeon, Harrogate

1246 Laurence Olivier and Vivien Leigh in *Lady Hamilton* (film)

1247 Old Cinema Ticket

1248 Pathé News Still

1249 Cinema Sign, The Odeon, Manchester

Centenary of Cinema

1996 (16 Apr.) *One phosphor band (19p) or two phosphor bands (others). Perf 14 × 14½*

1920	**1245**	19p multicoloured	50	25	☐	☐
1921	**1246**	25p multicoloured	70	25	☐	☐
1922	**1247**	30p multicoloured	90	1·00	☐	☐
1923	**1248**	35p black, red and silver	1·25	1·25	☐	☐
1924	**1249**	41p multicoloured	1·60	1·60	☐	☐
		Set of 5	4·50	4·00	☐	☐
		First Day Cover		4·75		☐
		Presentation Pack	4·75		☐	
		PHQ Cards (set of 5)	3·00	7·50	☐	☐
		Set of 5 Gutter Pairs	9·00		☐	

1250 Dixie Dean

1251 Bobby Moore

1252 Duncan Edwards

1253 Billy Wright

1254 Danny Blanchflower

European Football Championship

1996 (14 MAY) *One phosphor band* (19p) *or two phosphor bands* (others). *Perf* $14\frac{1}{2} \times 14$

1925	**1250**	19p multicoloured	40	20	☐	☐
1926	**1251**	25p multicoloured	70	20	☐	☐
1927	**1252**	35p multicoloured	1·25	1·50	☐	☐
1928	**1253**	41p multicoloured	1·40	1·40	☐	☐
1929	**1254**	60p multicoloured	1·75	1·75	☐	☐
		Set of 5	5·00	4·50	☐	☐
		First Day Cover		5·00		☐
		Presentation Pack	5·50		☐	
		PHQ Cards (set of 5)	3·00	8·00	☐	☐
		Set of 5 Gutter Pairs	10·00		☐	

1255 Athlete on Starting Blocks

1256 Throwing the Javelin

1257 Basketball

1258 Swimming

1259 Athlete celebrating and Olympic Rings

T **1255/9** were printed together, *se-tenant,* in horizontal strips of 5 throughout the sheet.

Olympic and Paralympic Games, Atlanta

1996 (9 JULY) *Two phosphor bands. Perf* $14\frac{1}{2} \times 14$

1930	**1255**	26p multicoloured	90	1·00	☐	☐
		a. Horiz strip of 5. Nos. 1930/4	5·00	5·00	☐	☐
1931	**1256**	26p multicoloured	90	1·00	☐	☐
1932	**1257**	26p multicoloured	90	1·00	☐	☐
1933	**1258**	26p multicoloured	90	1·00	☐	☐
1934	**1259**	26p multicoloured	90	1·00	☐	☐
		Set of 5	5·00	4·50	☐	☐
		First Day Cover		5·50		☐
		Presentation Pack	5·50		☐	
		PHQ Cards (set of 5)	3·00	7·50	☐	☐
		Gutter Strip of 10	10·00		☐	

1260 Prof. Dorothy Hodgkin (scientist)

1261 Dame Margot Fonteyn (ballerina)

1262 Dame Elisabeth Frink (sculptress)

1263 Dame Daphne du Maurier (novelist)

1264 Dame Marea Hartman (sports administrator)

Europa. Famous Women

1996 (6 AUG.) *One phosphor band* (20p) *or two phosphor bands* (others). *Perf* $14\frac{1}{2}$

1935	**1260**	20p dull blue-green, brownish grey and black	60	25	☐	☐
1936	**1261**	26p dull mauve, brownish grey and black . . .	75	25	☐	☐
1937	**1262**	31p bronze, brownish grey and black . . .	95	1·10	☐	☐

1938	**1263**	37p silver, brownish grey and black	1·25	1·40	☐	☐
1939	**1264**	43p gold, brownish grey and black	1·40	1·50	☐	☐
		Set of 5	4·50	4·50	☐	☐
		First Day Cover		5·00		☐
		Presentation Pack	5·00		☐	
		PHQ Cards (set of 5)	3·00	7·50	☐	☐
		Set of 5 Gutter Pairs	9·00		☐	

Nos. 1936/7 include the 'EUROPA' emblem.

1265 *Muffin the Mule*   **1266** *Sooty*

1267 *Stingray*   **1268** *The Clangers*

1270 Triumph TR3   **1271** MG TD

1272 Austin-Healey 100   **1273** Jaguar XK120

1274 Morgan Plus 4

Classic Sports Cars

1996 (1 OCT.) *One phosphor band* (20p) *or two phosphor bands* (*others*). *Perf* 14½

1945	**1270**	20p multicoloured	50	20	☐	☐
1946	**1271**	26p multicoloured	65	20	☐	☐
1947	**1272**	37p multicoloured	95	1·40	☐	☐
1948	**1273**	43p multicoloured	1·00	1·40	☐	☐
1949	**1274**	63p multicoloured	1·40	1·50	☐	☐
		Set of 5	4·00	4·25	☐	☐
		First Day Cover		5·25		☐
		Presentation Pack	5·25		☐	
		PHQ Cards (set of 5)	3·00	8·00	☐	☐
		Set of 5 Gutter Pairs	8·00		☐	

1269 *Dangermouse*

50th Anniversary of Children's Television

1996 (3 SEPT.)–**97** *One phosphor band* (20p) *or two phosphor bands* (*others*). *Perf* 14½ × 14

1940	**1265**	20p multicoloured	55	20	☐	☐
		a. Perf 15 × 14 (23.9.97)	1·75	1·75	☐	☐
1941	**1266**	26p multicoloured	80	20	☐	☐
1942	**1267**	31p multicoloured	1·00	1·50	☐	☐
1943	**1268**	37p multicoloured	1·40	1·60	☐	☐
1944	**1269**	43p multicoloured	1·60	1·75	☐	☐
		Set of 5	4·75	4·75	☐	☐
		First Day Cover		5·50		☐
		Presentation Pack	5·25		☐	
		PHQ Cards (set of 5)	3·00	7·50	☐	☐
		Set of 5 Gutter Pairs	9·50		☐	

No. 1940*a* comes from stamp booklets.

1275 The Three Kings   **1276** The Annunciation

1277 The Journey to Bethlehem

1278 The Nativity

1279 The Shepherds

Christmas

1996 (28 Oct.) *One phosphor band* (2nd) *or two phosphor bands* (others)

1950	**1275**	(2nd) multicoloured	. . .	75	20	□	□
1951	**1276**	(1st) multicoloured	. . .	1·00	20	□	□
1952	**1277**	31p multicoloured	. . .	1·10	1·40	□	□
1953	**1278**	43p multicoloured	. . .	1·25	1·25	□	□
1954	**1279**	63p multicoloured	. . .	1·60	1·60	□	□
	Set of 5	. . . .		5·25	4·25	□	□
	First Day Cover	. . . .			5·00		□
	Presentation Pack	. . . .		5·50		□	
	PHQ Cards (set of 5)	. . . . .		3·00	7·00	□	□
	Set of 5 Gutter Pairs	. . . . . .		10·50		□	

Collectors Pack 1996

1996 (28 Oct.) *Comprises Nos.* 1901/4 *and* 1915/54

	Collectors Pack	. . . .	55·00	□

Post Office Yearbook

1996 (28 Oct.) *Comprises Nos.* 1901/4 *and* 1915/54 *in hardback book with slip case*

	Yearbook	. . . .	65·00	□

1280 Gentiana acaulis (Georg Ehret)

1281 Magnolia grandiflora (Ehret)

1282 *Camellia japonica* (Alfred Chandler)

1283 *Tulipa* (Ehret)

1284 *Fuchsia 'Princess of Wales'* (Augusta Withers)

1285 *Tulipa gesneriana* (Ehret)

1286 *Guzmania splendens* (Charlotte Sowerby)

1287 *Iris latifolia* (Ehret)

1288 *Hippeastrum rutilum* (Pierre-Joseph Redoute)

1289 *Passiflora coerulea* (Ehret)

T **1280/9** were printed together, *se-tenant,* in booklet panes of 10 stamps and 20 half stamp-size labels.

Greeting Stamps. 19th-century Flower Paintings

1997 (6 Jan.) *Two phosphor bands. Perf* $14\frac{1}{2} \times 14$ (*with one elliptical hole on each vertical side*)

1955	**1280**	(1st) multicoloured	. . . .	70	70	□	□
		a. Booklet pane. Nos.					
		1955/64	. . . .	6·25		□	
1956	**1281**	(1st) multicoloured	. · . . .	70	70	□	□
1957	**1282**	(1st) multicoloured	. . . .	70	70	□	□
1958	**1283**	(1st) multicoloured	. . . .	70	70	□	□
1959	**1284**	(1st) multicoloured	. . . .	70	70	□	□
1960	**1285**	(1st) multicoloured	. . . .	70	70	□	□
1961	**1286**	(1st) multicoloured	. . . .	70	70	□	□
1962	**1287**	(1st) multicoloured	. . . .	70	70	□	□

1963	**1288**	(1st) multicoloured	70	70 □ □	
1964	**1289**	(1st) multicoloured	70	70 □ □	
		Set of 10	6·25	6·25 □ □	
		First Day Cover		8·00 □	
		Presentation Pack	7·00	□	
		PHQ Cards (set of 10)	6·00	10·00 □ □	

1290 'King Henry VIII'

1291 'Catherine of Aragon'

1292 'Anne Boleyn'

1293 'Jane Seymour'

1294 'Anne of Cleves'

1295 'Catherine Howard'

1296 'Catherine Parr'

T **1290/6** were printed together, *se-tenant*, in horizontal strips of 6 throughout the sheet.

450th Death Anniversary of King Henry VIII

1997 (21 JAN.) *Two phosphor bands. Perf* 15 (*No.* 1965) *or* 14 × 15 (*others*)

1965	**1290**	26p multicoloured	1·00	80 □ □	
1966	**1291**	26p multicoloured	1·25	85 □ □	
		a. Horiz strip of 6. Nos.			
		1966/71	7·50	7·50 □ □	
1967	**1292**	26p multicoloured	1·25	85 □ □	
1968	**1293**	26p multicoloured	1·25	85 □ □	
1969	**1294**	26p multicoloured	1·25	85 □ □	
1970	**1295**	26p multicoloured	1·25	85 □ □	
1971	**1296**	26p multicoloured	1·25	85 □ □	
		Set of 7	7·75	5·50 □ □	
		First Day Cover		8·50 □	
		Presentation Pack	8·50	□	
		PHQ Cards (set of 7)	5·00	11·00 □ □	
		Gutter Pair and Gutter Block of 12	17·00	□	

1297 St Columba in Boat

1298 St Columba on Iona

1299 St Augustine with King Ethelbert

1300 St Augustine with Model of Cathedral

Religious Anniversaries

1997 (11 MAR.) *Two phosphor bands. Perf* 14½

1972	**1297**	26p multicoloured	70	30 □ □	
1973	**1298**	37p multicoloured	1·00	1·40 □ □	
1974	**1299**	43p multicoloured	1·40	1·40 □ □	
1975	**1300**	63p multicoloured	1·90	1·90 □ □	
		Set of 4	4·50	4·50 □ □	
		First Day Cover		5·50 □	
		Presentation Pack	5·00	□	
		PHQ Cards (set of 4)	2·50	6·50 □ □	
		Set of 4 Gutter Pairs	9·00	□	

Nos. 1972/3 commemorate the 1400th death anniversary of St Columba and Nos. 1974/5 the 1400th anniversary of the arrival of St Augustine of Canterbury in Kent.

1301   1302

Self-adhesive Coil Stamps

1997 (18 MAR.) *Photo Enschedé. One centre phosphor band (2nd) or two phosphor bands (1st). Perf 14 × 15 die-cut (with one elliptical hole on each vertical side)*

1976	**1301**	(2nd) bright blue	1·25	1·25 ☐	☐
1977	**1302**	(1st) bright orange-red .	2·00	2·00 ☐	☐
	Set of 2		3·25	3·25 ☐	☐
	First Day Cover			4·50	☐
	Presentation Pack		4·00		☐

Nos. 1976/7, which were priced at 20p and 26p, were each sold in rolls of 100 with the stamps separate on the backing paper.

Royal Golden Wedding (*1st issue*)

1997 (21 APR.) *Designs as T 367 and 914 but colours changed. Printed in photogravure by Harrison (26p), Harrison or Walsall (1st). Two phosphor bands. Perf 15 × 14 (with one elliptical hole on each vertical side)*

1978	**367**	26p gold	70	70 ☐	☐
1979	**914**	(1st) gold	70	70 ☐	☐
	Set of 2		1·40	1·40 ☐	☐
	First Day Cover		3·00		☐
	Presentation Pack		2·25		☐

See also Nos. 2011/14.

1303   *Dracula*

1304   *Frankenstein*

1305   *Dr Jekyll and Mr Hyde*

1306   *The Hound of the Baskervilles*

Europa. Tales and Legends. Horror Stories

1997 (13 MAY) *Two phosphor bands. Perf 14 × 15*

1980	**1303**	26p multicoloured	90	40 ☐	☐
1981	**1304**	31p multicoloured	1·00	1·40 ☐	☐
1982	**1305**	37p multicoloured	1·25	1·50 ☐	☐
1983	**1306**	43p multicoloured	1·50	1·60 ☐	☐
	Set of 4		4·25	4·50 ☐	☐
	First Day Cover			5·50	☐
	Presentation Pack		4·75		☐
	PHQ Cards (set of 4)		3·00	6·50 ☐	☐
	Set of 4 Gutter Pairs		8·50		☐

Nos. 1980/3 commemorate the birth bicentenary of Mary Shelley (creator of Frankenstein) with the 26p and 31p values incorporating the 'EUROPA' emblem.

1307   Reginald Mitchell and Supermarine Spitfire MkIIA

1308   Roy Chadwick and Avro Lancaster MkI

1309   Ronald Bishop and De Havilland Mosquito B MkXVI

1310   George Carter and Gloster Meteor T Mk7

1311   Sir Sidney Camm and Hawker Hunter FGA Mk9

British Aircraft Designers

1997 (10 JUNE) *One phosphor band (20p) or two phosphor bands (others)*

1984	**1307**	20p multicoloured	55	40 ☐	☐
1985	**1308**	26p multicoloured	95	1·10 ☐	☐
1986	**1309**	37p multicoloured	1·10	1·10 ☐	☐
1987	**1310**	43p multicoloured	1·25	1·40 ☐	☐
1988	**1311**	63p multicoloured	1·75	1·90 ☐	☐
	Set of 5		5·00	5·25 ☐	☐
	First Day Cover			6·00	☐
	Presentation Pack		5·50		☐
	PHQ Cards		3·50	9·00 ☐	☐
	Set of 5 Gutter Pairs		10·00		☐

1312 Carriage Horse and Coachman

1313 Lifeguards Horse and Trooper

1314 Household Cavalry Drum Horse and Drummer

1315 Duke of Edinburgh's Horse and Groom

'All The Queen's Horses'. 50th Anniv of the British Horse Society

1997 (8 JULY) *One phosphor band (20p) or two phosphor bands (others). Perf 14½*

1989	1312	20p multicoloured	. . . .	70	40 ☐ ☐
1990	1313	26p multicoloured	. . . .	1·00	1·25 ☐ ☐
1991	1314	43p multicoloured	. . . .	1·25	1·40 ☐ ☐
1992	1315	63p multicoloured	. . . .	1·75	1·90 ☐ ☐
		Set of 4	. . . .	4·25	4·50 ☐ ☐
		First Day Cover	. . . .		5·50 ☐
		Presentation Pack	. . . .	4·75	☐
		PHQ Cards (set of 4)	. . . . .	2·50	6·50 ☐ ☐
		Set of 4 Gutter Pairs	. . . . . .	8·50	☐

CASTLE

Harrison printing (Nos. 1611/14)

CASTLE

Enschedé printing (Nos. 1993/6)

Differences between Harrison and Enschedé printings:
Harrison – 'C' has top serif and tail of letter points to right. 'A' has flat top. 'S' has top and bottom serifs.
Enschedé – 'C' has no top serif and tail of letter points upwards. 'A' has pointed top. 'S' has no serifs.

1997 (29 JULY) *Designs as Nos. 1612/14 with Queen's head in silhouette as T 1044, but re-engraved as above. Perf 15 × 14 (with one elliptical hole on each vertical side).*

1993	880	£1·50 deep claret and gold†	5·00	3·75 ☐ ☐
1994	881	£2 indigo and gold†	. . .	7·00	1·40 ☐ ☐

1995	1044	£3 violet and gold†	. . .	10·00	4·00 ☐ ☐
1996	882	£5 deep brown and gold†	18·00	12·00 ☐ ☐
		Set of 4	. . . .	35·00	19·00 ☐ ☐
		Set of 4 Gutter Pairs	. . . . .	70·00	☐
		Presentation Pack (P.O. Pack No. 40)	. . . .	40·00	☐

† The Queen's head on these stamps is printed in optically variable ink which changes colour from gold to green when viewed from different angles.

•1316 Haroldswick, Shetland

1317 Painswick, Gloucestershire

1318 Beddgelert, Gwynedd

1319 Ballyroney, County Down

Sub-Post Offices

1997 (12 AUG.) *One phosphor band (20p) or two phosphor bands (others). Perf 14½*

1997	1316	20p multicoloured	. . . .	65	40 ☐ ☐
1998	1317	26p multicoloured	. . . .	80	40 ☐ ☐
1999	1318	43p multicoloured	. . . .	1·25	1·40 ☐ ☐
2000	1319	63p multicoloured	. . . .	1·75	1·90 ☐ ☐
		Set of 4	. . . .	4·00	3·75 ☐ ☐
		First Day Cover	. . . .		5·00 ☐
		Presentation Pack	. . . .	4·75	☐
		PHQ Cards (set of 4)	. . . . .	2·50	6·50 ☐ ☐
		Set of 4 Gutter Pairs	. . . . . .	8·00	☐

Nos. 1997/2000 also mark the centenary of the National Federation of Sub-Postmasters.

Enid Blyton's *Noddy*

Enid Blyton's *Famous Five*

1320 Noddy

1321 Famous Five

Enid Blyton's *Secret Seven*		Enid Blyton's *Faraway Tree*
1322 Secret Seven		**1323** Faraway Tree

Enid Blyton's *Malory Towers*

1324 Malory Towers

Birth Centenary of Enid Blyton (children's author)

1997 (9 SEPT.) *One phosphor band* (20p) *or two phosphor bands* (*others*). *Perf* 14 × 14½

2001	**1320**	20p multicoloured	. . . .	55	40	□ □
2002	**1321**	26p multicoloured	. . . .	95	1·10	□ □
2003	**1322**	37p multicoloured	. . . .	1·10	1·10	□ □
2004	**1323**	43p multicoloured	. . . .	1·40	1·40	□ □
2005	**1324**	63p multicoloured	. . . .	1·90	1·90	□ □
		Set of 5	. . . .	5·25	5·25	□ □
		First Day Cover	. . . .		6·00	□
		Presentation Pack	. . . .	5·50		□
		PHQ *Cards* (*set of* 5)	. . . . .	3·50	9·00	□ □
		Set of 5 *Gutter Pairs*	. . . . . .	10·50		□

1325 Children and Father Christmas pulling Cracker	**1326** Father Christmas with Traditional Cracker

1327 Father Christmas riding Cracker	**1328** Father Christmas on Snowball

1329 Father Christmas and Chimney

Christmas. 150th Anniversary of the Christmas Cracker

1997 (27 OCT.) *One phosphor band* (2nd) *or two phosphor bands* (*others*)

2006	**1325**	(2nd) multicoloured	. . . .	70	20	□ □
2007	**1326**	(1st) multicoloured	. . . .	80	20	□ □
2008	**1327**	31p multicoloured	. . . .	90	1·25	□ □
2009	**1328**	43p multicoloured	. . . .	1·10	1·50	□ □
2010	**1329**	63p multicoloured	. . . .	1·50	1·75	□ □
		Set of 5	. . . .	4·50	4·50	□ □
		First Day Cover	. . . .		5·00	□
		Presentation Pack	. . . .	5·00		□
		PHQ *Cards* (*set of* 5)	. . . . . .	3·00	8·50	□
		Set of 5 *Gutter Pairs*	. . . . .	9·00		□

The 1st value was re-issued on 3 October 2000, in sheets of 10 each with a *se-tenant* label, in connection with 'customised' stamps available from the Philatelic Bureau. The labels show either Christmas greetings or a personal photograph.

1330 Wedding Photograph, 1947	**1331** Queen Elizabeth II and Prince Philip, 1997

Royal Golden Wedding (2nd issue)

1997 (13 NOV.) *One phosphor band* (20p) *or two phosphor bands* (*others*). *Perf* 15

2011	**1330**	20p gold, yellow-brown and grey-black	. . .	85	40	□ □
2012	**1331**	26p multicoloured	. . . .	1·10	60	□ □
2013	**1330**	43p gold, bluish green and grey-black	. . .	1·90	2·00	□ □
2014	**1331**	63p multicoloured	. . . .	2·50	2·75	□ □
		Set of 4	. . . .	5·75	5·25	□ □
		First Day Cover	. . . .		6·00	□
		Presentation Pack	. . . .	6·25		□
		Souvenir Book (*contains Nos.* 1979, 1989/92 *and* 2011/14)	. .	15·00		□
		PHQ *Cards* (*set of* 4)	. . . . .	2·50	7·00	□ □
		Set of 4 *Gutter Pairs*	. . . . .	12·00		□

Collectors Pack 1997

1997 (13 Nov.) *Comprises Nos. 1965/75, 1980/92 and 1997/2014*
  Collectors Pack . . . . 60·00 □

Post Office Yearbook

1997 (13 Nov.) *Comprises Nos. 1965/75, 1980/92 and 1997/2014 in hardback book with slip case*
  Yearbook . . . . 60·00 □

1332 Common Doormouse   1333 Lady's Slipper Orchid

1334 Song Thrush   1335 Shining Ram's-horn Snail

1336 Mole Cricket   . 1337 Devil's Bolete

Endangered Species

1998 (20 JAN.) *One side phosphor band* (20p) *or two phosphor bands* (others). *Perf* 14 × 14½

2015	1332	20p multicoloured	55	40	□	□
2016	1333	26p multicoloured	70	40	□	□
2017	1334	31p multicoloured	90	1·00	□	□
2018	1335	37p multicoloured	1·10	1·00	□	□

2019	1336	43p multicoloured	1·25	1·10	□	□
2020	1337	63p multicoloured	1·75	1·60	□	□
		Set of 6	5·50	5·00	□	□
		First Day Cover		5·50		
		Presentation Pack	6·00		□	
		PHQ Cards (Set of 6)	3·00	9·00	□	□
		Set of 6 Gutter Pairs	11·00		□	

1338 Diana, Princess of Wales (photo by Lord Snowdon)   1339 At British Lung Foundation Function, April 1997 (photo by John Stillwell)

1340 Wearing Tiara, 1991 (photo by Lord Snowdon)   1341 On Visit to Birmingham, October 1995 (photo by Tim Graham)

1342 In Evening Dress, 1987 (photo by Terence Donovan)

T **1338**/42 were printed together, *se-tenant,* in horizontal strips of 5 throughout the sheet.

Diana, Princess of Wales Commemoration

1998 (3 FEB.) *Two phosphor bands*

2021	1338	26p multicoloured	90	90	□	□
		a. Horiz strip of 5. Nos. 2021/5	4·00	4·00	□	□
2022	1339	26p multicoloured	90	90	□	□
2023	1340	26p multicoloured	90	90	□	□

2024	**1341**	26p multicoloured	90	90	□	□
2025	**1342**	26p multicoloured	90	90	□	□
		Set of 5	4·00	4·00	□	□
		First Day Cover		6·00		□
		Presentation Pack	15·00		□	
		Presentation Pack (Welsh) . . .	70·00		□	
		Gutter Strip of 10	8·00		□	

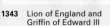

1343 Lion of England and Griffin of Edward III

1344 Falcon of Plantagenet and Bull of Clarence

1345 Lion of Mortimer and Yale of Beaufort

1346 Greyhound of Richmond and Dragon of Wales

1347 Unicorn of Scotland and Horse of Hanover

T **1343/7** were printed together, *se-tenant*, in horizontal strips of 5 throughout the sheet.

650th Anniversary of the Order of the Garter. The Queen's Beasts

1998 (24 Feb.) *Two phosphor bands*

2026	**1343**	26p multicoloured	90	90	□	□
		a. Horiz strip of 5. Nos.				
		2026/30	4·00	4·00	□	□
2027	**1344**	26p multicoloured	90	90	□	□
2028	**1345**	26p multicoloured	90	90	□	□
2029	**1346**	26p multicoloured	90	90	□	□
2030	**1347**	26p multicoloured	90	90	□	□
		Set of 5	4·00	4·00	□	□
		First Day Cover		5·00		□
		Presentation Pack	4·50		□	
		PHQ Cards (set of 5)	3·00	8·00	□	□
		Gutter Block of 10	8·00		□	

The phosphor bands on Nos. 2026/30 are only half the height of the stamps and do not cover the silver parts of the designs.

1348

Booklet Stamps

1998 (10 Mar.) *Design as T **157** (issued 1952–54), but with face values in decimal currency as T **1348**. One side phosphor band (20p) or two phosphor bands (others). Perf 14 (with one elliptical hole on each vertical side)*

2031	**1348**	20p light green	60	60	□	□
2032		26p red-brown	60	60	□	□
2033		37p light purple	2·00	2·00	□	□
		Set of 3	2·75	2·75	□	□

1349 St John's Point Lighthouse, County Down

1350 Smalls Lighthouse, Pembrokeshire

1351 Needles Rock Lighthouse, Isle of Wight, c 1900

1352 Bell Rock Lighthouse, Arbroath, mid-19th-century

1353 Eddystone Lighthouse, Plymouth, 1698

Lighthouses

1998 (24 Mar.) *One side phosphor band (20p) or two phosphor bands (others). Perf 14½ × 14*

2034	**1349**	20p multicoloured	. . . .	50		40 □	□
2035	**1350**	26p multicoloured	. . . .	70		50 □	□
2036	**1351**	37p multicoloured	. . . .	1·00		1·25 □	□
2037	**1352**	43p multicoloured	. . . .	1·40		1·40 □	□
2038	**1353**	63p multicoloured	. . . .	1·90		1·90 □	□
		Set of 5	. . . .	5·00		5·00 □	□
		First Day Cover	. . . .			5·75	□
		Presentation Pack	. . . .	5·50			□
		PHQ Cards (set of 5)	. . . . . .	3·50		8·50 □	□
		Set of 5 Gutter Pairs		10·00			□

Nos. 2034/8 commemorate the 300th anniversary of the first Eddystone Lighthouse and the final year of manned lighthouses.

Self-adhesive stamps

1998 (6 Apr.) *Photo Enschedé, Questa or Walsall. Designs as T **913/14**. One centre phosphor band (2nd) or two phosphor bands (1st). Perf 15 × 14 die-cut (with one elliptical hole on each vertical side)*

2039	(2nd) bright blue	. . . .	30		35 □	□
2040	(1st) bright orange-red	. . . . .	40		45 □	□
	Set of 2	. . . .	70		80 □	□

Nos. 2039/40 were initially priced at 20p and 26p, and were available in coils of 200 (Enschedé), sheets of 100 (Questa or Walsall) or self-adhesive booklets (Questa or Walsall).

1354 Tommy Cooper

1355 Eric Morecambe

1356 Joyce Grenfell

1357 Les Dawson

1358 Peter Cook

Comedians

1998 (23 Apr.) *One phosphor band (20p) or two phosphor bands (others). Perf 14½ × 14*

2041	**1354**	20p multicoloured	. . . .	50		50 □	□
2042	**1355**	26p multicoloured	. . . .	80		80 □	□
2043	**1356**	37p multicoloured	. . . .	1·10		1·10 □	□
2044	**1357**	43p multicoloured	. . . .	1·25		1·25 □	□
2045	**1358**	63p multicoloured	. . . .	1·90		1·90 □	□
		Set of 5	. . . .	5·00		5·00 □	□
		First Day Cover	. . . .			6·00	□
		Presentation Pack	. . . .	5·50			□
		PHQ Cards (set of 5)	. . . . . .	3·50		8·50 □	□
		Set of 5 Gutter Pairs	. . . . . .	10·00			□

1359 Hands forming Heart

1360 Adult and Child holding Hands

1361 Hands forming Cradle

1362 Hands taking Pulse

50th Anniversary of National Health Service

1998 (23 June) *One side phosphor band (20p) or two phosphor bands (others). Perf 14 × 14½*

2046	**1359**	20p multicoloured	. . . .	50		50 □	□
2047	**1360**	26p multicoloured	. . . .	70		70 □	□
2048	**1361**	43p multicoloured	. . . .	1·25		1·25 □	□
2049	**1362**	63p multicoloured	. . . .	1·90		1·90 □	□
		Set of 4	. . . .	3·75		3·75 □	□
		First Day Cover	. . . .			5·00	□
		Presentation Pack	. . . .	4·25			□
		PHQ Cards (set of 4)	. . . . . .	2·50		6·00 □	□
		Set of 4 Gutter Pairs	. . . . . .	7·50			□

For full information on all future British issues, collectors should write to Royal Mail, Freepost EH3647, 21 South Gyle Crescent, Edinburgh EH12 9PE.

1363 The Hobbit
(J. R. R. Tolkien)

1364 The Lion, The Witch
and the Wardrobe
(C. S. Lewis)

1365 The Phoenix and the
Carpet (E. Nesbit)

1366 The Borrowers
(Mary Norton)

1367 Through the Looking
Glass (Lewis Carroll)

Famous Children's Fantasy Novels

1998 (21 JULY) *One phosphor band* (20p) *or two phosphor bands* (others)

2050	1363	20p multicoloured	. . . .	50	40	☐	☐
2051	1364	26p multicoloured	. . . .	80	50	☐	☐
2052	1365	37p multicoloured	. . . .	1·10	1·40	☐	☐
2053	1366	43p multicoloured	. . . .	1·25	1·40	☐	☐
2054	1367	63p multicoloured	. . . .	1·90	1·90	☐	☐
		Set of 5	. . . .	5·00	5·00	☐	☐
		First Day Cover	. . . .		6·00		☐
		Presentation Pack	. . . .	5·50			☐
		PHQ Cards (set of 5)	. . . . . .	3·00	8·50	☐	☐
		Set of 5 Gutter Pairs	. . . . . .	10·00			☐

Nos. 2050/4 commemorate the birth centenary of C. S. Lewis and the death centenary of Lewis Carroll.

1368 Woman in Yellow
Feathered Costume

1369 Woman in Blue
Costume and Headdress

1370 Group of Children in
White and Gold Robes

1371 Child in 'Tree' Costume

Europa. Festivals. Notting Hill Carnival

1998 (25 AUG.) *One centre phosphor band* (20p) *or two phosphor bands* (others). *Perf* $14 \times 14\frac{1}{2}$

2055	1368	20p multicoloured	. . . .	70	40	☐	☐
2056	1369	26p multicoloured	. . . .	90	50	☐	☐
2057	1370	43p multicoloured	. . . .	1·40	1·50	☐	☐
2058	1371	63p multicoloured	. . . .	1·90	2·00	☐	☐
		Set of 4	. . . .	4·50	4·00	☐	☐
		First Day Cover	. . . .		4·75		☐
		Presentation Pack	. . . .	5·00			☐
		PHQ Cards (set of 4)	. . . . . .	2·50	6·00	☐	☐
		Set of 4 Gutter Pairs	. . . . . .	9·00			☐

Nos. 2055/6 include the 'EUROPA' emblem.

1372 Sir Malcolm Campbell's
Bluebird, 1925

1373 Sir Henry Segrave's
Sunbeam, 1926

1374 John G. Parry Thomas's
Babs, 1926

1375 John R. Cobb's
Railton Mobil Special, 1947

1376 Donald Campbell's
Bluebird CN7, 1964

British Land Speed Record Holders

1998 (29 Sept.–13 Oct.) *One phosphor band* (20p) *or two phosphor bands* (*others*). *Perf* 15 × 14

2059	**1372**	20p multicoloured (centre band)	70	20	☐	☐
		a. Perf 14½ × 13½ (*side band*) (13 Oct.) . . .	1·00	1·00	☐	☐
2060	**1373**	26p multicoloured	85	25	☐	☐
2061	**1374**	30p multicoloured	1·25	1·40	☐	☐
2062	**1375**	43p multicoloured	1·40	1·50	☐	☐
2063	**1376**	63p multicoloured	2·00	2·25	☐	☐
		Set of 5	5·50	5·00	☐	☐
		First Day Cover		5·25		☐
		Presentation Pack	6·00		☐	
		PHQ Cards (set of 5)	3·00	7·50	☐	☐
		Set of 5 Gutter Pairs	11·00		☐	

No. 2059*a*, which occurs with the phosphor band at the left or right of the stamp, comes from stamp booklets. There are minor differences of design between No. 2059 and No. 2059*a*, which also omits the copyright symbol and date.

Nos. 2059/63 commemorate the 50th death anniversary of Sir Malcolm Campbell.

1377 Angel with Hands raised in Blessing

1378 Angel praying

1379 Angel playing Flute

1380 Angel playing Lute

1381 Angel praying

Christmas. Angels

1998 (2 Nov.) *One phosphor band* (20p) *or two phosphor bands* (*others*)

2064	**1377**	20p multicoloured	70	40	☐	☐
2065	**1378**	26p multicoloured	85	40	☐	☐
2066	**1379**	30p multicoloured	1·25	1·40	☐	☐
2067	**1380**	43p multicoloured	1·40	1·50	☐	☐
2068	**1381**	63p multicoloured	2·00	2·00	☐	☐
		Set of 5	5·50	5·00	☐	☐
		First Day Cover		5·50		☐
		Presentation Pack	6·00		☐	
		PHQ Cards (set of 5)	3·00	7·50	☐	☐
		Set of 5 Gutter Pairs	11·00		☐	

Collectors Pack 1998

1998 (2 Nov.) *Comprises Nos.* 2015/30, 2034/8 *and* 2041/68

	Collectors Pack	50·00		☐

Post Office Yearbook

1998 (2 Nov.) *Comprises Nos.* 2015/30, 2034/8 *and* 2041/68 *in hardback book with slip case*

	Yearbook	55·00		☐

1382 Greenwich Meridian and Clock (John Harrison's chronometer)

1383 Industrial Worker and Blast Furnace (James Watt's discovery of steam power)

1384 Early Photos of Leaves (Henry Fox-Talbot's photographic experiments)

1385 Computer inside Human Head (Alan Turing's work on computers)

Millennium Series. The Inventors' Tale

1999 (12 Jan.–21 Sept.) *One centre phosphor band* (20p) *or two phosphor bands* (*others*). *Perf* 14 × 14½

2069	**1382**	20p multicoloured	50	50	☐	☐
2070	**1383**	26p multicoloured	70	80	☐	☐
2071	**1384**	43p multicoloured	1·10	1·25	☐	☐
2072	**1385**	63p multicoloured	1·75	1·90	☐	☐
		a. Perf 13½ × 14 (21 Sept.)	2·50	2·50	☐	☐
		Set of 4	3·75	4·00	☐	☐
		First Day Cover		5·50		☐
		Presentation Pack	4·75		☐	
		PHQ Cards (set of 4)	1·50	8·50	☐	☐
		Set of 4 Gutter Pairs	7·50		☐	

No. 2072*a* comes from stamp booklets.

1386 Airliner hugging Globe (International air travel)

1387 Woman on Bicycle (Development of the bicycle)

1388 Victorian Railway Station (Growth of public transport)

1389 Captain Cook and Maori (Captain James Cook's voyages)

Millennium Series. The Travellers' Tale

1999 (2 FEB.) *One centre phosphor band* (20p) *or two phosphor bands* (others). *Perf* 14 × 14½

2073	**1386**	20p multicoloured	50	50	□	□
2074	**1387**	26p multicoloured	70	80	□	□
2075	**1388**	43p grey-black, stone and bronze	1·10	1·25	□	□
2076	**1389**	63p multicoloured	1·75	1·90	□	□
	Set of 4		3·75	4·00	□	□
	First Day Cover			5·25		□
	Presentation Pack		4·75		□	
	PHQ Cards (set of 4)		1·50	8·00	□	□
	Set of 4 Gutter Pairs		7·50		□	

1390

1999 (16 FEB.) (*a*) *Embossed and litho Walsall. Self-adhesive. Die-cut perf* 14 × 15

2077 **1390** (1st) grey (face value) (Queen's head in colourless relief) (phosphor background around head) . . . . . 1·50 1·50 □ □

(*b*) *Recess Enschedé. Perf* 14 × 14½

2078 **1390** (1st) grey-black (2 phosphor bands) . . . . 1·50 1·50 □ □

(*c*) *Typo Harrison. Perf* 14 × 15

2079 **1390** (1st) black (2 phosphor bands) . . . . 1·50 1·50 □ □
Set of 3 . . . . 4·00 4·00 □ □

Nos. 2077/9 were only issued in £7·54 stamp booklets.

1391 Vaccinating Child (pattern in cow markings) (Jenner's development of smallpox vaccine)

1392 Patient on Trolley (nursing care)

1393 Penicillin Mould (Fleming's discovery of penicillin)

1394 Sculpture of Test-tube Baby (development of in vitro fertilization)

Millennium Series. The Patients' Tale

1999 (2 MAR.) *One centre phosphor band* (20p) *or two phosphor bands* (others). *Perf* 13½ × 14

2080	**1391**	20p multicoloured	50	50	□	□
2081	**1392**	26p multicoloured	70	80	□	□
2082	**1393**	43p multicoloured	1·10	1·25	□	□
2083	**1394**	63p multicoloured	1·75	1·90	□	□
	Set of 4		3·75	4·00	□	□
	First Day Cover			5·25		□
	Presentation Pack		4·75		□	
	PHQ Cards (set of 4)		1·50	6·75	□	□
	Set of 4 Gutter Pairs		7·50		□	

Minimum Price. The minimum price quoted is 10p. This represents a handling charge rather than a basis for valuing common stamps. Where the actual value of a stamp is less than 10p this may be apparent when set prices are shown, particularly for sets including a number of 10p stamps. It therefore follows that in valuing common stamps the 10p catalogue price should not be reckoned automatically since it covers a variation in real scarcity.

1395 Dove and Norman Settler (medieval migration to Scotland)

1396 Pilgrim Fathers and Red Indian (17th-century migration to America)

1397 Sailing Ship and Aspects of Settlement (19th-century migration to Australia)

1398 Hummingbird and Superimposed Stylised Face (20th-century migration to Great Britain)

Millennium Series. The Settlers' Tale

1999 (6 APR.) *One centre phosphor band* (20p) *or two phosphor bands* (others). *Perf* 14 × 14½

2084	**1395**	20p multicoloured	50	50	□	□
2085	**1396**	26p multicoloured	70	80	□	□
2086	**1397**	43p multicoloured	1·10	1·25	□	□
2087	**1398**	63p multicoloured	1·75	1·90	□	□
		Set of 4	3·75	4·00	□	□
		First Day Cover		5·25		□
		Presentation Pack	4·75		□	
		PHQ Cards (set of 4)	1·50	6·75	□	□
		Set of 4 Gutter Pairs	7·50		□	

1399 Woven Threads (woollen industry)

1400 Salts Mill, Saltaire (worsted cloth industry)

1401 Hull on Slipway (shipbuilding)

1402 Lloyd's Building (City of London finance centre)

Millennium Series. The Workers' Tale

1999 (4 MAY) *One centre phosphor band* (19p) *or two phosphor bands* (others). *Perf* 14 × 14½

2088	**1399**	19p multicoloured	50	50	□	□
2089	**1400**	26p multicoloured	70	80	□	□
2090	**1401**	44p multicoloured	1·10	1·25	□	□
2091	**1402**	64p multicoloured	1·75	1·90	□	□
		Set of 4	3·75	4·00	□	□
		First Day Cover		5·25		□
		Presentation Pack	4·75		□	
		PHQ Cards (set of 4)	1·50	6·75	□	□
		Set of 4 Gutter Pairs	7·50		□	

1403 Freddie Mercury (lead singer of Queen) ('Popular Music')

1404 Bobby Moore with World Cup, 1966 ('Sport')

1405 Dalek from *Dr Who* (science-fiction series) ('Television')

1406 Charlie Chaplin (film star) ('Cinema')

Millennium Series. The Entertainers' Tale

1999 (1 JUNE) *One centre phosphor band* (19p) *or two phosphor bands* (others). *Perf* 14 × 14½

2092	**1403**	19p multicoloured	50	50	□	□
2093	**1404**	26p multicoloured	70	80	□	□

2094	1405	44p multicoloured	1·10	1·25	□	□
2095	1406	64p multicoloured	1·75	1·90	□	□
		Set of 4	3·75	4·00	□	□
		First Day Cover		5·25		□
		Presentation Pack	4·75		□	
		PHQ Cards (set of 4)	1·50	6·75	□	□
		Set of 4 Gutter Pairs	7·50		□	

1407 Prince Edward and Miss Sophie Rhys-Jones **1408**
(from photos by John Swannell)

Royal Wedding

1999 (15 JUNE) *Two phosphor bands*

2096	1407	26p multicoloured	60	60	□	□
2097	1408	64p multicoloured	1·40	1·40	□	□
		Set of 2	2·00	2·00	□	□
		First Day Cover		3·50		□
		Presentation Pack	2·25		□	
		PHQ Cards (set of 2)	75	5·00	□	□
		Set of 2 Gutter Pairs	4·00		□	

1409 Suffragette behind Prison Window ('Equal Rights for Women')

1410 Water Tap ('Right to Health')

1411 Generations of School Children ('Right to Education')

1412 'MAGNA CARTA' ('Human Rights')

Millennium Series. The Citizens' Tale

1999 (6 JULY) *One centre phosphor band (19p) or two phosphor bands (others). Perf 14 × 14½*

2098	1409	19p multicoloured	50	50	□	□
2099	1410	26p multicoloured	70	80	□	□

2100	1411	44p multicoloured	1·10	1·25	□	□
2101	1412	64p multicoloured	1·75	1·90	□	□
		Set of 4	3·75	4·00	□	□
		First Day Cover		5·25		□
		Presentation Pack	4·75		□	
		PHQ Cards (set of 4)	1·50	6·75	□	□
		Set of 4 Gutter Pairs	7·50		□	

1413 Molecular Structures ('DNA decoding')

1414 Galapagos Finch and Fossilized Skeleton ('Darwin's theory of evolution')

1415 Rotation of Polarized Light by Magnetism (Faraday's work on electricity)

1416 Saturn (development of astronomical telescopes)

Millennium Series. The Scientists' Tale

1999 (3 AUG.–21 SEPT.) *One centre phosphor band (19p) or two phosphor bands (others). Perf 13½ × 14 (19p, 64p) or 14 × 14½ (26p, 44p)*

2102	1413	19p multicoloured	50	50	□	□
2103	1414	26p multicoloured	70	80	□	□
		b. Perf 14½ × 14 (21 Sept.)	2·00	2·00	□	□
2104	1415	44p multicoloured	1·10	1·25	□	□
		a. Perf 14½ × 14 (21 Sept.)	2·50	2·50	□	□
2105	1416	64p multicoloured	1·75	1·90	□	□
		Set of 4	3·75	4·00	□	□
		First Day Cover		5·25		□
		Presentation Pack	4·75		□	
		PHQ Cards (set of 4)	1·50	6·75	□	□
		Set of 4 Gutter Pairs	7·50		□	

Nos. 2103*b* and 2104*a* come from stamp booklets.

For full information on all future British issues, collectors should write to Royal Mail, Freepost EH3647, 21 South Gyle Crescent, Edinburgh EH12 9PE.

1416a

Solar Eclipse
1999 (11 Aug.) *Sheet* 89 × 121 *mm. Two phosphor bands. Perf* 14 × 14½

MS2106	**1416a**	64p × 4 multicoloured	12·00	12·00	□	□
		First Day Cover		12·00	□	

1417 Upland Landscape (Strip farming)

1418 Horse-drawn Rotary Seed Drill (Mechanical farming)

1419 Man peeling Potato (Food imports)

1420 Aerial View of Combine Harvester (Satellite agriculture)

Millennium Series. The Farmers' Tale
1999 (7 Sept.) *One centre phosphor band* (19p) *or two phosphor bands* (*others*). *Perf* 14 × 14½

2107	**1417**	19p multicoloured	50	50	□	□
2108	**1418**	26p multicoloured	70	80	□	□
2109	**1419**	44p multicoloured	1·10	1·25	□	□
2110	**1420**	64p multicoloured	1·75	1·90	□	□
		Set of 4	3·75	4·00	□	□
		First Day Cover		5·25		□
		Presentation Pack	4·75		□	
		PHQ Cards (set of 4)	1·50	6·75	□	□
		Set of 4 Gutter Pairs	7·50		□	

No. 2107 includes the 'EUROPA' emblem.

1421 Robert the Bruce (Battle of Bannockburn, 1314)

1422 Cavalier and Horse (English Civil War)

1423 War Graves Cemetery, The Somme (World Wars)

1424 Soldiers with Boy (Peace-keeping)

Millennium Series. The Soldiers' Tale
1999 (5 Oct.) *One centre phosphor band* (19p) *or two phosphor bands* (*others*). *Perf* 14 × 14½

2111	**1421**	19p black, stone and silver	50	50	□	□
2112	**1422**	26p multicoloured	70	80	□	□
2113	**1423**	44p grey-black, black and silver	1·10	1·25	□	□
2114	**1424**	64p multicoloured	1·75	1·90	□	□
		Set of 4	3·75	4·00	□	□
		First Day Cover		5·25		□
		Presentation Pack	4·75		□	
		PHQ Cards (set of 4)	1·50	6·75	□	□
		Set of 4 Gutter Pairs	7·50		□	

For full information on all future British issues, collectors should write to Royal Mail, Freepost EH3647, 21 South Gyle Crescent, Edinburgh EH12 9PE.

1425 'Hark the herald angels sing', and Hymnbook (John Wesley)

1426 King James I and Bible (Authorised Version of Bible)

1427 St Andrews Cathedral, Fife ('Pilgrimage')

1428 Nativity ('First Christmas')

Millennium Series. The Christians' Tale

1999 (2 Nov.) *One centre phosphor band* (19p) *or two phosphor bands* (others). *Perf* 14 × 14½

2115	**1425**	19p multicoloured	. . . .	50	50	□ □
2116	**1426**	26p multicoloured	. . . .	70	80	□ □
2117	**1427**	44p multicoloured	. . . .	1·10	1·25	□ □
2118	**1428**	64p multicoloured	. . . .	1·75	1·90	□ □
		Set of 4	. . . .	3·75	4·00	□ □
		First Day Cover	. . . .		5·25	□
		Presentation Pack	. . . .	4·75		□
		PHQ Cards (set of 4)	. . . . . .	1·50	6·75	□ □
		Set of 4 Gutter Pairs	. . . . . .	7·50		□

1429 'World of the Stage' (Allen Jones)

1430 'World of Music' (Bridget Riley)

1431 'World of Literature' (Lisa Milroy)

1432 'New Worlds' (Sir Howard Hodgkin)

Millennium Series. The Artists' Tale

1999 (7 Dec.) *One centre phosphor band* (19p) *or two phosphor bands* (others). *Perf* 14 × 14½

2119	**1429**	19p multicoloured	. . . .	50	50	□ □
2120	**1430**	26p multicoloured	. . . .	70	80	□ □
2121	**1431**	44p multicoloured	. . . .	1·10	1·25	□ □
2122	**1432**	64p multicoloured	. . . .	1·75	1·90	□ □
		Set of 4	. . . .	3·75	4·00	□ □
		First Day Cover	. . . .		5·25	□
		Presentation Pack	. . . .	4·75		□
		PHQ Cards (set of 4)	. . . . . .	1·50	6·75	□ □
		Set of 4 Gutter Pairs	. . . . . .	7·50		□

Collectors Pack 1999

1999 (7 Dec.) *Comprises Nos.* 2069/76, 2080/105 *and* 2107/22

	Collectors Pack	. . . .	40·00	□

Post Office Yearbook

1999 (7 Dec.) *Comprises Nos.* 2069/76, 2080/105 *and* 2107/22 *in hardback book with slip case*

	Yearbook	. . . .	45·00	□

1433a

135

Millennium Series. 'Millennium Timekeeper'

1999 (14 DEC.) *Sheet* 120 × 89 *mm. Multicoloured. Two phosphor bands. Perf* 14 × 14½

MS2123 **1433**a 64p Clock face and map
of North America; 64p Clock face
and map of Asia; 64p Clock face
and map of Middle East; 64p Clock
face and map of Europe . . . . . 6·00 6·00 ☐ ☐
First Day Cover . . . . 8·00 ☐
Presentation Pack . . . . 6·00 ☐
PHQ Cards (set of 5) . . . . . . 1·90 12·00 ☐ ☐

No. MS2123 also exists overprinted 'EARLS COURT, LONDON 22–28 MAY 2000 THE STAMP SHOW 2000' from Exhibition Premium Passes, costing £10, available from 1 March 2000.

1437 Queen Elizabeth II

New Millennium

2000 (6 JAN.) *Photo De La Rue, Questa or Walsall* (*No.* 2124); *Questa or Walsall* (*No.* 2124c). *Two phosphor bands. Perf* 15 × 14 (*with one elliptical hole on each vertical side*)

2124 **1437** (1st) olive-brown . . . . 40 45 ☐ ☐
        c. Perf 14 . . . . 40 45 ☐ ☐
First Day Cover . . . . 2·00 ☐
Presentation Pack . . . . 90 ☐
PHQ Card (23 May) . . . . 40 ☐

No. 2124 comes from sheets or stamp booklets and No. 2124c from booklets only.

1438 Barn Owl (World Owl Trust, Muncaster)

1439 Night Sky (National Space Science Centre, Leicester)

1440 River Goyt and Textile Mills (Torrs Walkway, New Mills)

1441 Cape Gannets (Seabird Centre, North Berwick)

Millennium Projects (1st series). 'Above and Beyond'

2000 (18 JAN.–26 MAY) *One centre phosphor band* (19p) *or two phosphor bands* (*others*). *Perf* 14 × 14½ (1st, 44p) *or* 13½ × 14 (*others*)

2125	**1438**	19p multicoloured . .	50	50	☐	☐
2126	**1439**	26p multicoloured . .	70	80	☐	☐
2126a		(1st) multicoloured				
		(26 May)	5·00	5·00	☐	☐
2127	**1440**	44p multicoloured . .	1·10	1·25	☐	☐
2128	**1441**	64p multicoloured . .	1·75	1·90	☐	☐
		Set of 4 (ex No. 2126a)	3·75	4·00	☐	☐
		First Day Cover		5·25		☐
		Presentation Pack	4·25		☐	
		PHQ Cards (set of 4)	1·50	6·25	☐	☐
		Set of 4 Gutter Pairs	7·50		☐	

No. 2126a was only issued in stamp booklets.

1442 Millennium Beacon (Beacons across the Land)

1443 Garratt Steam Locomotive No. 143 pulling Train (Rheilffordd Eryri, Welsh Highland Railway)

1444 Lightning (Dynamic Earth Centre, Edinburgh)

1445 Multicoloured Lights (Lighting Croydon's Skyline)

Millennium Projects (2nd series). 'Fire and Light'

2000 (1 FEB.) *One centre phosphor band* (19p) *or two phosphor bands* (*others*). *Perf* 14 × 14½

2129	**1442**	19p multicoloured	50	50	☐	☐
2130	**1443**	26p multicoloured	70	80	☐	☐
2131	**1444**	44p multicoloured	1·10	1·25	☐	☐
2132	**1445**	64p multicoloured	1·75	1·90	☐	☐
		Set of 4	3·75	4·00	☐	☐
		First Day Cover		5·25		☐
		Presentation Pack	4·25		☐	
		PHQ Cards (set of 4)	1·50	6·00	☐	☐
		Set of 4 Gutter Pairs	7·50		☐	

The Lighthouse
Great Britain Hingeless Album

Available in three beautiful volumes

From the birth of the Penny Black to the Millennium stamps of the year 2000, these works of art contain all the standard issues including commemoratives, definitives, regionals and postage dues, as released by the Philatelic Bureau. Each volume comes in a titled leatherette padded binder. Commemorative and definitive issues are all housed on separate pages with special attention given to the machin definitive period. For those of you who like to collect in even more detail we have additional specialised page sets to cover this.

Want to know more?

Then just turn the page.

1446   Queen Victoria and Queen Elizabeth II

2000 (15 FEB.) *Design T* **929**, *but redrawn with '1st' face value as*
T **1446**. *Two phosphor bands. Perf* 14 (*with one elliptical hole*
on each vertical side)

2133   **1446**   (1st) brownish black
              and cream   . . . . .   1·10   1·25 □ □
No. 2133 was only issued in stamp booklets.

1451   Reed Beds, River Braid   1452   South American
       (ECOS, Ballymena)   Leaf-cutter Ants
                                           ('Web of Life' Exhibition,
                                           London Zoo)

1447   Beach Pebbles   1448   Frog's Legs and Water
       (Turning the Tide,   Lilies (National Pondlife
       Durham Coast)   Centre, Merseyside)

1453   Solar Sensors (Earth   1454   Hydroponic Leaves
       Centre, Doncaster)   (Project SUZY, Teesside)

Millennium Projects (4th series). 'Life and Earth'

2000 (4 APR.) *One centre phosphor band* (2nd) *or two phosphor*
bands (*others*). *Perf* 14 × 14½

2138	**1451**	(2nd) multicoloured . . .	50	50	□	□
2139	**1452**	(1st) multicoloured . . .	70	80	□	□
2140	**1453**	44p multicoloured . . .	1·10	1·25	□	□
2141	**1454**	64p multicoloured . . .	1·75	1·90	□	□
	Set of 4		3·75	4·00	□	□
	First Day Cover			5·25		□
	Presentation Pack		4·25		□	
	PHQ Cards (*set of* 4)		1·50	6·00	□	□
	Set of 4 *Gutter Pairs*		7·50		□	

1449   Cliff Boardwalk   1450   Reflections in Water
       (Parc Arfordirol,   (Portsmouth Harbour
       Llanelli Coast)   Development)

Millennium Projects (3rd series). 'Water and Coast'

2000 (7 MAR.) *One centre phosphor band* (19p) *or two phosphor*
bands (*others*). *Perf* 14 × 14½

2134	**1447**	19p multicoloured	50	50	□	□
2135	**1448**	26p multicoloured	70	80	□	□
2136	**1449**	44p black, grey and silver	1·10	1·25	□	□
2137	**1450**	64p multicoloured	1·75	1·90	□	□
	Set of 4	. . . .	3·75	4·00	□	□
	First Day Cover			5·25		□
	Presentation Pack		4·25		□	
	PHQ Cards (*set of* 4)		1·50	6·00	□	□
	Set of 4 *Gutter Pairs*		7·50		□	

1455   Pottery Glaze   1456   Bankside Galleries
       (Ceramica Museum,   (Tate Modern, London)
       Stoke-on-Trent)

1457　Road Marking (Cycle Network Artworks)

1458　People of Salford (Lowry Centre, Salford)

Millennium Projects (5th series). 'Art and Craft'

2000 (2 MAY) *One centre phosphor band* (2nd) *or two phosphor bands* (others). *Perf* 14 × 14½

2142	**1455**	(2nd) multicoloured . . .	50	50	□	□
2143	**1456**	(1st) multicoloured . . .	70	80	□	□
2144	**1457**	45p multicoloured . . .	1·10	1·25	□	□
2145	**1458**	65p multicoloured . . .	1·75	1·90	□	□
		Set of 4	3·75	4·00	□	□
		First Day Cover		5·25	□	
		Presentation Pack	4·25		□	
		PHQ Cards (set of 4)	1·50	6·00	□	□
		Set of 4 Gutter Pairs	7·50		□	

'Stamp Show 2000' International Stamp Exhibition, London. Jeffrey Matthews Colour Palette

2000 (22 MAY) *Sheet,* 124 × 70 *mm, containing stamps as T* **367** *with two labels. Phosphorised paper. Perf* 15 × 14 (*with one elliptical hole on each vertical side*)

MS2146	4p new blue; 5p dull red-brown;			
	6p yellow-olive; 10p dull orange;			
	31p dp mauve; 39p brt magenta;			
	64p turq-green; £1 bluish violet	8·00	8·50	□ □
	First Day Cover		8·50	□
	Exhibition Card (wallet, sold at £4.99, containing one mint sheet and one cancelled on postcard)	15·00		□

The £1 value is printed in Iriodin ink which gives a shiny effect to the solid part of the background behind the Queen's head.

1459

'Stamp Show 2000' International Stamp Exhibition, London. 'Her Majesty's Stamps'

2000 (23 MAY) *Sheet* 121 × 89 *mm. Phosphorised paper. Perf* 15 × 14 (*with one elliptical hole on each vertical side of stamps as T* **1437**)

MS2147	**1459**	(1st) olive-brown (Type **1437**) × 4; £1 slate-green (as Type 163)	7·50	8·00	□ □
		First Day Cover		8·50	□
		Presentation Pack	8·00		□
		PHQ Cards (set of 2)	80		□

The £1 value is an adaptation of the 1953 Coronation 1s. 3d. stamp. It is shown on one of the PHQ cards with the other depicting the complete miniature sheet.

1460　Children playing (Millennium Greens Project)

1461　Millennium Bridge, Gateshead

1462　Daisies (Mile End Park, London)

1463　African Hut and Thatched Cottage ('On the Meridian Line' Project)

Millennium Projects (6th series). 'People and Places'

2000 (6 JUNE) *One centre phosphor band* (2nd) *or two phosphor bands* (others). *Perf* 14 × 14½

2148	**1460**	(2nd) multicoloured . . .	50	50	□	□
2149	**1461**	(1st) multicoloured . . .	70	80	□	□
2150	**1462**	45p multicoloured . . .	1·10	1·25	□	□
2151	**1463**	65p multicoloured . . .	1·75	1·90	□	□
		Set of 4	3·75	4·00	□	□
		First Day Cover		5·25	□	
		Presentation Pack	4·25		□	
		PHQ Cards (set of 4)	1·50	6·00	□	□
		Set of 4 Gutter Pairs	7·50		□	

1464 Raising the Stone (Strangford Stone, Killyleagh)

1465 Horse's Hooves (Trans Pennine Trail, Derbyshire)

1466 Cyclist (Kingdom of Fife Cycle Ways, Scotland)

1467 Bluebell Wood (Groundwork's 'Changing Places' Project)

Millennium Projects (7th series). 'Stone and Soil'

2000 (4 JULY) *One centre phosphor band* (2nd) *or two phosphor bands* (others). *Perf* 14 × 14½

2152	**1464**	(2nd) brownish black, grey-black and silver	50	50	☐	☐
2153	**1465**	(1st) multicoloured . . .	70	80	☐	☐
2154	**1466**	45p multicoloured . . .	1·10	1·25	☐	☐
2155	**1467**	65p multicoloured . . .	1·75	1·90	☐	☐
	Set of 4	. . . .	3·75	4·00	☐	☐
	First Day Cover	. . . .		5·25		☐
	Presentation Pack	. . . .	4·25		☐	
	PHQ Cards (set of 4)	. . . . . .	1·50	6·00	☐	☐
	Set of 4 Gutter Pairs	. . . . . .	7·50		☐	

1468 Tree Roots ('Yews for the Millennium' Project)

1469 Sunflower ('Eden' Project, St. Austell)

1470 Sycamore Seeds (Millennium Seed Bank, Wakehurst Place, Surrey)

1471 Forest, Doire Dach ('Forest for Scotland')

Millennium Projects (8th series). 'Tree and Leaf'

2000 (1 AUG.) *One centre phosphor band* (2nd) *or two phosphor bands* (others). *Perf* 14 × 14½

2156	**1468**	(2nd) multicoloured . . .	50	50	☐	☐
2157	**1469**	(1st) multicoloured . . .	70	80	☐	☐
2158	**1470**	45p multicoloured . . .	1·10	1·25	☐	☐
2159	**1471**	65p multicoloured . . .	1·75	1·90	☐	☐
	Set of 4	. . . .	3·75	4·00	☐	☐
	First Day Cover	. . . .		5·25		☐
	Presentation Pack	. . . .	4·25		☐	
	PHQ Cards (set of 4)	. . . . . .	1·50	6·00	☐	☐
	Set of 4 Gutter Pairs	. . . . . .	7·50		☐	

1472 Queen Elizabeth the Queen Mother

1472*a* Royal Family on Queen Mother's 99th Birthday (from photo by J. Swannell)

Queen Elizabeth the Queen Mother's 100th Birthday

2000 (4 Aug.) *Phosphorised paper plus two phosphor bands. Perf 14½*

2160	**1472**	27p multicoloured . . .	1·00	1·00	☐	☐
MS2161	121 × 89 mm.	**1472**a 27p				
		Queen Elizabeth II; 27p Prince				
		William; 27p Queen Elizabeth the				
		Queen Mother; 27p Prince Charles	2·50	3·00	☐	☐
		First Day Cover (**MS**2161)		4·25		☐
		Presentation Pack (**MS**2161) . .	4·50		☐	
		PHQ Cards (set of 5)	1·90		☐	

No. 2160 was only issued in stamp booklets and in No. **MS**2161.

The complete miniature sheet is shown on one of the PHQ cards with the others depicting individual stamps.

1473 Head of *Gigantiops destructor* (Ant) (Wildscreen at Bristol)

1474 Gathering Water Lilies on Broads (Norfolk and Norwich Project)

1475 X-ray of Hand holding Computer Mouse (Millennium Point, Birmingham)

1476 Tartan Wool Holder (Scottish Cultural Resources Access Network)

Millennium Projects (9th series). 'Mind and Matter'

2000 (5 Sept.) *One centre phosphor band* (2nd) *or two phosphor bands* (others). *Perf 14 × 14½*

2162	**1473**	(2nd) multicoloured . . .	50	50	☐	☐
2163	**1474**	(1st) multicoloured . . .	70	80	☐	☐
2164	**1475**	45p multicoloured . . .	1·10	1·25	☐	☐
2165	**1476**	65p multicoloured . . .	1·75	1·90	☐	☐
		Set of 4	3·75	4·00	☐	☐
		First Day Cover		5·25		☐
		Presentation Pack	4·25		☐	
		PHQ Cards (set of 4)	1·50	6·00	☐	☐
		Set of 4 Gutter Pairs	7·50		☐	

1477 Acrobatic Performers (Millennium Dome)

1478 Football Players (Hampden Park, Glasgow)

1479 Bather (Bath Spa Project)

1480 Hen's Egg under Magnification (Centre for Life, Newcastle)

Millennium Projects (10th series). 'Body and Bone'

2000 (3 Oct.) *One centre phosphor band* (2nd) *or two phosphor bands* (others). *Perf 14 × 14½* (2nd) *or 13½ × 14* (others)

2166	**1477**	(2nd) black, slate-blue and silver	50	50	☐	☐
2167	**1478**	(1st) multicoloured . . .	70	80	☐	☐
2168	**1479**	45p multicoloured . . .	1·10	1·25	☐	☐
2169	**1480**	65p multicoloured . . .	1·75	1·90	☐	☐
		Set of 4	3·75	4·00	☐	☐
		First Day Cover		5·25		☐
		Presentation Pack	4·25		☐	
		PHQ Cards (set of 4)	1·50	6·00	☐	☐
		Set of 4 Gutter Pairs	7·50		☐	

1481 Virgin and Child Stained Glass Window, St. Edmundsbury Cathedral (Suffolk Cathedral Millennium Project)

1482 Floodlit Church of St. Peter and St. Paul, Overstowey (Church Floodlighting Trust)

1483 12th-cent. Latin Gradual (St. Patrick Centre, Downpatrick)

1484 Chapter House Ceiling, York Minster (York Millennium Mystery Plays)

Millennium Projects (11th series). 'Spirit and Faith'

2000 (7 Nov.) *One centre phosphor band* (2nd) *or two phosphor bands* (others). *Perf* 14 × 14½

2170	**1481**	(2nd) multicoloured . . .	50	50	☐	☐
2171	**1482**	(1st) multicoloured . . .	70	80	☐	☐
2172	**1483**	45p multicoloured . . .	1·10	1·25	☐	☐
2173	**1484**	65p multicoloured . . .	1·75	1·90	☐	☐
	Set of 4	. . . .	3·75	4·00	☐	☐
	First Day Cover	. . . .		5·25		☐
	Presentation Pack	. . . .	4·25		☐	
	PHQ *Cards* (set of 4)	. . . . .	1·50	6·00	☐	☐
	Set of 4 Gutter Pairs	. . . . . .	7·50		☐	

Post Office Yearbook

2000 (7 Nov.) *Comprises Nos.* **MS**2123/6, 2127/32, 2134/45, 2148/59 *and* **MS**2161/81 *in hardback book with slip case*

Yearbook	. . . .	40·00	☐

The last two issues in the Millennium Projects Series were supplied for insertion into the above at a later date.

1485 Church Bells (Ringing in the Millennium)

1486 Eye (Year of the Artist)

1487 Top of Harp (Canolfan Mileniwm, Cardiff)

1488 Figure within Latticework (TS2K Creative Enterprise Centres, London)

Millennium Projects (12th series). 'Sound and Vision'

2000 (5 Dec.) *One centre phosphor band* (2nd) *or two phosphor bands* (others). *Perf* 14 × 14½

2174	**1485**	(2nd) multicoloured . . .	30	35	☐	☐
2175	**1486**	(1st) multicoloured . . .	45	50	☐	☐
2176	**1487**	45p multicoloured . . .	70	75	☐	☐
2177	**1488**	65p multicoloured . . .	1·00	1·10	☐	☐
	Set of 4	. . . .	2·40	2·50	☐	☐
	First Day Cover	. . . .		3·25		☐
	Presentation Pack	. . . .	2·75		☐	
	PHQ *Cards* (set of 4)	. . . . .	1·50	4·00	☐	☐
	Set of 4 Gutter Pairs	. . . . .	5·00		☐	

Collectors Pack 2000

2000 (5 Dec.) *Comprises Nos.* **MS**2123/6, 2127/32, 2134/45, 2148/59 *and* **MS**2161/81

Collectors Pack	. . . .	30·00	☐

1489 'Flower' ('Nurture Children')

1490 'Tiger' ('Listen to Children')

1491 'Owl' ('Teach Children')

1492 'Butterfly' ('Ensure Children's Freedom')

New Millennium. Rights of the Child. Face Paintings

2001 (16 Jan.) *One centre phosphor band* (2nd) *or two phosphor bands* (others). *Perf* 14 × 14½

2178	**1489**	(2nd) multicoloured . . .	30	35	☐	☐
2179	**1490**	(1st) multicoloured . . .	45	50	☐	☐
2180	**1491**	45p multicoloured . . .	70	75	☐	☐
2181	**1492**	65p multicoloured . . .	1·00	1·10	☐	☐
	Set of 4	. . . .	2·40	2·50	☐	☐
	First Day Cover	. . . .		3·25		☐
	Presentation Pack	. . . .	2·75		☐	
	PHQ *Cards* (set of 4)	. . . . .	1·50	4·00	☐	☐
	Set of 4 Gutter Pairs	. . . . .	5·00		☐	

1493 'Love'

1494 'THANKS'

1495 'abc' (New Baby)

1496 'WELCOME'

1497 'Cheers'

'Occasions' Greetings Stamps

2001 (6 FEB.) *Two phosphor bands. Perf* $14\frac{1}{2} \times 14$

2182	**1493**	(1st) multicoloured	45	50	☐	☐
2183	**1494**	(1st) multicoloured	45	50	☐	☐
2184	**1495**	(1st) multicoloured	45	50	☐	☐
2185	**1496**	(1st) multicoloured	45	50	☐	☐
2186	**1497**	(1st) multicoloured	45	50	☐	☐
		Set of 5	2·25	2·50	☐	☐
		First Day Cover		3·00		☐
		Presentation Pack (13 Feb.) . . .	2·50		☐	
		PHQ Cards (set of 5)	1·90	3·75	☐	☐
		Set of 5 *Gutter Pairs*	4·75		☐	

The silver-grey backgrounds are printed in Iriodin ink which gives a shiny effect.

Nos. 2182/6 were printed in photogravure. They were subsequently re-issued, as sheets of 20, including a *se-tenant* format, printed in lithography with each stamp accompanied by a half stamp-size label showing either postal symbols or a personal photograph.

1498 Dog and Owner on Bench

1499 Dog in Bath

1500 Boxer at Dog Show

1501 Cat in Handbag

1502 Cat on Gate

1503 Dog in Car

1504 Cat at Window

1505 Dog behind Fence

1506 Cat watching Bird

1507 Cat in Washbasin

T **1498/1507** were printed together in sheetlets of 10 (5 × 2), with the surplus self-adhesive paper around each stamp retained.

Cats and Dogs

2001 (13 FEB.) *Self-adhesive. Two phosphor bands. Die-cut perf* 15 × 14

2187	**1498**	(1st) black, grey and silver	45	50	☐	☐
		a. Sheetlet. Nos. 2187/96	4·50		☐	
2188	**1499**	(1st) black, grey and silver	45	50	☐	☐
2189	**1500**	(1st) black, grey and silver	45	50	☐	☐
2190	**1501**	(1st) black, grey and silver	45	50	☐	☐
2191	**1502**	(1st) black, grey and silver	45	50	☐	☐
2192	**1503**	(1st) black, grey and silver	45	50	☐	☐
2193	**1504**	(1st) black, grey and silver	45	50	☐	☐
2194	**1505**	(1st) black, grey and silver	45	50	☐	☐
2195	**1506**	(1st) black, grey and silver	45	50	☐	☐
2196	**1507**	(1st) black, grey and silver	45	50	☐	☐
		Set of 10	4·50	5·00	☐	☐
		First Day Cover		5·50		☐
		Presentation Pack	4·50		☐	
		PHQ Cards (set of 10)	2·50	6·25	☐	☐

1508 'RAIN'

1509 'FAIR'

1510 'STORMY'

1511 'VERY DRY'

Nos. 2197/200 show the four quadrants of a barometer dial which are combined on the miniature sheet.

The Weather

2001 (13 MAR.) *One side phosphor band (19p) or two phosphor bands (others). Perf* 14½

2197	**1508**	19p multicoloured	30	35	☐	☐
2198	**1509**	27p multicoloured	45	50	☐	☐
2199	**1510**	45p multicoloured	70	75	☐	☐
2200	**1511**	65p multicoloured	1·00	1·10	☐	☐
		Set of 4	2·40	2·50	☐	☐
		First Day Cover		3·25		☐
		Presentation Pack	2·75		☐	
		PHQ Cards (set of 4)	1·50	4·00	☐	☐
		Set of 4 Gutter Pairs	5·00		☐	
MS2201		105 × 105 mm. Nos. 2197/200	2·40	2·50	☐	☐
		First Day Cover		3·25		☐

The reddish violet on both the 27p and the miniature sheet is printed in thermochromic ink which changes from reddish violet to light blue when exposed to heat.

1512 *Vanguard* Class Submarine, 1992

1513 *Swiftsure* Class Submarine, 1973

1514 *Unity* Class Submarine, 1939

1515 'Holland' Type Submarine, 1901

1516 White Ensign

1517 Union Jack

1518 Jolly Roger flown by H.M.S. *Proteus* (submarine)

1519 Flag of Chief of Defence Staff

Centenary of Royal Navy Submarine Service

2001 (10 APR.–22 OCT.) *One centre phosphor band (2nd) or two phosphor bands (others).* (a) *Submarines. PVA gum. Perf* 15 × 14

2202	**1512**	(2nd) multicoloured	30	35	☐	☐
		a. Perf 15½ × 15 (22 Oct.)	60	65	☐	☐
2203	**1513**	(1st) multicoloured	45	50	☐	☐
		a. Perf 15½ × 15 (22 Oct.)	90	95	☐	☐
2204	**1514**	45p multicoloured	70	75	☐	☐
		a. Perf 15½ × 15 (22 Oct.)	1·50	1·60	☐	☐
2205	**1515**	65p multicoloured	1·00	1·10	☐	☐
		a. Perf 15½ × 15 (22 Oct.)	2·10	2·25	☐	☐
		Set of 4	2·40	2·50	☐	☐
		First Day Cover		3·25		☐
		Presentation Pack	2·75		☐	
		PHQ Cards (set of 4)	1·90	4·00	☐	☐
		Set of 4 Gutter Pairs	5·00		☐	

(b) *Flags. Sheet* 92 × 97 mm. PVA gum. Perf 14½

MS2206	**1516**	(1st) multicoloured;			
	1517	(1st) multicoloured; **1518**			
	(1st) multicoloured; **1519** (1st)				
	multicoloured (22 Oct.)	1·75	2·00	☐	☐
	First Day Cover		2·50		☐
	Presentation Pack	2·25		☐	
	PHQ Cards (set of 5)	1·90	3·25	☐	☐

(c) Self-adhesive. Die-cut perf $15\frac{1}{2} \times 14$ (No. 2207)
or $14\frac{1}{2}$ (others)

2207	**1513**	(1st) multicoloured (17 Apr.) 1·25		1·25	☐	☐
2208	**1516**	(1st) multicoloured (22 Oct.) 1·25		1·25	☐	☐
2209	**1518**	(1st) multicoloured (22 Oct.) 1·25		1·25	☐	☐

Nos. 2202a/5a only come from stamp booklets.

The five PHQ cards depict the four designs and the complete miniature sheet.

Nos. 2207/9 only come from two different £1.62 booklets.

1520 Leyland X2 Open-top, London General B Type, Leyland Titan TD1 and AEC Regent 1

1521 AEC Regent 1, Daimler COG5, Utility Guy Arab Mk II and AEC Regent III RT Type

1522 AEC Regent III RT Type, Bristol KSW5G Open-top, AEC Routemaster and Bristol Lodekka FSF6G

1523 Bristol Lodekka FSF6G, Leyland Titan PD3/4, Leyland Atlantean PDR1/1 and Daimler Fleetline CRG6LX-33

1524 Daimler Fleetline CRG6LX-33, MCW Metrobus DR102/43, Leyland Olympian ONLXB/1R and Dennis Trident

T **1520/4** were printed together, se-tenant, in horizontal strips of 5 throughout the sheet. The illustrations of the first bus on No. 2210 and the last bus on No. 2214 continue onto the sheet margins.

150th Anniversary of First Double-decker Bus

2001 (15 MAY) 'All-over' phosphor. Perf $14\frac{1}{2} \times 14$

2210	**1520**	(1st) multicoloured	. . .	45		50	☐ ☐
		a. Horiz strip of 5. Nos.					
		2210/14	. . . . . .	2·25		2·50	☐ ☐
2211	**1521**	(1st) multicoloured	. . .	45		50	☐ ☐
2212	**1522**	(1st) multicoloured	. . .	45		50	☐ ☐
2213	**1523**	(1st) multicoloured	. . .	45		50	☐ ☐
2214	**1524**	(1st) multicoloured	. . .	45		50	☐ ☐
	Set of 5	. . . .				2·50	☐ ☐
	First Day Cover	. . . .		2·25			
						3·00	☐
	Presentation Pack	. . . .		2·50			☐
	PHQ Cards (set of 5)	. . . . . .		2·25		3·75	☐ ☐
	Gutter Strip of 10	. . . .		5·00			☐
MS2215	120 × 105 mm. Nos. 2210/14			2·25		2·50	☐ ☐
	First Day Cover	. . . .				3·00	☐

In No. **MS**2215 the illustrations of the AEC Regent III RT Type and the Daimler Fleetline CRG6LX-33 appear twice.

1525 Toque Hat by Pip Hackett

1526 Butterfly Hat by Dai Rees

1527 Top Hat by Stephen Jones

1528 Spiral Hat by Philip Treacy

Fashion Hats

2001 (19 JUNE) 'All-over' phosphor. Perf $14\frac{1}{2}$

2216	**1525**	(1st) multicoloured	. . .	45		50	☐ ☐
2217	**1526**	(E) multicoloured	. . .	55		60	☐ ☐
2218	**1527**	45p multicoloured	. . .	70		75	☐ ☐
2219	**1528**	65p multicoloured	. . .	1·00		1·10	☐ ☐
	Set of 4	. . . .		2·50		2·75	☐ ☐
	First Day Cover	. . . .				3·75	☐
	Presentation Pack	. . . .		3·00			☐
	PHQ Cards (set of 4)	. . . . . .		1·50		4·50	☐ ☐
	Set of 4 Gutter Pairs	. . . . . .		5·25			☐

1529 Common Frog

1530 Great Diving Beetle

1531 Three-spined Stickleback

1532 Southern Hawker Dragonfly

1535 Mr. Punch

1536 Judy

1537 Beadle

1538 Crocodile

Europa. Pond Life

2001 (10 July) *Two phosphor bands*

2220	**1529**	(1st) multicoloured . . .	45	50	☐	☐
2221	**1530**	(E) multicoloured . . .	60	65	☐	☐
2222	**1531**	45p multicoloured . . .	70	75	☐	☐
2223	**1532**	65p multicoloured . . .	1·00	1·10	☐	☐
	Set of 4		2·75	3·00	☐	☐
	First Day Cover			3·75		☐
	Presentation Pack		3·00			☐
	PHQ Cards (*set of* 4)		1·50	4·50	☐	☐
	Set of 4 *Gutter Pairs*		5·75			☐

The 1st and E values incorporate the 'EUROPA' emblem.

The bluish silver on all four values is in Iriodin ink and was used as a background for those parts of the design below the water line.

1533 Policeman

1534 Clown

Nos. 2224/9 were printed together, *se-tenant*, in horizontal strips of 6 throughout the sheet.

Punch and Judy Show Puppets

2001 (4 Sept.) *Two phosphor bands.* (*a*) *PVA gum. Perf* 14 × 15

2224	**1533**	(1st) multicoloured . . .	45	50	☐	☐
		a. Horiz strip of 6.				
		Nos. 2224/9	2·50	3·00	☐	☐
2225	**1534**	(1st) multicoloured . . .	45	50	☐	☐
2226	**1535**	(1st) multicoloured . . .	45	50	☐	☐
2227	**1536**	(1st) multicoloured . . .	45	50	☐	☐
2228	**1537**	(1st) multicoloured . . .	45	50	☐	☐
2229	**1538**	(1st) multicoloured . . .	45	50	☐	☐
	Set of 6		2·50	3·00	☐	☐
	First Day Cover			3·50		☐
	Presentation Pack		3·00			☐
	PHQ Cards (*set of* 6)		2·25	4·25	☐	☐
	Gutter Block of 12		5·25			☐

(*b*) *Self-adhesive. Die-cut perf* 14 × 15½

2230	**1535**	(1st) multicoloured . . .	1·25	1·25	☐	☐
2231	**1536**	(1st) multicoloured . . .	1·25	1·25	☐	☐

Nos. 2230/1 were only issued in £1.62 stamp booklets.

For full information on all future British issues, collectors should write to Royal Mail, Freepost EH3647, 21 South Gyle Crescent, Edinburgh EH12 9PE.

1539 Carbon 60 Molecule (Chemistry)

1540 Globe (Economic Sciences)

1541 Embossed Dove (Peace)

1542 Crosses (Physiology or Medicine)

1543 Poem 'The Addressing of Cats' by T. S. Eliot in Open Book (Literature)

1544 Hologram of Boron Molecule (Physics)

Centenary of Nobel Prizes

2001 (2 OCT.) *One side phosphor band* (2nd) *or phosphor frame (others). Perf* $14\frac{1}{2}$

2232	**1539**	(2nd) black, silver and grey-black	30	35	☐	☐
2233	**1540**	(1st) multicoloured . . .	45	50	☐	☐
2234	**1541**	(E) black, silver and bright green	60	65	☐	☐
2235	**1542**	40p multicoloured . . .	60	65	☐	☐
2236	**1543**	45p multicoloured . . .	70	75	☐	☐
2237	**1544**	65p black and silver . .	1·00	1·10	☐	☐
	Set of 6	. . . .	3·50	4·00	☐	☐
	First Day Cover	. . . .		4·75		☐
	Presentation Pack	. . . .	4·00		☐	
	PHQ Cards (set of 6)	. . . . . .	2·25	4·75	☐	☐
	Set of 6 Gutter Pairs	. . . . . .	7·25		☐	

The grey-black on No. 2232 is printed in thermochromic ink which temporarily changes to pale grey when exposed to heat. The centre of No. 2235 is coated with a eucalyptus scent.

1545 Robins with Snowman

1546 Robins on Bird Table

1547 Robins skating on Bird Bath

1548 Robins with Christmas Pudding

1549 Robins in Paper Chain Nest

Christmas. Robins

2001 (6 NOV.) *Self-adhesive. One centre phosphor band* (2nd) *or two phosphor bands (others). Die-cut perf* $14\frac{1}{2}$

2238	**1545**	(2nd) multicoloured . . .	30	35	☐	☐
2239	**1546**	(1st) multicoloured . . .	45	50	☐	☐
2240	**1547**	(E) multicoloured . . .	60	65	☐	☐
2241	**1548**	45p multicoloured . . .	70	75	☐	☐
2242	**1549**	65p multicoloured . . .	1·00	1·10	☐	☐
	Set of 5	. . . .	3·00	3·25	☐	☐
	First Day Cover	. . . .		3·75		☐
	Presentation Pack	. . . .	3·50		☐	
	PHQ Cards (set of 5)	. . . . . .	1·90	4·00	☐	☐

Collectors Pack 2001

2001 (6 NOV.) *Comprises Nos.* 2178/2200, 2202/**MS**2206, 2210/14, 2216/29 *and* 2232/42

	Collectors Pack	. . . . 30·00	☐

Post Office Yearbook

2001 (6 NOV.) *Comprises Nos.* 2178/96, **MS**2201/6, **MS**2215/29 *and* 2232/42 *in hardback book with slip case*

	Yearbook	. . . . 42·00	☐

REGIONAL ISSUES

PERFORATION AND WATERMARK. All the following Regional stamps are perforated 15 × 14, unless otherwise stated.

For listing of First Day Covers see pages 157/9.

1 England

EN **1**   Three Lions

EN **2**   Crowned Lion with Shield of St. George

EN **3**   Oak Tree

EN **4**   Tudor Rose

2001 (23 APR.) *One centre phosphor band* (2nd) *or two phosphor bands* (others). *Perf* 15 × 14 (*with one elliptical hole on each vertical side*)

EN1	EN **1**	(2nd) slate-green and silver	30	35	☐	☐
EN2	EN **2**	(1st) lake-brown and silver	45	50	☐	☐
EN3	EN **3**	(E) olive-green and silver	55	60	☐	☐
EN4	EN **4**	65p deep reddish lilac and silver	1·00	1·10	☐	☐
		Presentation Pack (*P.O. Pack No.* 54)	2·75		☐	
		PHQ Cards (*set of* 4)	1·50	4·00	☐	☐

Nos. EN1/3 were initially sold at 19p, 27p and 36p, the latter representing the basic European airmail rate.

2 Northern Ireland

N **1**   N **2**   N **3**   N **4**

1958–67 *Wmk* **179**

NI1	N **1**	3d lilac	20	10	☐	☐
		p. One centre phosphor band	20	15	☐	☐
NI2		4d blue	20	15	☐	☐
		p. Two phosphor bands	20	15	☐	☐
NI3	N **2**	6d purple	25	25	☐	☐
NI4		9d bronze-green (2 phosphor bands)	40	80	☐	☐
NI5	N **3**	1s 3d green	40	80	☐	☐
NI6		1s 6d blue (2 phosphor bands)	40	80	☐	☐

1968–69 *One centre phosphor band* (*Nos.* NI8/9) *or two phosphor bands* (others). *No wmk*

NI7	N **1**	4d blue	20	15	☐	☐
NI8		4d sepia	20	15	☐	☐
NI9		4d vermilion	20	20	☐	☐
NI10		5d blue	20	20	☐	☐
NI11	N **3**	1s 6d blue	2·50	3·25	☐	☐
		Presentation Pack (*comprises Nos.* NI1*p*, NI4/6, NI8/10)	3·25		☐	

Decimal Currency

1971–91 *Type* N **4**. *No wmk*

  (a) *Printed in photogravure with phosphor bands*

NI12	2½p magenta (1 centre band)	80	30	☐	☐
NI13	3p ultramarine (2 bands)	25	15	☐	☐
NI14	3p ultramarine (1 centre band)	25	15	☐	☐
NI15	3½p olive-grey (2 bands)	20	20	☐	☐
NI16	3½p olive-grey (1 centre band)	20	25	☐	☐
NI17	4½p grey-blue (2 bands)	30	30	☐	☐
NI18	5p violet (2 bands)	1·50	1·50	☐	☐
NI19	5½p violet (2 bands)	20	20	☐	☐
NI20	5½p violet (1 centre band)	20	20	☐	☐
NI21	6½p blue (1 centre band)	20	20	☐	☐
NI22	7p brown (1 centre band)	35	25	☐	☐
NI23	7½p chestnut (2 bands)	2·25	2·25	☐	☐
NI24	8p rosine (2 bands)	40	40	☐	☐
NI25	8½p yellow-green (2 bands)	40	40	☐	☐
NI26	9p violet (2 bands)	40	40	☐	☐
NI27	10p orange-brown (2 bands)	50	50	☐	☐
NI28	10p orange-brown (1 centre band)	50	50	☐	☐
NI29	10½p blue (2 bands)	50	50	☐	☐
NI30	11p scarlet (2 bands)	50	50	☐	☐

(b) Printed in photogravure on phosphorised paper

NI31	12p yellowish green	50	50	□	□
NI32	13½p purple-brown	60	80	□	□
NI33	15p ultramarine	70	80	□	□

(c) *Printed in lithography. Perf* 14 (11½p, 12½p, 14p (*No.* NI38), 15½p, 16p, 18p, (*No.* NI45), 19½p, 20½p, 22p (*No.* NI53), 26p (*No.* NI60), 28p (*No.* NI62)) *or* 15 × 14 (*others*)

NI34	11½p drab (1 side band)	85	85	□	□
NI35	12p bright emerald (1 side band)	85	85	□	□
NI36	12½p light emerald (1 side band)	75	75	□	□
	a. Perf 15 × 14	4·50	4·25	□	□
NI37	13p pale chestnut (1 side band)	1·00	30	□	□
NI38	14p grey-blue (phosphorised paper)	75	75	□	□
NI39	14p deep blue (1 centre band)	90	75	□	□
NI40	15p bright blue (1 centre band)	1·10	75	□	□
NI41	15½p pale violet (phosphorised paper)	80	80	□	□
NI42	16p drab (phosphorised paper)	1·00	1·00	□	□
	a. Perf 15 × 14	10·00	9·00	□	□
NI43	17p grey-blue (phosphorised paper)	1·00	1·00	□	□
NI44	17p deep blue (1 centre band)	1·40	1·00	□	□
NI45	18p deep violet (phosphorised paper)	1·00	1·00	□	□
NI46	18p olive-grey (phosphorised paper)	1·00	90	□	□
NI47	18p bright green (1 centre band)	1·25	95	□	□
	a. Perf 14	2·50	2·25	□	□
NI48	18p bright green (1 side band)	2·75	2·75	□	□
NI49	19p bright orange-red (phosphorised paper) . . .	1·25	1·00	□	□
NI50	19½p olive-grey (phosphorised paper)	2·00	2·25	□	□
NI51	20p brownish black (phosphorised paper) . . .	1·25	1·00	□	□
NI52	20½p ultramarine (phosphorised paper)	4·00	4·00	□	□
NI53	22p blue (phosphorised paper)	1·40	1·25	□	□
NI54	22p yellow-green (phosphorised paper)	1·50	1·25	□	□
NI55	22p bright orange-red (phosphorised paper) . . .	1·60	1·00	□	□
NI56	23p bright green (phosphorised paper)	1·50	1·25	□	□
NI57	24p Indian red (phosphorised paper)	1·75	1·25	□	□
NI58	24p chestnut (phosphorised paper)	1·40	1·00	□	□
NI59	24p chestnut (2 bands)	3·00	2·75	□	□
NI60	26p rosine (phosphorised paper)	1·50	1·60	□	□
	a. Perf 15 × 14	5·00	3·75	□	□
NI61	26p drab (phosphorised paper)	1·75	1·25	□	□
NI62	28p deep violet-blue (phosphorised paper) . . .	1·40	1·25	□	□
	a. Perf 15 × 14	1·50	1·25	□	□

NI63	28p deep bluish grey (phosphorised paper) . . .	1·75	1·50	□	□
NI64	31p bright purple (phosphorised paper) . . .	1·75	1·75	□	□
NI65	32p greenish blue (phosphorised paper) . . .	2·00	1·75	□	□
NI66	34p deep bluish grey (phosphorised paper) . . .	2·00	2·00	□	□
NI67	37p rosine (phosphorised paper)	2·00	2·00	□	□
NI68	39p bright mauve (phosphorised paper) . . .	2·25	2·00	□	□

Nos. NI48 and NI59 were only issued in stamp booklets.

Presentation Pack (*P.O. Pack No.* 30) (*contains* 2½p (NI12), 3p (NI13), 5p (NI18), 7½p (NI23))	4·25		□
Presentation Pack (*P.O. Pack No.* 61) (*contains* 3p (NI14), 3½p (NI15), 5½p (NI19), 8p (NI24) *later with* 4½p (NI17) *added*) .	2·75		□
Presentation Pack (*P.O. Pack No.* 84) (*contains* 6½p (NI21), 8½p (NI25), 10p (NI27), 11p (NI30))	2·00		□
Presentation Pack (*P.O. Pack No.* 129d) (*contains* 7p (NI22), 9p (NI26), 10½p (NI29), 11½p (NI34), 12p (NI31), 13½p (NI32), 14p (NI38), 15p (NI33), 18p (NI45), 22p (NI53))	9·00		□
Presentation Pack (*P.O. Pack No.* 4) (*contains* 10p (NI28), 12½p (NI36), 16p (NI42), 20½p (NI52), 26p (NI60), 28p (NI62)) . .	10·00		□
Presentation Pack (*P.O. Pack No.* 8) (*contains* 10p (NI28), 13p (NI37), 16p (NI42a), 17p (NI43), 22p (NI54), 26p (NI60), 28p (NI62), 31p (NI64))	20·00		□
Presentation Pack (*P.O. Pack No.* 12) (*contains* 12p (NI35), 13p (NI37), 17p (NI43), 18p (NI46), 22p (NI54), 26p (NI60a), 28p (NI62a), 31p (NI64))	14·00		□

Combined Presentation Packs for Northern Ireland, Scotland and Wales

Presentation Pack (*P.O. Pack No.* 17) (*contains* 14p, 19p, 23p, 32p *from Northern Ireland, Scotland and Wales* (*Nos.* NI39, NI49, NI56, NI65, S54, S62, S67, S77, W40, W50, W57, W66))	16·00	□

Presentation Pack (*P.O. Pack No.* 20) (*contains* 15p, 20p, 24p, 34p *from Northern Ireland, Scotland and Wales* (*Nos.* NI40, NI51, NI57, NI66, S56, S64, S69, S78, W41, W52, W58, W67)) . . . . 18·00 □

Presentation Pack (*P.O. Pack No.* 23) (*contains* 17p, 22p, 26p, 37p *from Northern Ireland, Scotland and Wales* (*Nos.* NI44, NI55, NI61, NI67, S58, S66, S73, S79, W45, W56, W62, W68)) . . . . 18·00 □

Presentation Pack (*P.O. Pack No.* 26) (*contains* 18p, 24p, 28p, 39p *from Northern Ireland, Scotland and Wales* (*Nos.* NI47, NI58, NI63, NI68, S60, S70, S75, S80, W48, W59, W64, W69)) . . . . 18·00 □

1993 (7 DEC.)–**2000** (*a*) *Printed in lithography by Questa. Perf* 15 × 14 (*with one elliptical hole on each vertical side*)

NI69	N **4**	19p bistre (1 centre band)	1·00	75 □	□
NI70		19p bistre (1 side band) . .	2·50	2·00 □	□
NI71		20p bright green (1 centre band)	1·50	1·25 □	□
NI72		25p red (2 bands)	1·00	1·00 □	□
NI73		26p red-brown (2 bands) .	1·50	1·25 □	□
NI74		30p deep olive-grey (2 bands)	1·75	1·50 □	□
NI75		37p bright mauve (2 bands)	2·50	2·00 □	□
NI76		41p grey-brown (2 bands)	2·00	1·75 □	□
NI77		63p light emerald (2 bands)	3·25	3·00 □	□

(*b*) *Printed in photogravure by Walsall* (19p, 20p, 26p (*No.* NI81b), 38p, 40p, 63p, 64p, 65p), *Harrison or Walsall* (26p (*No.* NI81), 37p). *Perf* 14 (*No.* NI80) *or* 15 × 14 (*others*) (*both with one elliptical hole on each vertical side*)

NI78	N **4**	19p bistre (1 centre band)	30	35 □	□
NI79		20p bright green (1 centre band)	1·00	50 □	□
NI80		20p bright green (1 side band)	1·75	1·50 □	□
NI81		26p chestnut (2 bands) . .	1·25	45 □	□
		b. Perf 14	2·50	1·00 □	□
NI82		37p bright mauve (2 bands)	1·50	1·00 □	□
NI83		38p ultramarine (2 bands)	1·50	1·00 □	□
NI84		40p deep azure (2 bands)	60	65 □	□
NI85		63p light emerald (2 bands)	2·25	2·00 □	□
NI86		64p turquoise-green (2 bands)	2·25	2·00 □	□
NI87		65p greenish blue (2 bands)	1·00	1·10 □	□

Nos. NI70, NI80 and NI81b were only issued in stamp booklets. No. NI70 exists with the phosphor band at the left or right of the stamp.

Presentation Pack (*P.O. Pack No.* 47) (*contains* 19p, 26p, 38p, 64p (*Nos.* NI78, NI81, NI83 NI86)) . . . . 2·75 □

Presentation Pack (*P.O. Pack No.* 52) (*contains* 1st, 40p, 65p) (*Nos.* NI84, NI87, NI88b) . . 2·50 □

Combined Presentation Packs for Northern Ireland, Scotland and Wales

Presentation Pack (*P.O. Pack No.* 31) (*contains* 19p, 25p, 30p, 41p *from Northern Ireland, Scotland and Wales* (*Nos.* NI69, NI72, NI74, NI76, S81, S84, S86, S88, W70, W73, W75, W77)) . . . . 18·00 □

Presentation Pack (*P.O. Pack No.* 36) (*contains* 20p, 26p, 37p, 63p *from Northern Ireland, Scotland and Wales* (*Nos.* NI71, NI73, NI75, NI77, S83, S85, S87, S89, W72, W74 W76, W78)) . . . . 22·00 □

Presentation Pack (*P.O. Pack No.* 42) (*contains* 20p (1 *centre band*), 26p, 37p, 63p *from Northern Ireland, Scotland and Wales* (*Nos.* NI79, NI81/2, NI85, S90/3, W79/82)) 12·00 □

N **5**

2000 (15 FEB.–25 APR.) *Type N **4** redrawn with '1st' face value as Type N **5**. Two phosphor bands. Perf* 14 (*with one elliptical hole on each vertical side*)

NI88	N **5**	(1st) bright orange-red . .	1·10	1·10 □	□
		b. Perf 15 × 14 (25 Apr.)	40	45 □	□

No. NI88 was only issued in stamp booklets. No. NI88b was issued in sheets on 25 April.

N **6** Basalt Columns, Giant's Causeway

N **7** Aerial View of Patchwork Fields

N **8**   Linen Pattern

N **9**   Vase Pattern
from Belleck

2001 (6 MAR.) *One centre phosphor band (2nd) or two phosphor bands (others). Perf* 15 × 14 *(with one elliptical hole on each vertical side)*

NI89	N **6**	(2nd) black, new blue, bright magenta and greenish yellow . . .	30	35	☐	☐
NI90	N **7**	(1st) black, new blue and greenish yellow . . .	45	50	☐	☐
NI91	N **8**	(E) black, new blue and pale orange	55	60	☐	☐
NI92	N **9**	65p black, bright magenta and greenish yellow	1·00	1·10	☐	☐
		Presentation Pack (*P.O. Pack No.* 53)	2·75		☐	
		PHQ Cards (*set of* 4)	1·50	4·00	☐	☐

Nos. NI89, NI90 and NI91 were initially sold at 19p, 27p and 36p, the latter representing the basic European airmail rate.

3 Scotland

S **1**   S **2**   S **3**   S **4**

1958–67 *Wmk* **179**

S1	S **1**	3d lilac	20	15	☐	☐
		p. Two phosphor bands	16·00	2·00	☐	☐
		pa. One side band . . .	20	30	☐	☐
		pb. One centre band . .	20	15	☐	☐
S2		4d blue	20	10	☐	☐
		p. Two phosphor bands	20	20	☐	☐
S3	S **2**	6d purple	20	15	☐	☐
		p. Two phosphor bands	25	30	☐	☐
S4		9d bronze-green (2 phosphor bands) . .	40	50	☐	☐
S5	S **3**	1s 3d green	40	50	☐	☐
		p. Two phosphor bands	45	50	☐	☐
S6		1s 6d blue (2 phosphor bands)	45	50	☐	☐

No. S1*pa* exists with the phosphor band at the left or right of the stamp.

1967–70 *One centre phosphor band (Nos. S7, S9/10) or two phosphor bands (others). No wmk*

S7	S **1**	3d lilac	10	15	☐	☐
S8		4d blue	10	15	☐	☐
S9		4d sepia . . . . ⁓ . . .	10	10	☐	☐
S10		4d vermilion	10	10	☐	☐
S11		5d blue	20	10	☐	☐
S12	S **2**	9d bronze-green	4·75	6·00	☐	☐
S13	S **3**	1s 6d blue	1·50	1·50	☐	☐
		Presentation Pack (*containing Nos. S3, S5p, S7, S9/13*) . . .	10·00		☐	

Decimal Currency

1971–93 *Type* S **4**. *No wmk*

(*a*) *Printed in photogravure by Harrison and Sons with phosphor bands. Perf* 15 × 14

S14	2½p magenta (1 centre band) .		30	15	☐	☐
S15	3p ultramarine (2 bands) . . .		35	15	☐	☐
S16	3p ultramarine (1 centre band)		15	15	☐	☐
S17	3½p olive-grey (2 bands)		20	20	☐	☐
S18	3½p olive-grey (1 centre band)		20	20	☐	☐
S19	4½p grey-blue (2 bands)		30	20	☐	☐
S20	5p violet (2 bands)		85	1·00	☐	☐
S21	5½p violet (2 bands)		20	20	☐	☐
S22	5½p violet (1 centre band) . . .		20	20	☐	☐
S23	6½p blue (1 centre band)		20	20	☐	☐
S24	7p brown (1 centre band) . .		30	30	☐	☐
S25	7½p chestnut (2 bands)		95	1·25	☐	☐
S26	8p rosine (2 bands)		45	40	☐	☐

S27	8½p yellow-green (2 bands) ..	40	40	□	□
S28	9p violet (2 bands)	40	40	□	□
S29	10p orange-brown (2 bands) .	45	50	□	□
S30	10p orange-brown (1 centre band)	40	50	□	□
S31	10½p blue (2 bands)	45	50	□	□
S32	11p scarlet (2 bands)	50	50	□	□

(b) *Printed in photogravure by Harrison and Sons on phosphorised paper.* Perf 15 × 14

S33	12p yellowish green	40	50	□	□
S34	13½p purple-brown	70	80	□	□
S35	15p ultramarine	70	80	□	□

(c) *Printed in lithography by John Waddington. One side phosphor band (11½p, 12p, 12½p, 13p) or phosphorised paper* (others). Perf 14

S36	11½p drab	90	70	□	□
S37	12p bright emerald	2·25	1·75	□	□
S38	12½p light emerald	70	80	□	□
S39	13p pale chestnut	85	80	□	□
S40	14p grey-blue	80	80	□	□
S41	15½p pale violet	80	80	□	□
S42	16p drab	70	80	□	□
S43	17p grey-blue	1·25	1·00	□	□
S44	18p deep violet	1·00	1·00	□	□
S45	19½p olive-grey	1·90	1·75	□	□
S46	20½p ultramarine	4·00	4·00	□	□
S47	22p blue	1·25	1·25	□	□
S48	22p yellow-green	2·75	2·50	□	□
S49	26p rosine	1·25	1·25	□	□
S50	28p deep violet-blue	1·25	1·25	□	□
S51	31p bright purple	2·25	2·00	□	□

(d) *Printed in lithography by Questa.* Perf 15 × 14

S52	12p bright emerald (1 side band)	2·00	2·00	□	□
S53	13p pale chestnut (1 side band)	80	80	□	□
S54	14p deep blue (1 centre band)	60	70	□	□
S55	14p deep blue (1 side band) ..	90	1·00	□	□
S56	15p bright blue (1 centre band)	80	80	□	□
S57	17p grey-blue (phosphorised paper)	4·50	4·00	□	□
S58	17p deep blue (1 centre band)	1·25	80	□	□
S59	18p olive-grey (phosphorised paper)	1·25	90	□	□
S60	18p bright green (1 centre band)	1·50	80	□	□
	a. Perf 14	1·75	1·25	□	□
S61	18p bright green (1 side band)	2·50	2·50	□	□
S62	19p bright orange-red (phosphorised paper) . . .	90	90	□	□
S63	19p bright orange-red (2 bands)	2·00	1·75	□	□
S64	20p brownish black (phosphorised paper) . . .	1·40	1·00	□	□
S65	22p yellow-green (phosphorised paper)	1·25	1·00	□	□
S66	22p bright orange-red (phosphorised paper) . . .	1·40	1·00	□	□

S67	23p bright green (phosphorised paper)	1·75	1·50	□	□
S68	23p bright green (2 bands) ..	12·00	12·00	□	□
S69	24p Indian red (phosphorised paper)	1·75	1·25	□	□
S70	24p chestnut (phosphorised paper)	1·50	1·00	□	□
	a. Perf 14	2·75	2·50	□	□
S71	24p chestnut (2 bands)	2·75	2·25	□	□
S72	26p rosine (phosphorised paper)	3·00	2·75	□	□
S73	26p drab (phosphorised paper)	1·60	1·40	□	□
S74	28p deep violet-blue (phosphorised paper) . . .	1·50	1·25	□	□
S75	28p deep bluish grey (phosphorised paper) . . .	1·60	1·25	□	□
	a. Perf 14	5·00	4·00	□	□
S76	31p bright purple (phosphorised paper)	2·25	2·00	□	□
S77	32p greenish blue (phosphorised paper) . . .	1·75	1·50	□	□
S78	34p deep bluish grey (phosphorised paper) . . .	1·90	1·90	□	□
S79	37p rosine (phosphorised paper)	2·00	1·90	□	□
S80	39p bright mauve (phosphorised paper)	2·00	1·90	□	□
	a. Perf 14	3·00	2·75	□	□

Nos. S55, S61, S63, S68 and S71 were only issued in stamp booklets.

Presentation Pack (*P.O. Pack No.* 27) (*contains* 2½p (S14), 3p (S15), 5p (S20), 7½p (S25)) ..	4·25	□
Presentation Pack (*P.O. Pack No.* 62) (*contains* 3p (S16), 3½p (S17), 5½p (S21), 8p (S26), *later with* 4½p (S19) *added*) .	2·75	□
Presentation Pack (*P.O. Pack No.* 85) (*contains* 6½p (S23), 8½p (S27), 10p (S29), 11p (S32)) .	2·00	□
Presentation Pack (*P.O. Pack No.* 129b) (*contains* 7p (S24), 9p (S28), 10½p (S31), 11½p (S36), 12p (S33), 13½p (S34), 14p (S40), 15p (S35), 18p (S44), 22p (S47))	9·00	□
Presentation Pack (*P.O. Pack No.* 2) (*contains* 10p (S30), 12½p (S38), 16p (S42), 20½p (S46), 26p (S49), 28p (S50))	10·00	□
Presentation Pack (*P.O. Pack No.* 6) (*contains* 10p (S30), 13p (S39), 16p (S42), 17p (S43), 22p (S48), 26p (S49), 28p (S50), 31p (S51))	13·00	□

Presentation Pack (*P.O. Pack No.*
10) (*contains* 12p (S52), 13p
(S53), 17p (S57), 18p (S59),
22p (S65), 26p (S72), 28p (S74),
31p (S76)) . . . .   16·00   □

For combined packs containing values from all three Regions
see under Northern Ireland.

1993 (7 DEC.)–**98** (*a*) *Printed in lithography by Questa. Perf*
15 × 14 (*with one elliptical hole on each vertical side*)

S81	S **4**	19p bistre (1 centre band)	1·00	75	□	□
S82		19p bistre (1 side band) .	3·25	2·75	□	□
S83		20p bright green (1 centre band)	1·50	1·00	□	□
S84		25p red (2 bands)	1·50	1·00	□	□
S85		26p red-brown (2 bands)	1·50	1·00	□	□
S86		30p deep olive-grey (2 bands)	1·75	1·50	□	□
S87		37p bright mauve (2 bands)	2·40	2·00	□	□
S88		41p grey-brown (2 bands)	2·00	1·75	□	□
S89		63p light emerald (2 bands)	3·50	3·00	□	□

(*b*) *Printed in photogravure by Walsall* (20*p*, 26*p* (*No.* S91*a*),
63*p*), *Harrison or Walsall* (26*p* (*No.* S91), 37*p*). *Perf* 14 (*No.*
S90*a*) *or* 15 × 14 (*others*) (*both with one elliptical hole on
each vertical side*)

S90	S **4**	20p bright green (1 centre band)	50	50	□	□
S90*a*		20p bright green (1 side band)	1·75	1·50	□	□
S91		26p chestnut (2 bands) .	1·25	75	□	□
		a. Perf 14	2·25	1·50	□	□
S92		37p bright mauve (2 bands)	1·50	1·00	□	□
S93		63p light emerald (2 bands)	2·40	1·90	□	□

Nos. S82, S90*a* and S91*a* were only issued in stamp booklets.
For combined presentation packs for all three Regions, see
under Northern Ireland.

S **5** Scottish Flag

S **6** Scottish Lion

S **7** Thistle

S **8** Tartan

1999 (8 JUNE)–**2000** *One centre phosphor band* (2nd) *or two
phosphor bands* (*others*). *Perf* 15 × 14 (*with one elliptical hole
on each vertical side*)

S94	S **5**	(2nd) new blue, blue and silver	30	35	□	□
S95	S **6**	(1st) greenish yellow, deep rose-red, rose-red and silver	40	45	□	□
S96	S **7**	(E) bright lilac, deep lilac and silver	45	50	□	□
S97	S **8**	64p greenish yellow, bright magenta, new blue, grey-black and silver	2·50	2·00	□	□
S98		65p greenish yellow, bright magenta, new blue, grey-black and silver	1·00	1·10	□	□
		Presentation Pack (*P.O. Pack No.* 45) (contains 2nd, 1st, E, 64p) (*Nos.* S94/7))	4·00		□	
		Presentation Pack (*P.O. Pack No.* 50) (*contains* 65p) (*No.* S98)	1·50		□	
		PHQ *Cards* (*Nos.* S94/7)	1·50	3·75	□	□

Nos. S94, S95 and S96 were initially sold at 19p, 26p and 30p,
the latter representing the basic European airmail rate.

S **9**

2000 (15 FEB.) *Type* S **5** *redrawn with* '1st' *face value as Type*
S **9**. *Two phosphor bands. Perf* 14 (*with one elliptical hole on
each vertical side*)

S108	S **9**	(1st) bright orange-red . .	1·10	1·10	□	□

No. S108 was only issued in stamp booklets.

4 Wales and Monmouthshire

W **1**   W **2**   W **3**

1958–67 *Wmk* **179**

W1	W **1**	3d lilac	20	10	☐	☐
		p. One centre phosphor band	20	15	☐	☐
W2		4d blue	20	15	☐	☐
		p. Two phosphor bands	20	15	☐	☐
W3	W **2**	6d purple	50	20	☐	☐
W4		9d bronze-green (2 phosphor bands) . .	40	50	☐	☐
W5	W **3**	1s 3d green	40	50	☐	☐
W6		1s 6d blue (2 phosphor bands)	50	50	☐	☐

1967–69 *One centre phosphor band (Nos.* W7, W9/10) *or two phosphor bands (others). No wmk*

W7	W **1**	3d lilac	20	10	☐	☐
W8		4d blue	20	10	☐	☐
W9		4d sepia	20	10	☐	☐
W10		4d vermilion	20	20	☐	☐
W11		5d blue	20	10	☐	☐
W12	W **3**	1s 6d blue	3·50	3·50	☐	☐
		Presentation Pack (*comprises Nos.* W4, W6/7, W9/11)	3·75		☐	

W **4** With 'p'   W **5** Without 'p'

Decimal Currency
1971–92 *Type* W **4**. *No wmk*

(a) Printed in photogravure with phosphor bands

W13	2½p magenta (1 centre band) .	20	15	☐	☐
W14	3p ultramarine (2 bands) . . .	25	15	☐	☐
W15	3p ultramarine (1 centre band)	25	20	☐	☐
W16	3½p olive-grey (2 bands)	20	30	☐	☐
W17	3½p olive-grey (1 centre band)	20	30	☐	☐
W18	4½p grey-blue (2 bands) . . .	30	20	☐	☐
W19	5p violet (2 bands)	85	1·00	☐	☐
W20	5½p violet (2 bands)	20	30	☐	☐
W21	5½p violet (1 centre band) . . .	25	30	☐	☐
W22	6½p blue (1 centre band)	20	20	☐	☐
W23	7p brown (1 centre band) . .	30	30	☐	☐

W24	7½p chestnut (2 bands)	95	1·50	☐	☐
W25	8p rosine (2 bands)	40	40	☐	☐
W26	8½p yellow-green (2 bands) . .	40	40	☐	☐
W27	9p violet (2 bands)	40	40	☐	☐
W28	10p orange-brown (2 bands) .	45	40	☐	☐
W29	10p orange-brown (1 centre band)	40	40	☐	☐
W30	10½p blue (2 bands)	50	50	☐	☐
W31	11p scarlet (2 bands)	50	50	☐	☐

(b) Printed in photogravure on phosphorised paper

W32	12p yellow-green	45	50	☐	☐
W33	13½p purple-brown	75	80	☐	☐
W34	15p ultramarine	80	80	☐	☐

(c) Printed in lithography. Perf 14 (11½p, 12½p, 14p (*No.* W39), 15½p, 16p, 18p (*No.* W46), 19½p, 20½p, 22p (*No.* W54), 26p (*No.* W61), 28p (*No.* W63)) *or* 15 × 14 (*others*)

W35	11½p drab (1 side band)	1·10	80	☐	☐
W36	12p bright emerald (1 side band)	1·50	1·25	☐	☐
W37	12½p light emerald (1 side band)	1·00	80	☐	☐
	a. Perf 15 × 14	6·25	6·25	☐	☐
W38	13p pale chestnut (1 side band)	75	75	☐	☐
W39	14p grey-blue (phosphorised paper)	80	80	☐	☐
W40	14p deep blue (1 centre band)	90	80	☐	☐
W41	15p bright blue (1 centre band)	1·10	80	☐	☐
W42	15½p pale violet (phosphorised paper)	1·00	80	☐	☐
W43	16p drab (phosphorised paper)	1·90	1·50	☐	☐
	a. Perf 15 × 14	2·25	1·75	☐	☐
W44	17p grey-blue (phosphorised paper)	1·00	90	☐	☐
W45	17p deep blue (1 centre band)	1·25	90	☐	☐
W46	18p deep violet (phosphorised paper)	1·10	90	☐	☐
W47	18p olive-grey (phosphorised paper)	1·25	90	☐	☐
W48	18p bright green (1 centre band)	75	75	☐	☐
	b. Perf 14	3·25	3·00	☐	☐
W49	18p bright green (1 side band)	2·00	2·50	☐	☐
W50	19p bright orange-red (phosphorised paper) . . .	1·40	80	☐	☐
W51	19½p olive-grey (phosphorised paper)	2·10	2·00	☐	☐
W52	20p brownish black (phos-phorised paper)	1·40	1·00	☐	☐
W53	20½p ultramarine (phosphorised paper)	4·00	4·00	☐	☐
W54	22p blue (phosphorised paper)	1·25	1·25	☐	☐
W55	22p yellow-green (phosphorised paper)	1·40	1·40	☐	☐
W56	22p bright orange-red (phosphorised paper) . . .	1·40	1·25	☐	☐
W57	23p bright green (phosphorised paper)	1·50	1·40	☐	☐
W58	24p Indian red (phosphorised paper)	1·60	1·25	☐	☐

W59	24p chestnut (phosphorised					
	paper)	1·25	1·25	☐	☐
	b. Perf 14	3·00	2·75	☐	☐
W60	24p chestnut (2 bands)	1·50	1·50	☐	☐
W61	26p rosine (phosphorised					
	paper)	1·60	1·50	☐	☐
	a. Perf 15 × 14	5·50	5·00	☐	☐
W62	26p drap (phosphorised paper)	1·50	1·25	☐	☐
W63	28p deep violet-blue (phos-					
	phorised paper)	1·40	1·25	☐	☐
	a. Perf 15 × 14	1·60	1·25	☐	☐
W64	28p deep bluish grey					
	(phosphorised paper) . . .	1·60	1·25	☐	☐
W65	31p bright purple (phosphorised					
	paper)	1·50	1·50	☐	☐
W66	32p greenish blue (phos-					
	phorised paper)	2·00	1·90	☐	☐
W67	34p deep bluish grey					
	(phosphorised paper) . . .	1·75	1·75	☐	☐
W68	37p rosine (phosphorised					
	paper)	1·90	1·90	☐	☐
W69	39p bright mauve (phos-					
	phorised paper)	2·00	2·00	☐	☐

Nos. W49 and W60 were only issued in stamp booklets. The former exists with the phosphor band at the left or right of the stamp.

Presentation Pack (P.O. Pack No. 28) (contains 2½p (W13), 3p (W14), 5p (W19), 7½p (W24)) .	4·25	☐
Presentation Pack (P.O. Pack No. 63) (contains 3p (W15), 3½p (W16), 5½p (W20), 8p (W25), later with 4½p (W18) added) .	2·75	☐
Presentation Pack (P.O. Pack No. 86) (contains 6½p (W22), 8½p (W26), 10p (W28), 11p (W31))	2·00	☐
Presentation Pack (P.O. Pack No. 129c) (contains 7p (W23), 9p (W27), 10½p (W30), 11½p (W35), 12p (W32), 13½p (W33), 14p (W39), 15p (W34), 18p (W46), 22p (W53))	9·00	☐
Presentation Pack (P.O. Pack No. 3) (contains 10p (W29), 12½p (W37), 16p (W43), 20½p (W53), 26p (W61), 28p (W63))	10·00	☐
Presentation Pack (P.O. Pack No. 7) (contains 10p (W29), 13p (W38), 16p (W43a), 17p (W44), 22p (W55), 26p (W61), 28p (W63), 31p (W65))	12·00	☐
Presentation Pack (P.O. Pack No. 11) (contains 12p (W36), 13p (W38), 17p (W44), 18p (W47), 22p (W55), 26p (W61a), 28p (W63a), 31p (W65))	12·00	☐

For combined packs containing values from all three Regions see under Northern Ireland.

1993 (7 DEC.)–**96** *Printed in lithography by Questa. Perf* 15 × 14 (*with one elliptical hole on each vertical side*)

W70	W **4**	19p bistre (1 centre band)	1·00	75	☐	☐
W71		19p bistre (1 side band) .	3·00	2·75	☐	☐
W72		20p bright green (1 centre band)	1·50	1·00	☐	☐
W73		25p red (2 bands)	1·50	1·00	☐	☐
W74		26p red-brown (2 bands)	1·50	1·00	☐	☐
W75		30p deep olive-grey (2 bands)	1·25	1·50	☐	☐
W76		37p bright mauve (2 bands)	2·25	2·00	☐	☐
W77		41p grey-brown (2 bands)	2·50	2·00	☐	☐
W78		63p light emerald (2 bands)	3·75	3·50	☐	☐

No. W71 was only issued in stamp booklets.

For combined presentation packs for all three Regions see under Northern Ireland.

1997 (1 JULY)–**98** *Printed in photogravure by Walsall* (20p, 26p (*No.* W80a), 63p), *Harrison or Walsall* (26p (*No.* W80), 37p) *Perf* 14 (*No.* W79a) *or* 15 × 14 (*both with one elliptical hole on each vertical side*)

W79	W **5**	20p bright green (1 centre band)	1·00	90	☐	☐
W79a		20p bright green (1 side band)	2·00	1·50	☐	☐
W80		26p chestnut (2 bands) .	1·25	1·00	☐	☐
		a. Perf 14	2·00	2·00	☐	☐
W81		37p bright mauve (2 bands)	1·50	1·00	☐	☐
W82		63p light emerald (2 bands)	2·25	2·00	☐	☐
		Presentation Pack (P.O. Pack No. 39) (Nos. W79 and W80/2) . .	6·00		☐

Nos. W79a and W80a were only issued in stamp booklets.

W **6** Leek

W **7** Welsh Dragon

W **8** Daffodil

W **9** Prince of Wales Feathers

1999 (8 JUNE)–**2000** *One phosphor band* (2nd) *or two phosphor bands* (others). *Perf* 14 (*No.* W83a) *or* 15 × 14 (*others*) (*both with one elliptical hole on each vertical side*)

W83	W **6**	(2nd) orange-brown, yellow-orange and black (1 centre band) . . .	30	35	☐	☐
W83a		(2nd) orange-brown, yellow-orange and black (1 side band)	1·50	1·50	☐	☐
W84	W **7**	(1st) blue-green, greenish yellow, silver and black	40	45	☐	☐
W85	W **8**	(E) greenish blue, deep greenish blue and grey-black	45	50	☐	☐
W86	W **9**	64p violet, gold, silver and black	2·50	2·25	☐	☐
W87		65p violet, gold, silver and black	1·00	1·10	☐	☐
		Presentation Pack (*P.O. Pack No.* 46) (*contains* 2nd, 1st, E, 64p) (*Nos.* W83, W84/6))	4·00		☐	
		Presentation Pack (*P.O. Pack No.* 51) (*contains* 65p) (No. W87))	1·50		☐	
		PHQ Cards (*Nos.* W83, W84/6) .	1·50	3·75	☐	☐

Nos. W83, W84 and W85 were initially sold at 19p, 26p and 30p, the latter representing the basic European airmail rate.

No. W83a was only issued in stamp booklets.

W **10**

2000 (15 FEB.) *Type* W **4** *redrawn with* '1af/st' *face value as Type* W **10**. *Two phosphor bands. Perf* 14 (*with one elliptical hole on each vertical side*)

W97	W **10**	(1st) bright orange-red .	1·10	1·10	☐	☐

No. W97 was only issued in stamp booklets.

ISLE OF MAN

Regional Issues

1   2   3

1958–67 *Wmk* **179**. *Perf* 15 × 14

1	1	2½d red	50	1·25	☐ ☐
2	2	3d lilac	30	20	☐ ☐
		p. One centre phosphor band	30	50	☐ ☐
3		4d blue	1·50	1·50	☐ ☐
		p. Two phosphor bands	30	30	☐ ☐

1968–69 *One centre phosphor band* (*Nos.* 5/6) *or two phosphor bands* (*others*). *No wmk*

4	2	4d blue	25	30	☐ ☐
5		4d sepia	25	40	☐ ☐
6		4d vermilion	45	75	☐ ☐
7		5d blue	45	75	☐ ☐

Decimal Currency

1971 (7 JULY) *One centre phosphor band* (2½p) *or two phosphor bands* (*others*). *No wmk*

8	3	2½p magenta	20	15	☐ ☐
9		3p ultramarine	20	15	☐ ☐
10		5p violet	40	60	☐ ☐
11		7½p chestnut	40	75	☐ ☐
		Presentation Pack	2·75		☐

For comprehensive listings of the Independent Administration issues of the Isle of Man, see Stanley Gibbons *Collect Channel Islands and Isle of Man Stamps*.

CHANNEL ISLANDS

1 General Issue

C 1   Gathering Vraic   C 2   Islanders gathering Vraic

Third Anniversary of Liberation

1948 (10 MAY) *Wmk Type* **127**. *Perf* 15 × 14

C1	C 1	1d red	25	30	☐ ☐
C2	C 2	2½d blue	25	30	☐ ☐
		First Day Cover	35·00		☐

2 Guernsey

(a) War Occupation Issues

Stamps issued under British authority during the German Occupation.

1   2   3

1941–44 *Rouletted.* (*a*) *White paper. No wmk*

1	1	½d green	2·50	1·50	☐ ☐
2		1d red	2·00	75	☐ ☐
3		2½d blue	3·25	5·00	☐ ☐
		(*b*) *Bluish French bank-note paper. Wmk loops*			
4	1	½d green	21·00	18·00	☐ ☐
5		1d red	10·00	16·00	☐ ☐

(b) Regional Issues

1958–67 *Wmk* **179**. *Perf* 15 × 14

6	2	2½d red	35	40	☐ ☐
7	3	3d lilac	35	30	☐ ☐
		p. One centre phosphor band	25	25	☐ ☐
8		4d blue	30	30	☐ ☐
		p. Two phosphor bands	25	25	☐ ☐

1968–69 *One centre phosphor band* (*Nos.* 10/11) *or two phosphor bands* (*others*). *No wmk*

9	3	4d blue	10	30	☐ ☐
10		4d sepia	15	20	☐ ☐
11		4d vermilion	15	30	☐ ☐
12		5d blue	15	30	☐ ☐

For comprehensive listings of the Independent Postal Administration issues of Guernsey, see Stanley Gibbons *Collect Channel Islands and Isle of Man Stamps*.

3 Jersey

(a) War Occupation Issues

Stamps issued under British authority during the German Occupation.

1   2 Old Jersey Farm   3 Portelet Bay

4   Corbière Lighthouse

5   Elizabeth Castle

6   Mont Orgueil Castle

7   Gathering Vraic
    (seaweed)

1941–42 *White paper. No wmk Perf* 11

1	1	½d green	4·50	3·25	□	□
2		1d red	4·25	2·00	□	□

1943 *No wmk Perf* 13½

3	2	½d green	7·00	5·50	□	□
4	3	1d red	2·00	75	□	□
5	4	1½d brown	3·25	3·00	□	□
6	5	2d orange	4·75	3·25	□	□
7a	6	2½d blue	1·10	1·00	□	□
8	7	3d violet	1·25	2·75	□	□
		Set of 6	17·00	14·50	□	□

(b) Regional Issues

8

9

1958–67 *Wmk* **179**. *Perf* 15 × 14

9	8	2½d red	10	60	□	□
10	9	3d lilac	15	10	□	□
		p. One centre phosphor				
		band	10	30	□	□
11		4d blue	10	15	□	□
		p. Two phosphor bands . .	10	25	□	□

1968–69 *One centre phosphor band* (4d *values*) *or two phosphor bands* (5d). *No wmk*

12	9	4d sepia	10	30	□	□
13		4d vermilion	10	40	□	□
14		5d blue	10	60	□	□

For comprehensive listings of the Independent Postal Adminstration issues of Jersey, see Stanley Gibbons *Collect Channel Islands and Isle of Man Stamps.*

REGIONAL FIRST DAY COVERS

PRICES for First Day Covers listed below are for stamps, as indicated, used on illustrated envelopes and postmarked with operational cancellations (before 1964) or with special First Day of Issue cancellations (1964 onwards). First Day postmarks of 8 June 1964 and 7 February 1966 were of the machine cancellation 'envelope' type.

£sd Issues

18 Aug. 1958	Guernsey 3d (*No.* 7)	17·00 □
	Isle of Man 3d (*No.* 2)	32·00 □
	Jersey 3d (*No.* 10)	17·00 □
	Northern Ireland 3d (*No.* NI1) .	30·00 □
	Scotland 3d (*No.* S1)	12·00 □
	Wales 3d (*No.* W1)	12·00 □
29 Sept. 1958	Northern Ireland 6d, 1s 3d (*Nos.* NI3, NI5)	35·00 □
	Scotland 6d, 1s 3d (*Nos.* S3, S5)	25·00 □
	Wales 6d, 1s 3d (*Nos.* W3, W5)	25·00 □
8 June 1964	Guernsey 2½d (*No.* 6)	30·00 □
	Isle of Man 2½d (*No.* 1)	45·00 □
	Jersey 2½d (*No.* 9)	30·00 □
7 Feb. 1966	Guernsey 4d (*No.* 8)	8·00 □
	Isle of Man 4d (*No.* 3)	10·00 □
	Jersey 4d (*No.* 11)	8·00 □
	Northern Ireland 4d (*No.* NI2) .	7·00 □
	Scotland 4d (*No.* S2)	7·00 □
	Wales 4d (*No.* W2)	7·00 □
1 March 1967	Northern Ireland 9d, 1s 6d (*Nos.* NI4, NI6)	4·00 □
	Scotland 9d, 1s 6d (*Nos.* S4, S6)	4·00 □
	Wales 9d, 1s 6d (*Nos.* W4, W6)	4·00 □
4 Sept. 1968	Guernsey 4d, 5d (*Nos.* 10, 12)	3·00 □
	Isle of Man 4d, 5d (*Nos.* 5, 7) .	4·00 □
	Jersey 4d, 5d (*Nos.* 12, 14) . .	3·00 □
	Northern Ireland 4d, 5d (*Nos.* NI8, NI10)	3·00 □
	Scotland 4d, 5d (*Nos.* S9, S11) .	3·00 □
	Wales 4d, 5d (*Nos.* W9, W11) .	3·00 □
Decimal Issues		
7 July 1971	Isle of Man 2½p, 3p, 5p, 7½p (*Nos.* 8/11)	3·00 □
	Northern Ireland 2½p, 3p, 5p, 7½p (*Nos.* NI12/13, NI18, NI23) .	3·75 □
	Scotland 2½p, 3p, 5p, 7½p (*Nos.* S14/15, S20, S25)	3·00 □
	Wales 2½p, 3p, 5p, 7½p (*Nos.* W13/14, W19, W24)	3·00 □
23 Jan. 1974	Northern Ireland 3p, 3½p, 5½p, 8p (*Nos.* NI14/15, NI19, NI24) .	2·00 □
	Scotland 3p, 3½p, 5½p, 8p (*Nos.* S16/17, S21, S26)	2·00 □
	Wales 3p, 3½p, 5½p, 8p (*Nos.* W15/16, W20, W25)	2·00 □

6 Nov. 1974 — Northern Ireland 4½p (No. NI17) .... 2·00 □
Scotland 4½p (No. S19) .... 2·00 □
Wales 4½p (No. W18) ...... 2·00 □

14 Jan. 1976 — Northern Ireland 6½p, 8½p (Nos. NI21, NI25) .... 2·00 □
Scotland 6½p, 8½p (Nos. S23, S27) .... 2·00 □
Wales 6½p, 8½p (Nos. W22, W26) 2·00 □

20 Oct. 1976 — Northern Ireland 10p, 11p (Nos. NI27, NI30) .... 2·00 □
Scotland 10p, 11p (Nos. S29, S32) .... 2·00 □
Wales 10p, 11p (Nos. W28, W31) .... 2·00 □

18 Jan. 1978 — Northern Ireland 7p, 9p, 10½p (Nos. NI22, NI26, NI29) .... 2·00 □
Scotland 7p, 9p, 10½p (Nos. S24, S28, S31) .... 2·00 □
Wales 7p, 9p, 10½p (Nos. W23, W27, W30) .... 2·00 □

23 July 1980 — Northern Ireland 12p, 13½p, 15p (Nos. NI31/3) .... 2·25 □
Scotland 12p, 13½p, 15p (Nos. S33/5) .... 2·25 □
Wales 12p, 13½p, 15p (Nos. W32/4) .... 2·25 □

8 April 1981 — Northern Ireland 11½p, 14p, 18p, 22p (Nos. NI34, NI38, NI45, NI53) .... 3·50 □
Scotland 11½p, 14p, 18p, 22p (Nos. S36, S40, S44, S47) ... 3·50 □
Wales 11½p, 14p, 18p, 22p (Nos. W35, W39, W46, W54) ..... 3·75 □

24 Feb. 1982 — Northern Ireland 12½p, 15½p, 19½p, 26p (Nos. NI36, NI41, NI50, NI60) .... 5·00 □
Scotland 12½p, 15½p, 19½p, 26p (Nos. S38, S41, S45, S49) ... 4·50 □
Wales 12½p, 15½p, 19½p, 26p (Nos. W37, W42, W51, W61) . 4·50 □

27 April 1983 — Northern Ireland 16p, 20½p, 28p (Nos. NI42, NI52, NI62) .... 6·00 □
Scotland 16p, 20½p, 28p (Nos. S42, S46, S50) .... 5·50 □
Wales 16p, 20½p, 28p (Nos. W43, W53, W63) .... 6·50 □

23 Oct. 1984 — Northern Ireland 13p, 17p, 22p, 31p (Nos. NI37, NI43, NI54, NI64) .... 4·75 □
Scotland 13p, 17p, 22p, 31p (Nos. S39, S43, S48, S51) ... 7·50 □
Wales 13p, 17p, 22p, 31p (Nos. W38, W44, W55, W65) ..... 4·25 □

7 Jan. 1986 — Northern Ireland 12p (No. NI35) 1·50 □
Scotland 12p (No. S37) .... 1·50 □
Wales 12p (No. W36) .... 1·50 □

6 Jan. 1987 — Northern Ireland 18p (No. NI46) 1·50 □
Scotland 18p (No. S59) .... 1·50 □
Wales 18p (No. W47) .... 1·50 □

8 Nov. 1988 — Northern Ireland 14p, 19p, 23p, 32p (Nos. NI39, NI49, NI56, NI65) .... 4·00 □
Scotland 14p, 19p, 23p, 32p (Nos. S54, S62, S67, S77) ... 4·25 □
Wales 14p, 19p, 23p, 32p (Nos. W40, W50, W57, W66) ..... 4·50 □

28 Nov. 1989 — Northern Ireland 15p, 20p, 24p, 34p (Nos. NI40, NI51, NI57, NI66) .... 4·50 □
Scotland 15p, 20p, 24p, 34p (Nos. S56, S64, S69, S78) ... 4·75 □
Wales 15p, 20p, 24p, 34p (Nos. W41, W52, W58, W67) ..... 4·75 □

4 Dec. 1990 — Northern Ireland 17p, 22p, 26p, 37p (Nos. NI44, NI55, NI61, NI67) .... 4·75 □
Scotland 17p, 22p, 26p, 37p (Nos. S58, S66, S73, S79) ... 4·75 □
Wales 17p, 22p, 26p, 37p (Nos. W45, W56, W62, W68) ..... 4·75 □

3 Dec. 1991 — Northern Ireland 18p, 24p, 28p, 39p (Nos. NI47, NI58, NI63, NI68) .... 4·75 □
Scotland 18p, 24p, 28p, 39p (Nos. S60, S70, S75, S80) ... 4·75 □
Wales 18p, 24p, 28p, 39p (Nos. W48, W59, W64, W69) ..... 5·00 □

7 Dec 1993 — Northern Ireland 19p, 25p, 30p, 41p (Nos. NI69, NI72, NI74, NI76) .... 5·50 □
Scotland 19p, 25p, 30p, 41p (Nos. S81, S84, S86, S88) ... 5·50 □
Wales 19p, 25p, 30p, 41p (Nos. W70, W73, W75, W77) ..... 5·75 □

23 July 1996 — Northern Ireland 20p (1 centre band), 26p, 37p, 63p (Nos. NI71, NI73, NI75, NI77) .... 7·25 □
Scotland 20p (1 centre band), 26p, 37p, 63p (Nos. S83, S85, S87, S89) .... 7·25 □
Wales 20p, 26p, 37p, 63p (Nos. W72, W74, W76, W78) ..... 7·50 □

1 July 1997 — Wales 20p (1 centre band), 26p, 37p, 63p (Nos. W79/82) ... 4·00 □

8 June 1999 — Northern Ireland 38p, 64p (Nos. NI83, NI86) .... 3·50 □
Scotland 2nd, 1st, E, 64p (Nos S94/7) .... 3·75 □
Wales 2nd, 1st, E, 64p (Nos. W83, W84/6) .... 3·75 □

25 Apr 2000	Northern Ireland 1st, 40p, 65p		
	(Nos. NI84, NI87, NI88b)	3·00	☐
	Scotland 65p (No. S98)	1·75	☐
	Wales 65p (No. W87)	1·75	☐
6 Mar 2001	Northern Ireland 2nd, 1st, E, 65p (Nos. NI89/92)	3·25	☐
23 Apr 2001	England 2nd, 1st, E, 65p (Nos. EN1/4)	3·25	☐

159

POSTAGE DUE STAMPS

PERFORATION. All postage due stamps to No. D101 are perf 14 × 15.

D **1**

D **2**

1914–22 *Wmk Type* **100** *(Royal Cypher ('Simple')) sideways*

D1	D **1**	½d green	50	25 ☐ ☐
D2		1d red	50	25 ☐ ☐
D3		1½d brown	48·00	20·00 ☐ ☐
D4		2d black	50	25 ☐ ☐
D5		3d violet	5·00	75 ☐ ☐
D6		4d green	18·00	5·00 ☐ ☐
D7		5d brown	6·00	3·50 ☐ ☐
D8		1s blue	40·00	4·75 ☐ ☐
	Set of 8	. . . .	90·00	30·00 ☐ ☐

1924–31 *Wmk Type* **111** *(Block* G v R*) sideways*

D10	D **1**	½d green	1·25	75 ☐ ☐
D11		1d red	60	25 ☐ ☐
D12		1½d brown	45·00	18·00 ☐ ☐
D13		2d black	1·00	25 ☐ ☐
D14		3d violet	1·50	25 ☐ ☐
D15		4d green	15·00	3·00 ☐ ☐
D16		5d brown	32·00	28·00 ☐ ☐
D17		1s blue	10·00	1·00 ☐ ☐
D18	D **2**	2s 6d purple/*yellow*	45·00	2·00 ☐ ☐
	Set of 9	. . . .	£130	48·00 ☐ ☐

1936–37 *Wmk Type* **125** *(E 8 R) sideways*

D19	D **1**	½d green	7·50	8·00 ☐ ☐
D20		1d red	1·50	2·00 ☐ ☐
D21		2d black	7·00	11·00 ☐ ☐
D22		3d violet	1·50	2·25 ☐ ☐
D23		4d green	23·00	35·00 ☐ ☐
D24*a*		5d brown	16·00	23·00 ☐ ☐
D25		1s blue	11·00	9·00 ☐ ☐
D26	D **2**	2s 6d purple/*yellow*	£275	9·00 ☐ ☐
	Set of 8	. . . .	£325	90·00 ☐ ☐

1937–38 *Wmk Type* **127** *(G* vi R*) sideways*

D27	D **1**	½d green	9·00	5·00 ☐ ☐
D28		1d red	3·00	75 ☐ ☐
D29		2d black	2·50	75 ☐ ☐
D30		3d violet	12·00	1·00 ☐ ☐
D31		4d green	75·00	13·00 ☐ ☐
D32		5d brown	14·00	75 ☐ ☐
D33		1s blue	75·00	2·00 ☐ ☐
D34	D **2**	2s 6d purple/*yellow*	75·00	2·50 ☐ ☐
	Set of 8	. . . .	£250	23·00 ☐ ☐

1951–52 *Colours changed and new value (1½d) Wmk Type* **127** *(G* vi R*) sideways*

D35	D **1**	½d orange	1·00	3·00 ☐ ☐
D36		1d blue	1·50	1·50 ☐ ☐
D37		1½d green	1·75	3·00 ☐ ☐
D38		4d blue	32·00	12·00 ☐ ☐
D39		1s brown	38·00	14·00 ☐ ☐
	Set of 5	. . . .	70·00	30·00 ☐ ☐

1954–55 *Wmk Type* **153** *(Mult Tudor Crown and E 2 R) sideways*

D40	D **1**	½d orange	7·00	8·00 ☐ ☐
D41		2d black	5·00	5·50 ☐ ☐
D42		3d violet	55·00	38·00 ☐ ☐
D43		4d blue	20·00	23·00 ☐ ☐
D44		5d brown	30·00	6·00 ☐ ☐
D45	D **2**	2s 6d purple/*yellow*	£110	2·00 ☐ ☐
	Set of 6	. . . .	£200	75·00 ☐ ☐

1955–57 *Wmk Type* **165** *(Mult St Edward's Crown and E 2 R) sideways*

D46	D **1**	½d orange	1·25	4·00 ☐ ☐
D47		1d blue	6·00	1·75 ☐ ☐
D48		1½d green	6·00	7·00 ☐ ☐
D49		2d black	45·00	3·75 ☐ ☐
D50		3d violet . . . . : .	7·00	1·50 ☐ ☐
D51		4d blue	22·00	3·75 ☐ ☐
D52		5d brown	38·00	2·00 ☐ ☐
D53		1s brown	75·00	2·00 ☐ ☐
D54	D **2**	2s 6d purple/*yellow*	£150	10·00 ☐ ☐
D55		5s red/*yellow*	80·00	28·00 ☐ ☐
	Set of 10	. . . .	£375	55·00 ☐ ☐

1959–63 *Wmk Type* **179** *(Mult St Edward's Crown) sideways*

D56	D **1**	½d orange	15	1·25 ☐ ☐
D57		1d blue	15	50 ☐ ☐
D58		1½d green	90	3·50 ☐ ☐
D59		2d black	1·10	50 ☐ ☐
D60		3d violet	30	30 ☐ ☐
D61		4d blue	30	30 ☐ ☐
D62		5d brown	45	60 ☐ ☐
D63		6d purple	50	30 ☐ ☐
D64		1s brown	90	30 ☐ ☐
D65	D **2**	2s 6d purple/*yellow*	4·75	75 ☐ ☐
D66		5s red/*yellow*	6·50	1·00 ☐ ☐
D67		10s blue/*yellow*	10·00	5·50 ☐ ☐
D68		£1 black/*yellow*	40·00	7·50 ☐ ☐
	Set of 13	. . . .	60·00	20·00 ☐ ☐

1968–69 *Design size 22½ × 19 mm. No wmk*

D69	D **1**	2d black	25	75 ☐ ☐
D70		3d violet	30	75 ☐ ☐
D71		4d blue	40	75 ☐ ☐
D72		5d orange-brown	5·00	10·00 ☐ ☐
D73		6d purple	60	1·00 ☐ ☐
D74		1s brown	2·00	1·00 ☐ ☐
	Set of 6	. . . .	7·50	12·00 ☐ ☐

1968–69 *Design size 21½ × 17½ mm. No wmk*

D75	D **1**	4d blue	6·00	6·00 ☐ ☐
D76		8d red	1·25	1·00 ☐ ☐

D **3**   D **4**

Decimal Currency

1970–77 *No wmk*

D77	D 3	½p turquoise-blue . . .	15	50	□	□
D78		1p reddish purple . . .	15	15	□	□
D79		2p myrtle-green	20	15	□	□
D80		3p ultramarine	20	15	□	□
D81		4p yellow-brown	25	15	□	□
D82		5p violet	25	15	□	□
D83		7p red-brown	35	80	□	□
D84	D 4	10p red	30	30	□	□
D85		11p green	50	1·00	□	□
D86		20p brown	60	25	□	□
D87		50p ultramarine	1·75	25	□	□
D88		£1 black	3·25	50	□	□
D89		£5 orange-yellow and black	35·00	1·50	□	□
	Set of 13		38·00	5·00	□	□

Presentation Pack (*P.O. Pack No. 36*) (*Nos.* D77/82, D84, D86/8)   10·00   □

Presentation Pack (*P.O. Pack No. 93*) (*Nos.* D77/88) . . . .   10·00   □

D **5**   D **6**   D **7**

1982 *No wmk*

D90	D **5**	1p lake	10	30	□	□
D91		2p bright blue	30	30	□	□
D92		3p deep mauve	15	40	□	□
D93		4p deep blue	15	50	□	□
D94		5p sepia	20	30	□	□
D95	D **6**	10p light brown	30	30	□	□
D96		20p olive-green	50	30	□	□
D97		25p deep greenish blue .	75	1·00	□	□
D98		50p grey-black	1·50	50	□	□
D99		£1 red	3·00	50	□	□
D100		£2 turquoise-blue . . .	6·00	50	□	□
D101		£5 dull orange	14·00	50	□	□
	Set of 12		24·00	5·00	□	□
	Set of 12 *Gutter Pairs*		48·00		□	
	Presentation Pack		26·00		□	

For full information on all future British issues, collectors should write to Royal Mail, Freepost EH3647, 21 South Gyle Crescent, Edinburgh EH12 9PE.

1994 (15 FEB.) *Perf* 15 × 14 (*with one elliptical hole on each vertical side*)

D102	D **7**	1p red, yellow and black	10	50	□	□
D103		2p magenta, purple and black	10	50	□	□
D104		5p yellow, red-brown and black	15	35	□	□
D105		10p yellow, emerald and black	30	45	□	□
D106		20p blue-green, violet and black	50	70	□	□
D107		25p cerise, rosine and black	60	75	□	□
D108		£1 violet, magenta and black	2·25	2·50	□	□
D109		£1.20 greenish blue, blue-green and black	2·75	3·50	□	□
D110		£5 greenish black, blue-green and black	12·00	12·00	□	□
	Set of 9		17·00	20·00	□	□
	Presentation Pack		18·00		□	

ROYAL MAIL POSTAGE LABELS

These imperforate labels were issued as an experiment by the Post Office. Special microprocessor-controlled machines were installed at post offices in Cambridge, London, Shirley (Southampton) and Windsor to provide an after-hours sales service to the public. The machines printed and dispensed the labels according to the coins inserted and the buttons operated by the customer. Values were initially available in ½p steps to 16p and in addition, the labels were sold at philatelic counters in two packs containing either 3 values (3½, 12½, 16p) or 32 values (½p to 16p).

From 28 August 1984 the machines were adjusted to provide values up to 17p. After 31 December 1984 labels including ½p values were withdrawn. The machines were taken out of service on 30 April 1985.

Machine postage-paid impression in red on phosphorised paper with grey-green background design. No watermark. imperforate.

1984 (1 MAY–28 AUG.)

Set of 32 (½p to 16p)	13·00	22·00 ☐ ☐
Set of 3 (3½p, 12½p, 16p)	2·50	3·00 ☐ ☐
Set of 3 on First Day Cover		
(1 May)		6·50 ☐
Set of 2 (16½p, 17p) (28 August)	4·00	3·00 ☐ ☐

OFFICIAL STAMPS

Various stamps of Queen Victoria and King Edward VII overprinted in Black.

I.R.	I. R.	O.W.
OFFICIAL	**OFFICIAL**	**OFFICIAL**
(O 1)	(O 2)	(O 3)
ARMY	**ARMY**	
OFFICIAL	**OFFICIAL**	**GOVᵀ PARCELS**
(O 4)	(O 5)	(O 7)

BOARD OF EDUCATION (O 8)	**R.H. OFFICIAL** (O 9)	ADMIRALTY **OFFICIAL** (O 10)

1 Inland Revenue

Overprinted with Types O 1 or O 2 (5s, 10s, £1)

1882–1901 *Queen Victoria*

O 1	52	½d green	20·00	20·00 ☐ ☐
O 5		½d blue	35·00	22·00 ☐ ☐
O13	67	½d vermilion	2·50	1·50 ☐ ☐
O17		½d green	6·00	4·50 ☐ ☐
O 3	57	1d lilac (Die II)	3·00	2·00 ☐ ☐
O 6	64	2½d lilac	£150	55·00 ☐ ☐
O14	70	2½d purple on blue	70·00	6·00 ☐ ☐
O 4	43	6d grey (Plate 18)	£190	50·00 ☐ ☐
O18	75	6d purple on red	£175	45·00 ☐ ☐
O 7	65	1s green	£2750	£575 ☐ ☐
O15	78	1s green	£240	40·00 ☐ ☐
O19		1s green and red	£850	£250 ☐ ☐
O 9	59	5s red	£1600	£475 ☐ ☐
O10	60	10s blue	£3000	£650 ☐ ☐
O11	61	£1 brown (Wmk Crowns)	£22000	☐
O12		£1 brown (Wmk Orbs) . .	£30000	☐
O16		£1 green	£4000	£600 ☐ ☐

1902–04 *King Edward VII*

O20	79	½d blue-green	22·00	3·00 ☐ ☐
O21		1d red	15·00	2·00 ☐ ☐
O22	82	2½d blue	£475	£100 ☐ ☐
O23	79	6d purple	£90000	£70000 ☐ ☐
O24	89	1s green and red	£600	£150 ☐ ☐
O25	91	5s red	£4750	£2000 ☐ ☐
O26	92	10s blue	£17000	£10000 ☐ ☐
O27	93	£1 green	£14000	£8000 ☐ ☐

2 Office of Works

Overprinted with Type O 3

1896–1902 *Queen Victoria*

O31	67	½d vermilion	£110	60·00 ☐ ☐
O32		½d green	£190	95·00 ☐ ☐
O33	57	1d lilac (Die II)	£190	60·00 ☐ ☐
O34	74	5d dull purple and blue .	£900	£210 ☐ ☐
O35	77	10d dull purple and red . .	£1500	£300 ☐ ☐

1902–03 *King Edward VII*

O36	79	½d blue-green	£425	£110 ☐ ☐
O37		1d red	£425	£110 ☐ ☐
O38	81	2d green and red	£750	£110 ☐ ☐
O39	82	2½d blue	£850	£300 ☐ ☐
O40	88	10d purple and red	£5500	£2000 ☐ ☐

3 Army

Overprinted with Types O 4 ($\frac{1}{2}d$, 1d) or O 5 ($2\frac{1}{2}d$, 6d)

1896–1901 *Queen Victoria*

O41	67	$\frac{1}{2}$d vermilion	2·50	1·50	□	□
O42		$\frac{1}{2}$d green	2·50	4·50	□	□
O43	57	1d lilac (Die II)	2·50	1·50	□	□
O44	70	2$\frac{1}{2}$d purple on blue	6·00	3·50	□	□
O45	75	6d purple on red	18·00	20·00	□	□

Overprinted with Type O 4

1902 *King Edward VII*

O48	79	$\frac{1}{2}$d blue-green	3·00	1·50	□	□
O49		1d red	3·00	1·50	□	□
O50		6d purple	80·00	35·00	□	□

4 Government Parcels

Overprinted with Type O 7

1883–1900 *Queen Victoria*

O69	57	1d lilac (Die II)	30·00	9·00	□	□
O61	62	1$\frac{1}{2}$d lilac	£125	30·00	□	□
O65	68	1$\frac{1}{2}$d purple and green . . .	25·00	3·00	□	□
O70	69	2d green and red	50·00	8·00	□	□
O71	73	4$\frac{1}{2}$d green and red	£125	80·00	□	□
O62	63	6d green	£825	£300	□	□
O66	75	6d purple on red	60·00	12·00	□	□
O63	64	9d green	£675	£190	□	□
O67	76	9d purple and blue	70·00	16·00	□	□
O64	44	1s brown (Plate 13)	£450	80·00	□	□
O64c		1s brown (Plate 14)	£775	£125	□	□
O68	78	1s green	£150	80·00	□	□
O72		1s green and red	£175	55·00	□	□

1902 *King Edward VII*

O74	79	1d red	17·00	6·00	□	□
O75	81	2d green and red	70·00	18·00	□	□
O76	79	6d purple	£110	18·00	□	□
O77	87	9d purple and blue	£250	60·00	□	□
O78	89	1s green and red	£375	90·00	□	□

5 Board of Education

Overprinted with Type O 8

1902 *Queen Victoria*

O81	74	5d dull purple and blue .	£600	£140	□	□
O82	78	1s green and red	£1100	£450	□	□

1902–04 *King Edward VII*

O83	79	$\frac{1}{2}$d blue-green	35·00	10·00	□	□
O84		1d red	35·00	9·00	□	□
O85	82	2$\frac{1}{2}$d blue	£600	70·00	□	□
O86	85	5d purple and blue	£2400	£1100	□	□
O87	89	1s green and red	£40000		□	

6 Royal Household

Overprinted with Type O 9

1902 *King Edward VII*

O91	79	$\frac{1}{2}$d blue-green	£170	£110	□	□
O92		1d red	£150	£100	□	□

7 Admiralty

Overprinted with Type O 10

1903 *King Edward Vii*

O107	79	$\frac{1}{2}$d blue-green	12·00	7·00	□	□
O102		1d red	7·00	4·00	□	□
O103	80	1$\frac{1}{2}$d purple and green . . .	70·00	55·00	□	□
O104	81	2d green and red	£140	70·00	□	□
O105	82	2$\frac{1}{2}$d blue	£150	55·00	□	□
O106	83	3d purple on yellow . . .	£140	55·00	□	□

GB or All World
we've got what
you're looking for!

Looking to fill those awkward gaps in your collection through a reliable, one-stop supplier, without any fuss or bother?
Rick Warren Approvals are the solution.
We offer over 1/2 million individually priced stamps/sets so whatever you're looking for, we've probably got it. However, offering the best selection is only part of our service - take a look at what we offer!

- Selections when you want them.
- View at your leisure, at home, no pressure, no fuss.
- Prompt, personal service.
- Generous loyalty scheme.
- All major credit cards taken.
- See before you buy.

SPECIAL OFFER £50 to start you off

Fill those gaps in your collection with - Rick Warren Approvals

The Stanley Gibbons

"Celebration Collection"

An elegant collection representing a great period in philatelic history